LEADERSHIP AND NATIONAL DEVELOPMENT
IN NORTH AFRICA

Leadership and National Development in North Africa

A Comparative Study

Elbaki Hermassi

UNIVERSITY OF CALIFORNIA PRESS

BERKELEY, LOS ANGELES, LONDON

UNIVERSITY OF CALIFORNIA PRESS
BERKELEY AND LOS ANGELES, CALIFORNIA
UNIVERSITY OF CALIFORNIA PRESS, LTD.
LONDON, ENGLAND
COPYRIGHT © 1972, BY
THE REGENTS OF THE UNIVERSITY OF CALIFORNIA
LIBRARY OF CONGRESS CATALOG CARD NUMBER: 70–182279
FIRST PAPERBACK EDITION, 1975
ISBN: 0-520-02170-3 (CLOTHBOUND)
0-520-02894-5 (PAPERBOUND)

PRINTED IN THE UNITED STATES OF AMERICA
DESIGNED BY DAVE COMSTOCK

*To the friends with whom I lived through
the bellicose dreams of early youth.*

CONTENTS

TABLES

PREFACE

This book emerged from my desire to understand the political revolutions of the Maghrib. These revolutions have shaped my autobiography: first as a participant and later as a sociologist vitally interested in how social science could enhance the capacities of maghribi societies to pursue national goals.

The national liberation movements in the area, especially the Algerian Revolution, raised high expectations and stimulated the well known works of Frantz Fanon, Albert Memmi, Mostefa Lacheraf and Kateb Yacine, only to be followed thereafter by disillusionment and bewilderment. In many respects, the disillusionment was justified. The changes that were insignificant in Morocco, too gradual in Tunisia, and even spectacular in Algeria constitute in no way an innovative departure from the social structures of the past. Moreover, despite allusions to the "greater Maghrib," the ruling elites have systematically refused to coordinate their national policies, leaving a tremendous potential unemployed. Thus, they have decreased the chances for achieving in common what no maghribi society can achieve on its own.

In other respects, however, great expectations, such as those of the European left, were simply misplaced. It has rarely been understood that there are qualitative differences between early and late processes of nation building. European revolutions involved primarily class conflicts. These revolutions occurred in societies which had benefited from centuries of independent development, and in which national unity and industrialization had long ceased to be problematical. Third World revolutions, however, confront simultaneously problems of even greater magnitude and complexity, such as national liberation, national unification and the building of new economic, social, and cultural orders. These problems arise in a context that restricts severely the leaders' courses of action and which calls for new rules in the game of nations.

Thus, the criteria for evaluating these late processes of nation building cannot be drawn from developed societies, whose democratic or socialistic forms represent an imperialism of categories for the Maghrib. That is, not only does the Maghrib cease to be studied for itself, but new and significant changes are not even perceived.

The more I have been immersed in this study, the more I have felt the need for a new theoretical perspective to identify the problems for the purpose of analyzing and comparing the different formations of national societies. Specifically, I have wanted to consider the following questions:

Why is it that a civic polity has emerged only in Tunisia up to the present?

Why is Algeria attaining a much higher rate of economic growth than its neighbors?

Why does Morocco find itself in a political, economic, and cultural stalemate?

Why are all maghribi societies free from ethnic, cultural, and regional disintegration?

In order to answer these questions, I have had to examine: (1) the formations of Algeria, Morocco and Tunisia as distinct national societies; (2) the patterns of colonial domination and colonial change; (3) the ways in which (1) and (2) have influenced maghribi political institutions and their elites' postures toward the basic challenges to their nations; (4) finally, the strategies and costs of national choices, given the various political actors' structural contexts and their situational facilities.

In view of the complex problems treated in this book, I have avoided the often arbitrary specialization of academic departments in attempting to bring together modes of inquiry that the literature usually segregates. My intention is to give the reader an overall perspective of the Maghrib which is denied to him by the hasty and partial snapshots of economic reports and ethnological monographs.

I am deeply grateful to my teachers in the Department of Sociology at the University of California, Berkeley: Professor Neil Smelser, who taught me how to study social change while being theoretically systematic; Professor Robert Bellah, who permitted me to combine intellectual rigor with passion; and Professor Arthur Stinchcombe, whose critical eye helped me realize the implications of my own questions. I would like especially to thank Professor Ernest Gellner of the London School of Economics. These pages have not escaped his creative inspiration.

A word of acknowledgment to my friends, Dean Tipps, Mostefa

Lacheraf, Abdallah Laroui, Ali Mahsas, and M. S. Sfia, from whose intelligent discussion I have learned a great deal.

Finally, to Karen Hermassi, who has been with me from the beginning, when this book was but a dim vision, and throughout a difficult journey, I wish to say more than can be said here.

E. H.

Carthage, Tunisia

INTRODUCTION

By focusing on the North African societies, this work attempts to analyze some of the basic issues confronting new nations. To the extent that these issues have been identified in the past, they have been treated as aspects of modernization, a process conceived of as total in its impact, progressive in its effects, and transformational in all areas of human thought and activity. It is precisely such a vision that is fundamentally in crisis today.

Modernization theory can first be criticized on ideological grounds. Many scholars have shared the hope that the entrance of African and Asian nations into modern social scientific consciousness would stimulate redefinitions of the conceptual apparatus of modernization theory. Although Western in origin, the new conceptual apparatus would gain legitimacy from its applicability to world societies that are evolving with rhythms, modalities, and ideologies different from those of Western societies. Instead, the emergence of new nations has come to be conceived as the grand process of modernization that bridges the Victorian dichotomy between traditional (i.e., non-European) and modern (i.e., European) societies. It can be argued that by implicitly or explicitly subscribing to Marx's view that "the country that is more developed industrially shows to the less developed the image of its own future," [1] evolutionists, functionalists, and Marxists alike have displayed a remarkable self-confidence as to ethnocentric achievement. Evaluating the particular advances of new nations exclusively by the degree to which they approximate the characteristics of industrial societies leaves us without means to conceptualize either the contributions of new nations or the profound dilemma which accompanies the formation and transformation of national societies.

Rather than seizing the opportunity to reassess the analytical construct in the face of empirical reality, modernization theory has resurrected the dichotomy between modernity and tradition, defining it essentially by its asymmetry and, hence, raising a host of

[1] Karl Marx, *Capital* (New York: The Modern Library, 1936), pp. 12–13.

theoretical and empirical difficulties. As Samuel Huntington noted, "The modern ideal is set forth and then everything which is not modern is labeled traditional." [2] On the one hand, traditional society is perceived as changeless, a perspective which is rendered untenable merely by familiarity with historical empires and available anthropological evidence. Moreover, because the transformation of new nations is assumed to be a simple by-product of contact with European societies, the entire history of new nations is denied relevance to their ongoing present. Thus, the illusion of changelessness is reinforced.

On the other hand, the overemphasis upon similarities among traditional societies and the reduction of historical and societal varieties to stages in a universal and uniform process of growth condemn old and new societies, save the European, to a residual category in which the most diverse social structures have been arbitrarily thrown together. Indeed, it is difficult to see what so-called traditional societies such as China, the Maghrib, medieval Europe, Tokugawa Japan, and Congo-Kinshasa have in common other than the label. Ignoring the diversity which characterizes these societies, in terms of national formation, culture, and socio-economic development, modernization theory fails to grasp the specific pattern of these societies' transformations.

Among the many characteristics assigned to the modernizing process, special emphasis is placed upon the systemic and global aspects of the transformation. These include industrialization, urbanization, secularization, increasing literacy, and expansion of political participation. The various elements are described as closely associated because, as Daniel Lerner writes, "in some historic sense, they *had* to go together." [3] The contention that modernity, being total and indivisible, produces a chain reaction of mutually reinforcing consequences rules out not only the historic possibility of innovation but also involution and decay. On the contrary, one can easily argue that significant advances within one dimension are entirely compatible with backwardness and decay in other spheres.

[2] Samuel P. Huntington, "The Change to Change: Modernization, Development, and Politics," *Comparative Politics*, III:3 (April, 1971), 294.

[3] Daniel Lerner, *The Passing of Traditional Society* (Beverly Hills, Calif.: Glencoe Press, 1958), p. 438.

It had been assumed, for instance, that rapid economic development would lead to political progress. In fact, modernization has been negatively correlated with the stability of political institutions.[4] The introduction of new elements can even serve to inhibit, rather than precipitate, an overall transformation of the society. For example, modern means of communication, such as radio, television, and film, have helped to strengthen and renovate former cultural segments and have, thus, encouraged traditionalization of the society.

In conformity with a long-standing sociological tradition based on the assumption that change is immanent in the thing changing, modernization theory has focused exclusively on the internal processes of change, particularly in explaining backwardness and has neglected the larger setting in which societies exist. The endogenous culture is considered, then, an obstacle to be overcome if change is to occur, and little attention is paid to crusades, wars, conquest, and international trade and pressure. Given these premises, it is doubtful whether the social and political struggles of new societies can be understood, let alone explained.

Finally, the most glaring defect of modernization theory is its pervasive preoccupation with the direction and goals of change—a preoccupation which should give way to attempts at an exacting depiction of the specific mechanisms of change. In our opinion, this defect results from the absence of an appropriate paradigm as well as from the lack of a scientific objective. Indeed, the fever of historical development seems to have gripped so many minds that decades have been spent in articulating transhistorical laws and documenting evolutionary universals, stages, and trends instead of focusing on a discrete range of phenomena to discover the scope, the tempo, and the rate of change of specific societies. The concept of modernization, as well as the Hegelian idea and Comte's notion of progress, falls within the scope of Durkheim's criticism: "The existence of [this] assumed evolution can be established only by an already completed science. It cannot, then, constitute the immediate subject of research, except as a conception of the mind and not as a thing." He adds that "it is only the individual societies which are

[4] Samuel P. Huntington, "Political Development and Political Decay," *World Politics,* XVII:3 (1965), 386–430.

born, develop, and die that can be observed and therefore have objective existence." [5]

In order to study the formation and transformation of national societies, we reject modernization theory as a surrogate paradigm. In fact, this work, through the problems it raises and the evidence it presents, represents an effort to construct some elements of an alternative paradigm. In our new framework, the unit of analysis for the formation and transformation of societies is neither the individual, nor the culture, but the nation-state; for it is "within and between the nation-states of the world that the effective means of power, and hence to a considerable extent of history-making, are now, for better or for worse, tightly organized." [6] This posture permits us to pursue the major issues confronting national societies, which we identify as the problems of national integration, institutional competence, economic development, and distributive justice. The nation-state is the framework in which these issues tend to be empirically aggregated and in which social scientists and, even more often, social actors feel the need to formulate these problems.

It is difficult, and even misleading, to pretend to construct models of universal applicability for an analysis of the ways in which different societies meet these issues. It is hoped, however, that explanatory models will provide (a) a body of propositions pertaining to the formation and transformation of national societies; and (b) a grounded explanation for regional differences in the pace and the style of development and decay during the process of nation building. Naturally, these models exclude so-called post-industrial societies, a discussion of which would be premature.

Once we have delimited our domain to an intelligible and autonomous field of study, we must develop further the models

[5] Emile Durkheim, *The Rules of Sociological Method* (New York: The Free Press, 1938), p. 19.

[6] C. Wright Mills, *The Sociological Imagination* (London and New York: Oxford University Press, 1959), p. 135. Concerning the national society as the unit of analysis in comparative research, see Terence K. Hopkins and Immanuel Wallerstein, "The Comparative Study of National Societies," *Information sur les Sciences Sociales*, VI:5 (October, 1967), 25–58; Stein Rokkan, "Models and Methods in the Comparative Study of Nation-Building," *Acta Sociologica*, XII:2 (June, 1969), 53–73; Bernard-Pierre Lécuyer, "Contribution of the Social Sciences to the Guidance of National Policy," *International Social Science Journal*, XXII:2 (1970), 264–300.

designed to explain variations in national formations and socio-economic development. Such explanatory models should proceed in two steps. First, the historical tradition of a given national unit should be studied along with its impact upon actual or potential national development. To understand what Marx has called the principle of historical specificity, comparative study should be based on long-term periods—that is, on decades, generations, and centuries —rather than on short-term occurrences. It should avoid the tendencies of most scholars who have studied new nations to locate the drama of these nations in the few years preceding and succeeding independence. This has been particularly true of studies of Africa in which reliance upon short-term occurrences has condemned research to faulty predictions and displaced typologies as regimes were toppled and structural change lagged behind. To eschew this sorry legacy, we shall devote attention in Part I to the historical political traditions of the Maghrib and the actual transformation of the precolonial societies.

Secondly, these models should enable us to evaluate the options of the emerging political system regarding the basic problems we have identified as integration, institutionalization, economic development, and distributive justice. To prevent the unfortunate imposition of the social scientist's selected commitments upon social and political actors, it is important to keep in mind that these problems can be understood only in relation to one another. Economists treat economic growth and political scientists focus on political stability as if each were an isolated variable and an end in itself. Most critical issues, however, confront the state simultaneously and inseparably. Any government, whatever its effectiveness, is capable of handling only a limited number of problems and resolving only a limited number of conflicts if it is to maintain itself at a particular level of institutionalization.[7] Very often, nothing short of a revolution can precipitate the transformation of a society; this should be sufficient to remind us that regime stability has its cost and that the definition of political development should not be restricted to the stability of a given regime. The key point is that the basic problems are institutional dilemmas and that the compounding of challenges is such that the mode of resolution for one (e.g., national integra-

[7] Joseph La Palombara and Myron Weiner, *Political Parties and Political Development* (Princeton, N.J.: Princeton University Press, 1966).

tion) determines the style and tempo of change in other areas (such as the economic sphere).

An evaluation of the options should include both endogenous and exogenous factors and lead to a determination of their differential weights in shaping institutional constellations and alternative policies. Instead of taking foreign domination and international pressure as unquestionable givens, it is fundamental to take into consideration how these elements participate in the making, maintenance, and disappearance of the endogenous social structures (Part II). Finally, an objective analysis of the paths of development among the new nations cannot be accomplished solely by applying either liberal or Marxist criteria. True, these have been genuine guidelines in their time. The new nations, however, represent very different kinds of social and cultural structures in which the accumulation of tasks, the structures of dependency, the involution of the economy, and, most importantly, the historical failure of the bourgeoisie and the correlative weakness of the proletariat preclude application of either the clear-cut liberal or Marxist positions.[8] The outcome can be only a social creation in part, whatever syncretist features it may incorporate. To perceive this social creation, we must direct our attention to the structure and posture of the ruling elites, their geopolitical contexts, and mainly their links to their various social groups. It is this kind of focus that can help us discern whether the elites are able to take decisive measures to transform their societies—to break from dependency on the outside and restructure privileges at home—and whether they are able to build the kinds of institutions which will sustain these transformations.

Apropos of this issue, Parts III and IV deal specifically with the political and developmental capabilities of the different national elites and the institutional contexts in which they operate. Economic development and distributive justice, particularly, depend not only on statesmanship but also on the situational facilities of the given country, its natural resources, and the structure of opportunities. Thus, these factors must be incorporated in any explanatory model.

It is hoped that our research strategy will cast some light upon an

---

[8] José A. Silva Michelena, *The Illusion of Democracy in Dependent Nations*, Vol. III of *The Politics of Change in Venezuela* (Cambridge, Mass. and London: M.I.T. Press, 1971); Barrington Moore, Jr., *Social Origins of Dictatorship and Democracy* (Boston: Beacon Press, 1967).

area known for its unusual capacity to invite and then frustrate standard sociological approaches. The work that the serious reader is to begin addresses itself simultaneously to a comparative analysis of past and present Maghrib and to the comparison of maghribi societies with one another. Anticipating the risk of openendedness which accompanies such a broad schema, we wish to add that such a beginning seems to us indispensable for gaining insight into the Maghrib and into the tragic, and often insoluble, problems of new nations.

Part I

THE HISTORICAL TRADITIONS OF
THE MAGHRIBI STATE

Chapter 1: THE STATE
MEDIEVAL AND PATRIMONIAL

The objective of this part is an inquiry into the political traditions of the historical Maghrib. Because the sociologist must rely upon works of historians and anthropologists in order to accomplish this task, the reader will find himself concerned with complex and diverse materials, which, we trust, will provide him with a grounded introduction to the area itself. Traditional maghribi society contained a paradox. Although the society was conceptually and normatively unified, the central authority did not exert equal control over the whole territory. Like many precapitalist societies, but in very specific ways, maghribi society was divided into zones of power and degrees of authority which varied significantly from the center to the periphery.

If, for heuristic reasons, one were to construct a model of the traditional maghribi state, it would be useful to present three concentric circles. The first circle would represent the locus of central power, which was based in the cities and which had a threefold vocation: military, commercial, and religious. In these urban zones, dynasties of a patrimonial kind were established. To defend themselves and to control the rest of the country, they relied upon tax-exempt tribes whose members gradually began to assume military responsibilities. Surrounding this circle of protected cities and privileged tribes, there existed an intermediary zone composed of subject tribes, which were administered either by local notabilities or by agents from the center and which were submitted to the heaviest system of taxation and exploitation. Finally, there was a third, peripheral circle with varying boundaries. Within this circle were regularly dissident and semidissident tribes. These marginal units not only constituted a challenge to the central authority through their dissidence but also constantly invaded the state and established dynasties, of which there is historical record. Such dynasties were, however, replaced by dynasties established by other tribes having equal ambition. The model of the maghribi state is, then, composed of three elements: people who raise taxes, those who submit to exploitation, and those who refuse it. One may justifiably perceive in this a symbol of the human condition.[1]

Once we have presented this model, many questions immediately come to mind. How do we interpret the structure of the maghribi society if the state was frequently invaded by dissident tribes? By what dynamic were the tribal units able to take over the state? Moreover, knowing that institutionalization of the political order presupposes development of a civic realm beyond primordial attachments, how can we define the relationship between the central power and the tribal society in North Africa?

The colonial ethnological school has attempted to answer some of these questions. It undertook microscopic and multiple inquiries into the tribes and villages of the Maghrib, but these culminated mainly in one empirical generalization: the famous theory of moieties.[2] The essence of this theory lies in the assessment that order in the maghribi society, to the extent that it was maintained, was assured primarily by the institutionalized hostility between opposed pairs of leagues, rather than by the central state authority. These leagues, called *leff-s* in Morocco and *soff-s* in Algeria and Tunisia, were supposedly in constant conflict and were, therefore, able to neutralize each other through their internal struggles and alliances. Within the framework of this theory, central authority was defined negatively. For the most part, the state was described as a remnant of ancient times, exploiting populations and playing upon inner divisions. In brief, it was perceived as a residual category. One other assumption of this theory was vulgarized by the French

[1] Ernest Gellner, "Tribalism and Social Change in North Africa," in W. H. Lewis, ed., *French-Speaking Africa: The Search for Identity* (New York: Walker, 1965), pp. 107–118.

[2] This theory was put forward by Robert Montagne in his *Les Berbères et le Makhzen dans le Sud du Maroc: Essai sur la transformation politique des Berbères sédentaires (groupe Chleuh)* (Paris: Felix Alcan, 1930). His thesis is also summarized in a small book designed to initiate French civil servants who were to serve in North Africa, *La vie sociale et politique des Berbères* (Paris: Alcan, 1931).

university and army. The assumption, presented sometimes as a hypothesis but more often as a fact, was that the maghribi tribe was fundamentally antistate.

However, one must account for the existence of the state and its centuries of uninterrupted historical continuity. Neglecting this purpose, colonial theory composed a monumental evolutionary scheme designed to answer all questions concerning the problem of power. The theory proposed that the emergence of the personal power of chiefs provided the foundation on which the empire was gradually built. The colonial approach usually began with documentation of a segment of origin which has been constituted by the reunion of patriarchal families and which has functioned as a spontaneous democracy called *les républiques berbères.* In order to explain the emergence of personal power and empire from tribal foundations, the leff-s theory tended to invoke simple laws of equilibrium and disequilibrium based on man's egoism and the inherent competition among groups. This colonial theory, which accounted for the oscillation between the chiefs' oppressive power and the ordered anarchy of the tribal society, has been, up to the present, the predominant interpretation of the political history of the entire Maghrib.

Commenting on a century of research related to the Maghrib, Jacques Berque did not fail to notice the simplistic aspect of this theory, which "seduces the honest man who suddenly reads total clarity into the past of the Maghrib, gives a political lever to the officers in action, and rallies the sociologist forth to this explanation of luminous simplicity. *Les Berbères et le Makhzen* (1930) appeared under the auspices of *l'Année Sociologique.* I still hear the late Marcel Mauss celebrating Robert Montagne as the equal of Granet." [3]

[3] Jacques Berque, "Cent vingt-cinq ans de sociologie maghrébine," *Annales Economies Sociétiés Civilizations* [hereinafter cited as *Annales, E.S.C.*], XI:3 (July–September, 1956), 296–335. The most serious objections to the theory of the leff-s have been formulated by Jacques Berque and by Ernest Gellner. The first author has questioned, since 1948, the degree of generality of binary organization, which is the touchstone of the whole theory; see his thesis on the Seksawa, *Structures sociales du Haut Atlas* (Paris: Presses Universitaires de France, 1955). Gellner has shown, as well, that the theory of the leff-s is incapable of explaining in what way the social order is maintained in the interior of these structures; see *Saints of the Atlas* (Chicago: University of Chicago Press, 1969). Jeanne

Evidently a key question arising from this theory is whether it is possible to infer the character of the state merely by studying tribal sociability. More specifically, can we deduce the dynamic of the political system, past and present, in the whole of North Africa from anthropological research pertaining to southern Morocco in the nineteenth century? (The leff-s theory acquired most of its material from this area.) It is undeniable that the maghribi society, especially the rural society, remained profoundly tribal in its orientations throughout the nineteenth and early twentieth centuries. Most decisions of importance were made within the framework of kinship groups. Individual loyalties were predominantly oriented toward the kinship group; and the community, in its turn, was oriented toward the protection of its members. Thus, the problem is not simply one of discerning tribal orientation within the rural society but rather of defining the North African tribe and determining its specific relationship to the central authority. If by tribe, we mean a self-sufficient social unit constituting a world unto itself—perceiving itself as the whole of mankind and recognizing no right or obligation beyond its limits—then tribes do not exist in North Africa. Furthermore, we do not see by what dialectical leap or miracle hundreds of social units, considered tribes by ethnologists, could come to recognize the authority of a state that was fundamentally exterior to them. That, historically, some tribal units have consented to the authority of the state, that others have accepted its religious legitimacy while rejecting its political control, and that a sizable number have refused to submit to it altogether renders the problem all the more complex and demands of us a greater sociological vigilance.

In recent scholarship on the subject, Ernest Gellner has attempted to interpret the maghribi rural society by applying Durkheim's concept of segmentarity. According to this perspective, the structural principle of organization in the Maghrib can be represented as a tree whose common trunk is the society itself, whose major branches are the important tribes, and whose minor branches represent the clans themselves. Such segmentation assumes a potential opposition

---

Favret gives a good exposition of the contribution of Ernest Gellner to maghribi anthropology and analyzes the deficiencies of French ethnology on North Africa in "La segmentarité au Maghreb," *L'Homme, Revue française d'Anthropologie,* VI:2 (April–June, 1966), 105–111.

between the parties: Each unit's members tend to unite against adjacent segments and to ally with these against even larger sections. Equilibrium is attained through contradictory tendencies toward fission and fusion and consists essentially in poles of opposition and solidarities, which ultimately achieve the economy of power and authority. Similar forms of organization have been analyzed for other cultural areas. For example, Georges Balandier has demonstrated that the logic of alternative solidarities and oppositions was at work among the Tiv in Nigeria. Among the Tiv, "The homologous groups of the same unit oppose each other (−), yet find themselves associated and in solidarity (+) within the unit immediately superior to them, which is itself in a relationship of opposition to its homologues." [4] In the maghribi context, at any rate, people express this structural principle in their cultural and political values. Hence, the man from Kabylia would say, "I hate my brother, but I hate even more he who hates him." The Arab proverbs tend to be more general and pervasive: "I against my brother; my brother and I against our cousins; our cousins, brothers, and I against the world."

This principle of segmentation militates against power concentration and political specialization because loyalties and oppositions are distributed along a continuum of ordered scales. A single shared residence can place brothers in opposition; the inheritance of land, cousins; an irrigation system, the village; and the use of pastoral land, the whole confederation. It is as if given this dynamic of fission and fusion, internal cohesion and reactivation of solidarities are not so much ensured by recognized authorities as by the awareness of external threat: a powerful confederation, a central government, or foreign occupation. It is only to be expected that the peripheral regions where tribes are in situations of marginality afford the best refuge for the maintenance of segmentary structures; thus, it has been argued that many tribal units, consciously or un-

---

[4] Georges Balandier, *Anthropologie politique* (Paris: Presses Universitaires de France, Collection SUP, 1969), p. 63. For a description of segmentary societies, see also Edward Evans-Pritchard, *The Nuer* (Oxford: Clarendon Press, 1940), a description of the modes of livelihood and political institutions of a Nilotic people; and M. Fortes, *The Dynamics of Clanship Among the Tallensi* (Oxford: Oxford University Press, 1945); A. W. Southall, *Alur Society: A Study in Processes and Types of Domination* (Cambridge, England: W. Heffer & Sons, 1954).

consciously, have encouraged division and fragmentation to avoid being governed by the central power.

Ernest Gellner is keenly aware that the notion of segmentation applies only to rural society and that, even there, marginality is at least partially voluntary. In this situation, the social units with which we are dealing, whatever their degree of segmentation and marginality, are part of a larger Arab-Moslem civilization. They participate in a universalistic system of values and norms, and they perceive themselves as an integral part of a vast community. Even the tribe's decision to declare dissidence attests to the fundamental reference of the larger community, regardless of the particular regime.

From the beginning of this work, we shall put forth the methodological principle that an understanding of the political and societal bifurcation of the maghribi societies depends on an understanding of the spiritual and economic unity of the societies. Thus, economic and religious aspects will be treated at various times and in different ways throughout this work. We have already indicated that there was religious unity; contrary to current stereotypes of the characteristics of traditional societies, there was also economic unity. There is enough evidence to show that the links between the maghribi cities and the rural tribal areas, both in terms of defense and of markets, were deeply organic. The point is that if political bifurcation was indeed a profound empirical reality to be investigated, bifurcation was not incompatible with the unity of the society. Only if we can confront this anthropological paradox—one in which social units with a structural disposition toward segmentation and autonomy have broad normative references reaching out to the entire community—is it possible to present a grounded interpretation of maghribi history and society. Otherwise, it is impossible to understand any maghribi society and especially to explain the mechanisms by which such tribes as the Kutama, the Sanhaja, and the Masmuda were able to found the most significant empires known to the area—empires which constitute the area's essential historical horizon.

The perspective of this thesis gives at least a partial answer to the question of emergence of authority. Although the propensity for segmentation tends to prevent power concentration, one can argue that the propensity for cohesion, activated both by feelings of external threat and the reference to a larger community and its cultural model, favors greatly the emergence of unifying leadership. Southall has illustrated that segmentary organizations and leadership institutions, far from being mutually exclusive, are frequently combined and integrated consistently within the framework of a common political system.[5]

As a matter of fact, it is curious to see how most of the anthropologists who studied political fragmentation in North Africa were satisfied to juxtapose a central state whose genesis is not explained and a society which is fundamentally tribal and segmentary in its orientation. Apparently, the tribal origin of most of these states from the eighth to the seventeenth centuries did not seem sufficiently striking to alter theoretical perspectives. Ironically, a result of this oversight is that some anthropologists still insist upon the fundamental incompatibility between central state and tribal organization, even though they have been confronted with facts as to the origin of the state. When they mention the rural origin of a given state, they do not recognize that this is an answer to a question they never raised. Only within a new framework that redefines the structure of the maghribi tribe and its relationship to the state is it feasible to analyze the ability of the tribal structure, despite its segmentarity and marginality, to provide dynasties and the basis for state organization.

Fresher views are now being presented, and new theoretical starting points promise to be more fruitful. In *Islam Observed,* Clifford Geertz writes,

> The formative period both of Morocco as a nation and of Islam as its creed (roughly 1050 to 1450) consisted of the peculiar process of tribal edges falling in upon an agricultural center and civilizing it. It was the periphery of the country, the harsh and sterile frontiers, that nourished and in fact created the advanced society which developed at its heart. . . . The critical feature of Morocco is that its cultural center of gravity lay not, paradoxical as this may seem, in the great cities, but in the mobile, aggressive, now federated, now fragmented tribes who not only harassed and exploited them but also shaped their growth.[6]

[5] Southall, *op. cit.,* p. 243.
[6] Clifford Geertz, *Islam Observed: Religious Development in Morocco and Indonesia* (New Haven and London: Yale University Press, 1968), pp. 5–9.

For a complete treatment of these formative years, however, we must turn to a work composed six centuries ago, undistorted by cultural content and sociological despair—the work of Ibn Khaldun.

On the theoretical and methodological levels, Ibn Khaldun's work is the most consistent ever written on North Africa and the Arab world. So far as theoretical vision is concerned, in its dynamic and specificity, it presents the only attempt to take seriously the relationship between state and rural society. Its mode of analysis recognizes both the normative unity of the society as a whole and the tensions and inherent contradictions between the hierarchical tendencies of the state and the autonomist, equalitarian proclivities of the tribal world. We shall analyze Ibn Khaldun's political theory by selecting the essential variables, the combination and interrelationships of which will constitute an explanatory model to account for political development and political decay in the medieval Maghrib. Schematically, these strategic variables are the conditions under which an empire can be founded from tribal movements.

1. The creation of a state and its institutionalization depend primarily upon what Ibn Khaldun calls *asabiyah*, often translated as group feeling, or tribal spirit. It would be theoretically sounder, however, to render this concept as the propensity for cohesion and segmentation. An exploration of the concept of asabiyah reveals that it contains contradictory elements. First, asabiyah indicates tribal cohesion. By this, Ibn Khaldun wants to illustrate that the establishment of central power within a culturally pluralistic and segmentary society is inconceivable without a minimum of cohesion among and within some tribal units. He also shows that cohesion was more common to the rural areas, in which people were accustomed to hard conditions of living and to political marginality, than it was to the urban centers, in which the population underwent processes of detribalization, individuation, and submission.

Asabiyah also indicates the propensity for segmentation. Thus, although Ibn Khaldun uses it when he speaks of the difficulties of establishing dynasties in heterogenous societies, he is not referring to social cohesion. The meaning of segmentation emanates clearly from this passage:

> The Berber tribes in the West are innumerable. All of them are
> Bedouins and members of groups and families. Whenever one tribe
> is destroyed, another takes its place and is as refractory and rebellious

as the former one had been. Therefore, it has taken the Arabs a long time to establish their dynasty in the land of Ifriqiyah [Tunisia] and the Maghrib. . . . On the other hand, it is easy to establish a dynasty in lands that are free from group feelings [asabiyah]. . . . This is the case in the contemporary Egypt . . . because it has few dissidents or people who represent tribal groups.[7]

That Ibn Khaldun feels free to use both meanings for the one concept, asabiyah, clearly indicates that he has perceived the contradictory tendencies of any segmentary system toward simultaneous fission and fusion. It indicates as well that he has perceived the full political implications of this structural principle of segmentarity: Tribal cohesion leads to empire building, just as tribal segmentation leads to its erosion. It is unfortunate that most of his translators, who had no anthropological background, failed to render the double meaning of asabiyah, thereby missing the contemporary quality of Ibn Khaldun's vision and revealing themselves to be beneath his level of comprehension.

At any rate, the articulation of a tribal, cohesive base necessary for empire building presupposes the reduction of inner dissensions and the domination of a tribe by a clan, and, in its turn, the domination of other tribes by this tribe. But once the tribe has achieved a domineering vocation, the type and the means of domination will depend upon the peculiar historical circumstances of the society in question. For Ibn Khaldun, "It is evident that royal authority is the goal of group feeling. Where group feeling attains that goal, the tribe [representing that group feeling] obtains royal authority, either by seizing actual control or by giving assistance to the ruling dynasty. It depends upon the circumstances prevailing at a given time [which of the two alternatives applies]. If the group feeling encounters obstacles on its way to the goal, it stops where it is." [8] In short, tribal cohesion is a necessary, but not sufficient, condition for empire building.

2. The emergence of a ruling structure assuming leadership functions represents another condition. In a segmentary society,

[7] Ibn Khaldun, *Prolegomenon: An Introduction to History*, trans. by Frantz Rosenthal (Princeton, N.J.: Princeton University Press, 1967), 3 vols. Throughout our text, we shall use Rosenthal's translation for its excellent rendering of Ibn Khaldun's thought and style.

[8] *Ibid.*, p. 278.

which tends to minimize central authority, the emergence of leadership requires some degree of differentiation. Many qualities, some of them universal and some peculiar to medieval Arab society, are required for the leadership to be accepted and successful. Ibn Khaldun supplies us with a long list:

> Desire for goodness and good qualities such as generosity, forgiveness of error, tolerance toward the weak, hospitality toward guests, the support of dependents, patience in adverse circumstances, faithful fulfillment of obligations, liberality with money for the preservation of honor, respect for the religious law, and for the scholars who are learned in it . . . great respect for old men and teachers, acceptance of the truth in response to those who call for it, fairness to and care of those who are too weak to take care of themselves, attentiveness to the complaints of supplicants . . . avoidance of fraud, cunning, deceit, and of not fulfilling obligations. . . . These are the qualities of leadership.[9]

All these qualities are obviously anchored in the Islamic value system, which defines the state primarily in terms of its capacity to protect its rational substantive justice in the Weberian sense, and to maintain reverence for tradition. Ibn Khaldun considers these attributes of the ruling elite, as well as tribal cohesion, to be so vital that their absence would lead to a monarchy that either ruled by naked power or was incapable of governing.

3. Another complementary factor facilitating the construction of political order consists of religion and religious prophecy.[10] Religion includes both the original Islam under which particularist tribes were unified into a large community (the *umma*) and the later religious movements, animated by sects and tribes, that took North Africa as their privileged terrain. After the conflicts and dissensions over the succession of the califate in the Middle East, the Maghrib

[9] *Ibid.*, p. 285.

[10] Saunders argues that Islam permitted the Arabs to build an empire and a civilization in contrast with the Mongols who, lacking a religious prophecy, melted into the societies they conquered by adopting the cultures and religions of these societies. See John Joseph Saunders, "The Nomad as Empire Builder: A Comparison of the Arab and Mongol Conquests," *Diogenes*, no. 52 (Winter, 1965), pp. 79–103. For a profound treatment of the present crisis of Islam, see Robert N. Bellah, "Islamic Tradition and the Problem of Modernization," in *Beyond Belief* (New York: Harper & Row, 1970), pp. 146–167.

became a refuge for heretics and sect initiators; these heretics along with local reformers began to preach new religious prophecies. The prophecies minimized intertribal and intratribal dissensions and provided an explosive basis for cohesion and a vision of the world that encouraged many tribes to acquire a position of political leadership. The best illustration of the functions of religion according to the Khaldunian thesis is the Almoravid and Almohad dynasties, founded by religious reformers in the ninth and twelfth centuries. Analyzing the two tribe-sects which founded these dynasties, Khaldun noted, "In the Maghrib, there existed many tribes equaling or surpassing them in numbers and group feeling. However, their religious organization doubled the strength of their group feeling through [their] feeling of having the right religious insight and their willingness to die . . . and nothing could withstand them." [11]

Tribal cohesion, leadership, and religious ideology are the strategic variables, the cultural and structural conditions, that allow a society, though segmentary, to build a central state. Although Ibn Khaldun's mode of logic leaves many aspects implicit in his reasoning (several readings are necessary for these aspects to become explicit), the logic is modern in the way variables are combined according to the principle of the value-added approach. In sociology, the intellectual apparatus of this approach, as it has been applied to the study of collective behavior,[12] essentially consists of a systematic ordering of the determinants of action. Each determinant is seen as operating in an established framework of previous determinations and adding its specific value; all these conditions constitute the necessary and sufficient elements that combine to produce a given instance of behavior. When applied to the analysis of social movements in a segmentary, tribal society, this approach demonstrates that the first structural condition for emergence of a political movement is a minimum of cohesion within a tribal unit.

Cohesion, however, can have varying results. It can bring a tribe to power, but it can also lead to regular raids (*razzia-s*) against other tribes or to the concentration of the local assembly's prerogatives in the hands of a single chief. In general, cohesion creates a fertile context for the emergence of local leadership. As

[11] Khaldun, *op. cit.*, p. 311.
[12] Neil J. Smelser, *Theory of Collective Behavior* (New York: The Free Press, 1962).

we discussed earlier, Ibn Khaldun shows how leadership and religious prophecy contribute to empire building. A fourth condition absent from his theoretical model, though prominent in his treatment of historical material, is the degree of vigilance and strength of the established power.

In the typology of Ibn Khaldun, we have an indispensable theoretical key for the interpretation of the significant sociopolitical movements and episodes that characterize the medieval Maghrib. One might add that contrary to colonial ethnology, the author refuses to focus upon secondary forms of collective behavior, like banditism, raids, and localized insurrections. Instead, he treats them as a residual category and chooses to focus upon the conditions under which movements oriented toward empire building succeeded or failed. By so doing, he provides us with a fruitful sociological perspective for analyzing political processes in the area.

Khaldun, in addition to providing insight into the genesis of the state, gives us specific information about the structure of the medieval state. We learn that the medieval state is structurally condemned to an insurmountable political instability. The dynamic of the system is such that there is a constant tribal circulation of elites, in which the circulating units are neither elites in the sense of Pareto, nor classes in the sense of Marx, but simply tribes. The essence of Khaldun's theory, as well as his personal tragedy as scholar and political man, is closely related to the regularity with which a tribe, having emerged from dissidence and having armed itself with a superior religious cohesion, took power, only to succumb to another tribe following the same pattern. Such occurrences took place every few generations. Maghribi medieval history, then, can be interpreted as a succession of political crystallizations, none of which brought about any fundamental change in the recurrent cycle.

Thus, it is tempting to describe the medieval maghribi state as a segmentary state, because a structural limitation, essentially tribal, affects its territorial sovereignty, its degree of centralization, and its means of stability.[13] Such an assertion is valid only as a limiting case and only if one never loses sight of the normative unity of the society. A peculiarity of segmentarity within the Arab-Moslem

---

[13] Southall, *op. cit.* (n. 4), pp. 246–249.

context is that the tribal base constantly oscillates between withdrawal into itself and enthusiastic identification with the larger community of faithfuls. In the first case, the tribe defines itself in terms of the defense of its identity and its autonomy. In the second, it sees itself in its identification with the nation or community (both of which concepts are elastic enough to refer to a political state like Tunisia or Algeria or to the entire Arab-Moslem world). This dual alignment constitutes the source of two fundamental forms of primordialism that are corrosive of the state. The local primordialism undermines the state from within; the communitarian and boundless primordialism transcends the existing states, and, like the eschatology of St. Augustine, culminates in the devaluation of political loyalty. Both of these orientations converge to shatter the consolidation of the national state, as it is conceived today.

Contemporary scholarship regarding state creation in the historical Maghrib has not advanced much beyond the perception of Ibn Khaldun. It is ironic that most of the available research has been dedicated either to the study of elementary units (tribes, villages, etc.) or to the analysis of the Arab-Moslem culture as a whole. Very little attention has been paid to the essential constituent of this thesis—the nation-state. We would belabor the obvious if we insisted that the sole possibility for political development is intimately related to the appearance and reinforcement of political institutions at the state level and that this enterprise is successful only when a state captures for itself, in line with its historical continuity, the various potentialities of primordialism.

Those who have focused on the culture as a whole have been historians, theologians, and Orientalists who, by adopting a unitary perspective, have tended to identify the maghribi societies mainly with their value system as embodied in Islam. The Arab-Moslem area owes much to this scripturalist orientation, which clarifies the cultural and universalistic elements of a pluralistic and heterogeneous world. One cannot help feeling, however, that this perspective overemphasizes the religious aspects of the societies, as if the entire Moslem population were preoccupied exclusively with the centuries-old dilemmas of the Koran.

More recent research, dating from the colonial penetration, has isolated the Maghrib as a terrain for separate investigation and has adopted a conflictive model, of which the famous antagonisms between Arabs and Berbers and between tribes and the state are the best examples. The theory of the leff-s is perhaps the most representative product of this orientation. It has utilized and popularized the Khaldunian thesis concerning tribal organization and segmentarity and has neglected his vital treatment of the political order; it does not realize that tribal organization is only one of many causes of the political instability and decay of the medieval state.

Ibn Khaldun suggests other significant factors for the instability and decay. One of these—the weakness of the cities and urban zones—is a major theme of his work. In this light, we can comprehend his fundamental pessimism concerning the basic antinomy between cohesion and civilization, that is, between community and society. For Ibn Khaldun, the tribe can build empires, but only the city can ultimately perpetuate civilization. If it is true that city and tribe are indispensable to each other for defense and economy, it is equally true that they are fatal to each other: the city is doomed to degenerate in luxury, and the tribe is an ever-watchful invader of weakening dynasties. Added to the frailty of urban life is the vulnerability of the capitalist who, according to Ibn Khaldun, finds himself the victim "of confiscations under any legal pretext" and whose enterprise is virtually impossible without his personal ties to men in power. For this reason, Ibn Khaldun demands the protection of the capitalist and holds the government responsible for the economic destinies of the country. In a Keynesian fashion, Ibn Khaldun writes,

> Cities in remote parts of the realm, even if they have an abundant civilization, are found to be predominantly Bedouin and remote from sedentary culture in all their ways. This is in contrast with [the situation in] towns that lie in the middle, the center and seat of dynasty. The only reason is that the government is near them and pours its money into them, like the water [of a river] that makes everything around it green, and fertilizes the soil adjacent to it, while in the distance everything remains dry. We have stated before that dynasty and government are the world's market place.[14]

In view of these considerations, it is obvious that the segmentarity

[14] Khaldun, *op. cit.*, II, 287. On the relation between Islam and politics, consult also C. A. O. Van Nieuwenhuijze, *Social Stratification and the Middle East* (Leiden: E. J. Brill, 1965); of great interest here also is Robert Bellah's paper, "Islamic Tradition and Problems of Modernization," *op. cit.*

of the rural society was far from being incompatible with the construction of a central state. The model we have put forward and our sketch of Ibn Khaldun's work indicate two things: the unifying vocation of social movements of a tribal origin and the fundamental instability of the political structures of that time.[15] Nevertheless, our immediate purpose is to evaluate the impact of historical developments upon contemporary political structures in North Africa. For this purpose, we shall show that the accepted notion of the immutability of traditional society is completely without foundation and that, in fact, the nineteenth-century maghribi state endured many phases of political and social change and emerged with a more secure basis for stability and authority, even prior to colonial occupation.

In view of these purposes, we shall first discuss the structure of the nineteenth-century state and contrast it with the medieval model to determine the most distinctive traits of the transformation. At this juncture, may I reemphasize that we shall not attempt a detailed historical description; instead, we shall concentrate on building a model of the nineteenth-century state and contrasting it with that of Ibn Khaldun. In order to substantiate our hypothesis concerning the impact of state traditions upon contemporary national development, we shall then focus on the differential degrees of government, or on a comparative analysis of the extension of central authority and supralocal institutions within each society.

The student of the nineteenth-century state finds that the configuration of central power had undergone an extensive transformation and had evolved into what may be called a form of patrimonial domination. Ideally, this type of domination is exercised by a military monarchy. As Max Weber has shown, "In the Oriental states, and since the beginning of modern times also in the Occident, we observe a characteristic phenomenon: the opportunities for the

---

[15] The best historical approach to medieval North Africa is the recent book by Abdallah Laroui, *L'Histoire du Maghreb* (Paris: Maspero, 1970). This book offers ample information about the role of external forces such as the Crusades, struggles for the domination of the Mediterranean, and the Iberian conquests, and their impact upon internal maghribi developments. Important though these factors are, we did not judge it useful, from our theoretical perspective, to include this historical evidence here because it can be easily consulted elsewhere and because we offer sufficient discussion of the European impact in Chapter II.

military monarchy of a despot backed by mercenaries increase significantly with the advance of money economy. In the Orient, the military monarchy has since remained the typical national form of domination." [16]

The ideal type of patrimonial domination includes distinctive traits which differentiate it from other forms of domination like the patriarchal and the feudal. First, there is private appropriation by the master of the army and the administration. This has led Max Weber to consider sultanism as the embodiment of patrimonial domination, par excellence: "Sultanism tends to emerge wherever traditional domination develops an administration and a military force which are purely the instruments of the master." [17] We note that in nineteenth-century North Africa, the previous dependence upon the tribe had been transformed into a structural dependence upon the army.

Another trait of patrimonialism concerns the high degree to which offices are stereotyped and monopolized, the beneficiaries of which tend to be arbitrarily replaceable. The final two characteristics deal with central and peripheral modes of government. The area surrounding the patrimonial residence was usually administered directly by officials from the court and, hence, was subject to dynastic appropriation of land (*Hausmacht*). More distant provinces were administered by governors who tended to exert their power in a patrimonial fashion. Because of the distance and the increasing difficulties of communication, governors tended to become more and more independent in their use of extractive and military capacities for administering their provinces.

It is possible to show that all these traits of patrimonialism— private appropriation of army and administration, total discretion in appointments of offices, dynastic appropriation of the land, and imitation of the same traits in the provinces—were present in every maghribi political system, allowing, of course, for some disparities among localities. Indeed, the whole government apparatus was considered an extension of the private domain of the men in power, whether it was established externally, as were the governments of Turkish origin in Tunisia and Algeria, or internally, as was the

[16] Max Weber, *Economy and Society*, ed. by Guenther Roth, and Claus Wittich (New York: Bedminster Press, 1968), III, 1017.
[17] *Ibid.*

Alawite dynasty, which emanated from the heart of Morocco. Even though the personal exercise of power was tempered and circumscribed by religious and traditional restraints, it continued to be arbitrary and total, as Ibn Abi Dhiyaf [18] recorded for all the North African rulers of the nineteenth century.

Another constraint on the exercise of patrimonial domination emanated from the tribal grounding of the rural society. Because of this, the ruling strata, and its military and administrative apparatus, represented a superstratification constantly involved in territorial and social unification. To a great extent, the state apparatus can be described as an instrument of conquest because of the highly mobile character of its units which strove always to integrate and control the scattered parts of the society. Thus, the primacy of military arrangements in the structuring of the state has been conspicuous as much for the Tunisian dynasty and the Turks of Algeria as for the Moroccan sultan who later borrowed most of the Tunisian and Turkish techniques.

During the nineteenth century, the strength of each state depended both upon the amount of support provided by those tribes which pursued a military vocation [19] and upon the organization and composition of the regular army. In Algeria, the military caste closed its ranks to Algerians, relying instead on regular recruits from Anatolia. In contrast, the Tunisian army recruited from the

[18] Ahmed Ibn Abi Dhiyaf, *Athaf Ahl ez-zaman bi Akhbar Tunis wa 'Ahd el-Aman*, 8 vols., a work written in Arabic on the history of Tunisian kings. New publication by the Secrétariat d'Etat à l'Information et à la Culture (1963), I, 1–30.

[19] Marcel Emerit, "Au début du XIXe siècle: les tribus privilégiées en Algérie," *Annales, E.S.C.*, XXI:1 (January, 1966), 44–58. This study offers a good description of the Coulouglis, a mixed element of Turkish and Algerian origins, whose task is mainly the surveillance of the towns and fortresses but, in time of war, includes entry into the infantry; the study also offers a presentation of a tentative list of Algerian tribes with war vocations *(Makhzen)*. Marcel Emerit notes that this organization was so effective that under the influence of Bugeaud, France made a special effort to adopt it. Jean Le Coz offers an even more systematic study of the military tribal organization of Morocco; see his "Les tribus guichs au Maroc: Essai de géographie agraire" (Paris: C.N.R.S. and Rabat: C.U.R.S.), extract from *La Revue de géographie du Maroc*, no. 7 (1965), 52 pp. In Tunisia, the Makhzen tribes have played a secondary role; see André Martel, "Le Makhzen du Sud Tunisien," *Les Cahiers de Tunisie*, no. 32 (1958), pp. 7–32.

country itself and principally from the coastal region of the Sahel. Morocco, which was late in setting up an army, remained dependent upon armed tribes (*Guish*) until the middle of the nineteenth century.

These brief notes on the military have a relationship to the administrative infrastructure and the political organization of each state. Administratively, the center was supposed to delegate its agents (*qaids*) to the whole of the subject territory. Wherever local communities found themselves able to resist forcefully total submission while preserving their customary laws and political institutions, whether they were local chiefs or democratic assemblies, the central power was satisfied to maintain a simple zone of influence. The Moroccan Establishment (*Makhzen*), a relic of the Middle Ages, continued to be a rudimentary apparatus in its means of organization, and eventually it would have failed to command any respect if there had not existed the most venerated personage of the entire country, an institution unto himself, the sultan. The Turkish government in Algeria which had been fragmented into four subdivisions, Dar es-Sultan and the three beyliks of Medea, Wahran, and Constantine, was structurally incapacitated, and in the midst of a greatly segmented society, it suffered a dysfunctional decentralization of authority. Such multiple poles of power encouraged competition, led to the risk of instability, and deprived the central state of a main portion of its public funds; the inequality in the extractive capacities was such that the beylik of Constantine's budget was estimated to be three times that of all Algeria.[20]

For the same period, Tunisia's administration was far more comprehensive and centralized. The entire population was administered by about sixty qaids, in the Tunisian context similar to governors, all of whom were appointed or removed by the dynasty. Administrative uniformity was extended to the whole territory, and hardly any distinction was made between the twenty-two district qaids and the forty rural qaids. As a matter of fact, as administrative standardization increased, power became more concentrated, and the numerical units of government decreased. Beneath the governors, and their representatives, were the 2,000 sheikhs who were in daily contact with the urban and rural population. Most sheikhs

[20] Yves Lacoste, André Nouschi, and André Prenant, *L'Algérie Passé et Présent* (Paris: Editions Sociales, 1960), p. 152.

were local notables whose position as intermediaries was extremely critical because they were torn between the contradictory pressures of the state, on the one hand, and the community they represented, on the other.

Later, we shall see the effects of these structural differences in the states of North Africa; but, for now, the point to remember is that, for the most part, the nineteenth-century state, with its bureaucratic and military apparatus, was able to govern its population and hold the society together. This was true even in Algeria, where central authority was the least entrenched. In discussing Algeria, the historian Marcel Emerit made this comparison: "From 1955 to 1962, a French army of 400,000 men, endowed with a crushing superiority of arms and materiel, did not succeed in obtaining results which the Turkish enjoyed with 3,661 men." [21]

The previous three centuries provided the maghribi state with various opportunities to master the art of governance. In the controlled regions, as we have seen, the central power acquired land, dominated subject tribes (*ra'iyah*), and raised maximum taxes. In the hostile or semihostile regions, however, the rulers were shrewd enough to preserve a delicate balance and exert only as much control as the region would bear. In fact, the rulers became expert at the manipulation of tribal hostilities, and we can credit their knowledge of the mechanisms of their societies for centuries of political stability. Such stability was in sharp contrast with the medieval dynasties, which endured merely a few generations.[22] Not only was the bureaucratic-military apparatus substituted for the tribe as a basis for stability and support, but the techniques of social control became more diverse. As we shall see, this does not mean that political dissidence disappeared; instead, the marginal areas, to the extent that they avoided governmental interference and succeeded in maintaining their separate jurisdiction and forms of self-government, became increasingly vulnerable. To match the elaborate strategy of withdrawal and avoidance that the marginal areas had

[21] Marcel Emerit, *op. cit.*, p. 45.

[22] Evoking in his memoirs his policy regarding the population of North Africa, Ahmed Bey writes, "The man who wishes to govern must entertain the taste for war among them and excite the rivalries among tribes of different origins." See "Les Mémoires d'Ahmed Bey," *Revue Africaine*, XCIII (1949), 88.

developed over the centuries, the state developed counterstrategies such as the policy of the marketplace.

Contrary to the stereotyped image of traditional society, neither the North African tribe nor the region could have existed with a closed economy. It was vitally necessary for the populations of both the north and the south to make regular visits to places of exchange. The Kabylia region, overpopulated and recalcitrant to central control, needed wheat products for subsistence; to that end, it had to commercialize its oil and figs in the marketplaces of the Tell, and it became greatly dependent upon its relationship to this market. The tribes of the south also depended upon the market; there, they exchanged their wool, livestock, and dates for grain and other items produced in the fertile regions of the north.

The marketplace, strategic as it was for exchange, was also instrumental in cementing social relationships for an otherwise dispersed and fragmented population. Historians have been unanimous in recognizing the peculiar significance of this institution. E. Doutté has noted,

> It is no exaggeration to say that the life of the tribe almost in its entirety happens in the market. It is the place where the natives meet; not only do they provide for their daily needs through sales in the market but it is also the spot where ideas are exchanged, political information is passed on, the announcements of the authorities are made and the reaction to these are formed, where decisions about peace and war are taken, political conspiracies started, public outcries raised, broadminded proposals mooted, and crimes hatched.[23]

Because of its political, economic, and cultural functions, the market (*suq*) became central in sustaining dissidence while maintaining the dissidents' link with the rest of the community.

For the state, the implications of this nerve center are equally important. Whenever the state's military and bureaucratic institu-

---

[23] E. Doutté, *Merrakech* (1905), p. 144. Francisco Benet presents abundant material to test his hypothesis that in a society characterized by weak political centralization, "market exchanges usually gain great significance and, indeed, play an integrative role that may transcend the economic sphere itself." See his "Explosive Markets: The Berber Highlands," in Karl Polanyi et al., eds., *Trade and Market in the Early Empires* (New York: The Free Press, 1957), pp. 188–217.

tions faltered, it was able to use the market as a means of social control. By enforcing economic blockades and often by practicing actual blackmail, the state was able to levy taxes and exert pressure. It would have been unable to do this if the market had not existed. It became extremely difficult, even for the most determined dissidents, entirely to avoid contact with representatives of central power.

> For the government, the place of each of these markets constituted one of the highest administrative compositions. . . . All of these tribes, which given the inaccessibility of their mountains, the remoteness of their territory or their nomadic habits, thought they could escape the action of the central authority and live independently, had, however, to pay for their rights to the market to compensate for the other taxes to which they managed to escape submission. How many times, after having braved and even defeated the troops of the beys, did these populations, dependent as they were upon the markets of the interior, beg for grace and accept the harshest of conditions? This state of affairs makes clear why the Turks' main efforts were always to achieve a vigorous organization of the agricultural tribes and to intelligently establish Makhzens [here, meaning garrisons] near the important markets and principal roads.[24]

Having achieved a minimum of stability by definitely curtailing, if not tribal dissidence, at least tribal competition for power, the nineteenth-century maghribi state had to face very specific problems related to the social and economic costs of its bureaucratic-military apparatus. As in any patrimonial political system, the fundamental dilemma of the Maghrib was increasingly becoming one of maintaining a taxation system capable of meeting the material needs of the bureaucracy and the army, even though the economy was still predominantly quasi-subsistent.[25] Any scholar familiar with the area knows the extent to which the problems of taxation and maintenance of the bureaucracy have been intricately related. In

[24] Pierre Boyer, *L'Evolution de l'Algérie médiane* (Paris: Adrien-Maisonneuve, 1960), pp. 48–53.

[25] For this interpretation—a Marxist reading of the Weberian texts on primordialism—we owe much to David Lockwood's "Social Integration and System Integration," in George K. Zollschan and Walter Hirsh, eds., *Explorations in Social Change* (Boston: Houghton Mifflin, 1964), pp. 244–257.

general, every state policy initiative, especially those involving army improvements and economic innovations, had to be met with increased taxation in both money and goods. With the intensification of taxation, intermediaries multiplied and, consequently, corruption increased. The result was fiscal evasion and the ultimate weakening of central power.

In this regard, the most significant pressures on the political system had two origins: first, the tendency of officials to appropriate for themselves the resources conferred upon them by virtue of their positions; and second, the constant struggle of local communities to obtain immunity from taxation. Marxists who have studied precapitalist and patrimonial political systems have tended to ascribe to these inherent contradictions a potential for the development of feudalism.[26] Whatever validity this interpretation may have in other areas, the basic elements of feudal institutions were missing in North Africa. It is true that in a legal sense the traditional state did have institutions resembling those of feudalism; for example, Guish and Makhzen tribes received land in return for an obligation of military service. Nevertheless, nothing of that stable hierarchy which characterizes the feudal systems of Europe and Japan predominated in North Africa. From Weber, we know that it is only when the people acquire some rights limiting the arbitrary will of the ruler that patrimonialism can evolve into feudalism.[27] If in an attempt to secure a degree of autonomy from official intervention, people tried to commit some revenues to public and religious institutions (*Habous*), this effort never seriously limited the arbitrary use of power or created even a religious kind of feudality. Instead, it led to what Weber calls an artificial mobilization of wealth.

In reality, the contradictions of the political systems of North Africa continued without solution, and these contradictions were even further from solution with the advent of European domination. From the outset of the nineteenth century, North Africa was never again to experience an autonomous form of political and economic development, whether feudalistic, capitalistic, or what-

[26] Lacoste, Nouschi, and Prenant, *op. cit.*, p. 150; see also René Gallissot and Lucette Valensi, "Le Maghreb précolonial," *Le Pensée*, no. 142 (December, 1968), pp. 57–93.

[27] Reinhard Bendix, *Nation-Building and Citizenship* (New York: John Wiley & Sons, 1964), p. 108.

ever, because the entire area was to be subjected to the infamous policy of *la canonnière*. After the Congress of Aix-la-Chapelle in 1819, the European states compelled the North African governments to terminate their practice of piracy and to open their markets to European products. For the study of structural and historical change of societies, it becomes important to take into consideration both the endogenous and the exogenous aspects of this change. From the time of Turkish domination and, even more decisively, after European conquest, political and economic change in the Maghrib should not be considered exclusively in terms of endogenous factors. Critical decisions made in foreign capitals were increasingly involved in the shaping of these societies.

Intensified by the European challenge, the crisis of patrimonial systems everywhere developed according to the same pattern. Confronted with meager extractive capacities, the Algerian central government raised taxes, multiplied the official troops who would extract taxes through force (*Mahalla*), and increasingly monopolized trade. Parallel to this, contracts were arranged with foreign companies, and as these companies' budgets enlarged, Algerian resources decreased proportionately. When French colonialism was finally established in 1830, it was estimated that Algeria's resources had diminished by more than half in the previous two centuries.[28]

The situation in Tunisia and Morocco was identical except for complications caused by their desperate attempts to avoid the fate of Algeria. For its part, Tunisia experienced the same phenomenon of commercial disequilibrium and monetary collapse. The historian Mohammed Cherif estimated that between 1816 and 1829, imports increased by 100 percent, while exports increased only 45 percent.[29] Aside from the quasi-institutional reflex of monopolizing trade, the ruling dynasty committed itself to a costly policy of modernization. Relying mainly upon heavy loans from Europe, the dynasty installed a telegraph system, modernized its army, and created some industries. Public debt and increasing consumption stimulated by

[28] Lacoste, *op. cit.*, p. 155.

[29] This was a half century before the real colonial occupation. My friend Mohammed Cherif, who has studied precolonial Tunisia, has placed at my disposal two or three papers which cover the period from 1815 to 1830; see: "Expansion européenne et difficultés tunisiennes," *Annales, E.S.C.*, XXV:3 (May–June, 1970), 714–746.

European goods led the King's Court to double the taxes. Increased taxation was the fundamental reason for the generalized insurrection of 1864. Antifiscal movements seem to have been relatively frequent in nineteenth-century Tunisia. Although it found itself unable to prevent bankruptcy or foreign occupation, Tunisia's central power was structured enough to preserve the country from internal rebellion and decay.

Morocco, even in its impenetrability to foreign influences,[30] could not forever remain isolated. When, late in 1901, the sultan tried to redress the financial situation by replacing the so-called multiple Koranic taxes with a unique and uniform mode of taxation, the population at large seized the occasion to reject both the previous and newly instituted systems. In addition, the most vigorous opposition to the new system came from the notability, which had been accustomed to exemption from taxation. Aside from this opposition within the Makhzen, there was some generalized rebellion sponsored by the grand chiefs who were emerging from the usually marginal zones. In face of this, the sultan had no other recourse but to make use of French assistance to maintain his empire.

In a sense, then, the three maghribi societies found themselves well entrenched in a situation of colonizability, but it should be clear by now that no metaphysical or cultural weakness can be inferred from this. The ensuing conquest of their states was as much the product of their lack of readiness for the exigencies of modern organizations as of the aggression of a triumphant imperialism. As we shall see time and again in this work, there can be no satisfactory explanation of the historical events which have led to economic backwardness in the societies of the Third World without an analysis of the patterns of external and internal forces that shaped the destiny of each society. In the Maghrib, late developments coinciding with colonialism should not be permitted to obscure the great progress that had been made since medieval times. The

[30] Concerning the European impact on precolonial Morocco, consult M. L. Miège, *Le Maroc et l'Europe, 1830–1894* (Paris: Presses Universitaires de France, 1962–   ), 5 vols. expected, 3 published to date. A critical account by Marcel Emérit, "Une grande enquête historique: Le Maroc et l'Europe jusqu'en 1885," *Annales, E.S.C.,* XX:3 (May–June, 1965), 635–642.

relationship between the state and the society had evolved so significantly since the Middle Ages that it is impossible to speak of the maghribi traditional state without specific reference to its particular configurations during the medieval periods and the nineteenth century. Were we to sum up the transformations of the political order between the medieval period and the precolonial era, we would describe them in terms of a stabilization of the political system which permitted the state to strengthen its control over a society which had become less and less segmentary. It has already been shown that the marginal tribes became less successful in challenging central authority and lost completely their potential for taking central power. The monarchical regimes established between the sixteenth and seventeenth centuries not only set the current boundaries of the present political societies but were also able to sustain their own positions of power. Some regimes retained power until the colonial occupation and others still retain power today.

Chapter 2: DIVERSITY AND DIMENSION
OF NATIONAL FORMATION

Up to this point, we have focused primarily on the evolving structure of the maghribi state as it increasingly became the central unit
of cultural integration as well as the major source of power. This
power was far more despotic[31] than was necessary for unification.
Although it did not entirely eliminate all forms of dissidence, the
state provided the contours of the present societies. Some of the
most distinctive elements of their political systems also took shape
during this historical period. Along with the elimination of tribal
dynasties, the emergence of the complex of the grand chiefs deserves particular treatment. The grand chiefs were men of political,
military, and religious standing who surged out of the usually
marginal zones. Their power rested in the intermediary positions
they occupied between central authority and the remaining dissidents.

A thorough analysis of the implications of the emergence of the
grand chiefs, as well as the study of the specific political traditions
which have a significant bearing on contemporary political developments, requires that we go beyond the common traits of
these societies and investigate more closely the differences among
them. Unfortunately, as we try to determine the strength of the
state by inquiring into the social forms parallel or antagonistic to it,
the scholarship becomes controversial. The paucity of solid information regarding rural society and the extent of dissident areas
has reinforced the propensity for distortion and groundless generalizations. In fact, for a long time, the history and the structure
of North African societies were the domain of the sifting sands of
prejudgments. For more than a century, research on political traditions contented itself with grandiose generalizations about the
different political behavior of the Arabs *qua* Arabs and of the
Berbers *qua* Berbers, as if these peoples lived in different worlds. A
Berber specialist attested to the faultiness of this perspective by
demonstrating that it is in the very nature of the Berbers to defy a
rigorous self-definition: "With its infinite particularism, what is
true here about the Berber phenomenon is not true there. . . .

[31] Ahmed Ibn Abi Dhiyaf, *op. cit.* (n. 18), I, 1–30.

Apropos to this, some truths are only partial, and some of these partial truths are elsewhere even countertruths."

Since our main task is the study of the differential degrees of government and the residue of organization each state has inherited from its past, we shall first focus on the degree to which tribal and cultural pluralism limited the extension of the nineteenth-century state. The significance of this issue does not arise simply from the existence of dissident tribes but from the persistence of tribal organization even within controlled and taxed areas; such persistence shows that social control had not been definitely displaced from local groups to the central power. By approaching the problem through the concept of cultural and tribal pluralism, we shall avoid one of the most serious pitfalls of the ethnic thesis on political behavior. Secondly, we intend to present the idea that each maghribi political system displayed distinctive forms of power concentration and power dispersion. To substantiate this idea, we shall examine how, in each instance, the three institutional complexes of power, mainly the central power (Makhzen), the intermediary chiefs, and the dissident factions, were combined.

Cultural and Tribal Pluralism

We have indicated that for many decades, research on political power in North Africa has not transcended ethnic generalizations.[32]

[32] Only conceptual confusion and ideologically oriented racist biases could permit colonial ethnology to formulate the most contradictory propositions concerning the maghribi communities; the popular and popularized thesis of an antagonism between the nomads and the sedentaries—as some would have it, an antagonism between the Arabs and the Berbers—came more and more to impose itself and take on, under the pen of Gautier, the dimension of a cosmic confrontation. These passages from his *Histoire de l'Afrique du Nord ou les Siècles obscurs du Maghreb* (Paris: Payot, 1937), pp. 72, 374, 114, illustrate well its approach. Maghribi history is supposed to be dominated by a permanent confrontation between "two biological parts fundamentally opposed in their eternal comportment. . . . Traversing the entirety of two thousand years since antiquity until our day, the Maghrib has always been cut into two irreconcilable halves, the nomads and the sedentaries. . . . The great nomad has instincts exactly opposite [to those of people who are sedentary]. He is a communist by his style of life. The hardship of his existence makes of him, at least on the day of battle, a disciplined soldier under the princely chiefs. But it leaves him eternally unsatisfied, ardent in his desires. Politically, he is an anarchist, a nihilist; he has a profound preference for disorder, which leaves him open

One paradox is that the more one emphasizes the diversity among cultural areas, the more one risks missing altogether the very real, though concealed, unity of the whole society. Historically, the Arab element was superimposed upon the local Berber population, influencing, particularly between the ninth and fourteenth centuries, the near totality of Tunisia, the western part of Algeria, and the Oriental and Atlantic Morocco. As of today, the Berber element has almost disappeared from Tunisia, but it continues to represent 30 percent of the Algerian population, half of whom are rural, and more than 40 percent of the Moroccan population, representing two-thirds of the total rural population.

An impressive melting pot emerged from the general adoption of Islam and the increasing Arabization of the Maghrib. However, structural conditions, modes of life, and manners by which groups define themselves and one another have contributed to the formation of some specific identities within the larger culture. What is even more important is that neither the Berber nor the Arab elements afford the integrated unity so often ascribed to them. The Moroccan Berbers, for example, boast of not one, but of three languages: the Tachelhit, or the language of the Chleuhs, native to the south of the country; the Tamazirht, or the language of the "free men" of the Middle Atlas; and, finally, the Rif dialect spoken in the northern region and the eastern oasis. A man from any one of

---

to these perspectives. He is a destructor, a negator. Even his victory is not an accomplishment, because he annihilates himself in the flame of an unaccustomed ecstasy." Having assumed all along that Berbers were sedentary, it is not necessary to go very far to reach the fatal conclusion that "La Berbérie [the Maghrib] has not only never been a nation, but it has never been an autonomous state. It has always been part of an empire. . . . The Maghribis are only the eternal conquered who have never succeeded in expulsing their masters." The epoch which began permitted not only ethnologists but also every retired colonel to put forth his personal theory on the Berbers and the Arabs, all variations on the same theme, and all filled with distortions. How can this theory be justified without disregarding the Berber nomadic element and the urban Arab, that is to say, without doing violence to reality? Was it necessary to exaggerate to this point the democratic aptitudes of the Berbers and the aristocratic structures of the Arabs? If it was, what explanation could be given for the emergence of what even these theoreticians call "the Berber feudalities"? Does the fact that these mythical constructions have become the commonplace, obligatory problem of all discourse on the Maghrib justify the man of science, in his turn, conceding to such a facile theory?

these regions would be at great pains to understand a man from another region. With a few differences, the same observation holds true for Algeria; there is diversity not only among the Arabs, of whom there are peoples as different as the Bedouins and urban dwellers, but also among the Berber units whose multiple languages and social structure, like the Kabyles, Chawia-s, Mzab-s (to cite only the essential), constitute a genuine cultural mosaic. If one adds the Arabized Berbers and the Berberized Arabs, one has an idea of the extent to which plurality and unity exist in the maghribi culture. As an anthropologist has written, "In the Maghrib, there is no unique and closed world and, hence, [no world that is] pure and intact; no group—however isolated, however withdrawn—thinks of itself or judges itself without reference to foreign models. Each group seeks and constitutes its identity in the difference; but if the analysis must tend to these differences, it is in order to discover beyond them the identity." [33]

For the analyst of political structure, the point is not whether a given social unit is Arab or Berber but rather that almost all social units in the rural society, whether Berber-speaking or Arab-speaking, whether subject to central power or traditionally dissident, have remained predominantly tribal, preserving their social structures intact until the beginning of the twentieth century. Carette has estimated that out of a total population in 1853 of 3 million in Algeria, 2,670,410 still belonged to a tribal form of organization.[34] Regardless of ethnic origin—in the broad sense, Arab or Berber—the organization of these units along tribal lines meant a common pattern in the articulation of basic solidarities. Everywhere, "descendant" is defined in a patrilinear fashion; relationships between units are based upon a more mythical than real genealogy. The segment, dominated as it was by the temptation to identify and the will to distinguish itself, constantly redefined the lines of alliance and opposition; thus, at different times, political

[33] Pierre Bourdieu, *Sociologie de l'Algérie* (Paris: Presses Universitaires de France, 1963). This little book represents by far the best summary of ethnological research on North Africa. An enlarged version may be found in Bourdieu's *The Algerians* (Boston: Beacon Press, 1962).

[34] Carette, *Recherches sur l'origine et les migrations des principales tribus de l'Afrique septentrionale* (Paris: 1853), p. 341.

organization engaged different levels and different political units. In a system such as this one, it is only to be expected that the capacity for societal integration and societal control by the central power would be very much affected by the strength or weakness of the tribal organization of the society.

Even in a segmentary society, all levels of tribal organization are crucial; a subsegment of a tribe is as politically relevant as an entire tribe. Therefore, we need some measure by which to evaluate and compare the segmentary and tribal structures of the societies. One way of transcending the dispute among anthropologists and colonial officers concerning whether the tribe or the confederation constitutes the basic political unit would be to take the number of tribes as an indicator of segmentarity. We must, however, remember that this is somewhat arbitrary. Indeed, one can argue that the fraction, or clan, is a vital socioeconomic unit, whose members, instead of exerting vengeance upon one another, minimize conflict among families; the clan's function, then, falls short of the political. On the other extreme, the confederation is an alliance for war, uniting many tribes which face a common external threat. The tribe, however, is composed of many federations; it involves the identity of the group in relating to a common ancestor and commits the whole group, both for major decisions and for external relationships, to a common destiny.[35]

That the tribe is the political unit in rural society and that the proportion of the population organized along tribal lines increases as we proceed from Tunisia to Morocco to Algeria (Table 1) lead us to infer that urban life is weakest in Algeria and strongest in

[35] Our definition concurs with the views of Augustin Bernard, who writes: "The aggregation of families designated under the name of tribe can be considered a political unit, that is as responsible for the external actions of the members of the collectivity vis-à-vis the neighboring agglomerations. The tribe will be, then, the political unit of the indigenous people, as the family is the social unit." *L'Evolution du nomadisme en Algérie* (Algiers: Imprimerie Orientale, 1906), p. 277. Also, E. Doutté, "A group much more extensive than the clan, its attributions [the tribe's] concern above all what one would call the 'external affairs,' the relations with other tribes, questions of alliance, the *horma* (honor) of the tribe, its limitations, and everything concerning armaments and war." "L'Organisation domestique et sociale chez les Haha (Maroc)," *Bulletin de l'Afrique française, Supplement* (1905), p. 10.

TABLE 1
NUMBER OF TRIBES BY SOCIETY

	Number of tribes	Year of estimation	Date of colonial occupation
Tunisia	93	1902	1881
Morocco	600+	1954	1912–1934
Algeria	744+	1865	1830

Tunisia. We are also led to infer indirectly the range of constraints upon the capacity for power concentration of each central state.[36] The sense in which the strength of tribal organization is able to constitute an obstacle to the political unification of a society alters according to historical configurations. The point is that the number of tribes indicates the general potential of social units for achieving an institutional closure, i.e., for segmenting or for joining the marginal areas once possessing the attributes of self-sufficiency: a common language, the practice of customary law, and an environment, to some degree, inaccessible. In the medieval era, the propensity for institutional closure on the part of tribal units led to tribal circulation within positions of power, and as we have seen, to the general political instability of the medieval state. But the sole avenues remaining for the cultural segments during the nineteenth

[36] The figures contained in this table are approximate for many reasons: the data are spread out and are not exhaustive. In addition, the information was recorded on different dates, mainly for administrative purposes, and the units of analysis were rarely made explicit. As a result, we do not know whether the figures stand for factions, clans, tribes, or confederations of tribes. But, hopefully, we have reduced the shortcomings as much as possible by relating the figures to the size of the population in each country and by comparing the greatest number of sources possible. Some of our sources are the following: Vincent Monteil gives the excessive figure of 1,200 tribes for Algeria in "Les bureaux arabes dans le Maghrib (1833–1861)," *Esprit* (November, 1961), pp. 575–606; Henri Brenot, *Le Douar, cellule administrative* (Algiers: Imprimerie V. Heintz, 1938), makes a more conservative evaluation; also *Nomenclature et repartition des tribus en Tunisie* (Chalon-sur-Saône: 1900); "Note sur les tribus de la régence," *Revue Tunisienne* (1902), pp. 3–23, 185–194, 277–282, represents the only useful material on Tunisia's tribal structure. For Morocco, see especially *L'Encyclopédie mensuelle d'Outre-mer* (1954); and the *Revue Hespéris-Tamuda*, published since World War I and sponsored now by Morocco's Centre Universitaire de la Recherche Scientifique.

century were those that led to the joining of the penumbra of institutionalized dissidence.

As we turn now to the study of the different forms of counter-powers, we shall supply additional evidence of the relationship between the degree of state organization and the extent of segmentation and dissidence.

States and Counterpowers

It is necessary at the outset to provide a methodological clarification of some basic concepts and to devise relatively precise indicators before we proceed to an analysis of the major legacies and political traditions of each maghribi state. First, we must clarify the concept of dissidence. Works dealing with North Africa have used and abused a distinction native to the area—*Bled el-Makhzen* and *Bled es-Siba*, or "land of government" and "land of dissidence"—to the point that the distinction has become trivialized, and, even worse, an ideological weapon designed to discredit or even deny maghribi capacities for self-government and to justify colonial rule. Having borrowed the distinction from the maghribis themselves, ethnologists and colonial historians did not go beyond the delusions and illusions of spontaneous knowledge, and they proved quite elliptical when it came to precision in delineating the limits and the extent of dissidence. No one, to our knowledge, tried to submit the notion of *siba* to a logical and lexicological critique, which is, after all, indispensable for the controlled elaboration of scientific notions. And no one, despite the profusion of big words used to describe the maghribi state's deficiencies, has taken the problem of political bifurcation seriously enough to treat it as an empirical question.

The notion of *siba* covers at least two forms of dissidence, one spatial and one temporal. The spatial form relates to a geographical portion of the territory, which, given the intensity of tribal connections, the difficulties of means of communication, and the oscillation between nomadic and sedentary forms of life,[37] has historically served to shelter marginal populations from the central power. The frontiers of this form of dissidence have been in con-

[37] X. de Planthol, *Les fondements géographiques de l'histoire de l'Islam* (Paris: Flammarion, 1968).

tinual fluctuation and have, to an extent, varied with the fortitude or frailty of the government.

Siba also refers to dissidence generalized to the whole population; it includes both the subjected and the recalcitrant portions of the country and tends to occur in weak dynasties during crises of succession. Clearly, it is in this sense that Robert Montagne, an expert on the region, employs the concept: "As soon as a sovereign dies and a dynastic crisis opens up among pretenders to power, those tribes which are vigorous enough to liberate themselves return to their laws, and one can see a rebirth in a great part of Morocco of the Berber republics." Or again, "The death of the Sultan Moulay 'Abd er Rahman was a signal for a *siba* lasting five years which desolated the entire plain." [38] Having made this distinction between *siba* as, first, a regular and ritualized form of anarchy arising during crises of succession, and, secondly, *siba* as the pulling away of a marginal area from central control, we shall use dissidence in this second sense. Our choice may be justified on the grounds that disorders engendered by crises of succession had neither the frequency nor the intensity to endanger the political stability of the nineteenth-century maghribi state. Thus, if we use *siba* as an indirect measure of the degree to which a state had succeeded in integrating its marginal populations within the boundaries of a delimited territory, we have a good indicator of both national unification and state centralization. In this context, the best indicator of degrees of dissidence is the proportion of units that refused taxation.

Another critical concept is that of *chefferie*. As an institution, the emergence of chiefs was a phenomenon that took place after the medieval period, and it does not constitute in any way, contrary to what many ethnologists have implied, a feudalization of North Africa. It is not enough, as Doutté has remarked,[39] that a chief lived in a castle, had pages, hunted with a falcon, that people prostrated themselves in his presence, and that he rendered justice, for him to be called a feudal baron, even if one adds quotation marks to the word feudal.

In North Africa, the conditions under which this intermediary leadership emerged and the relationship it had with the state were far from uniform. This form of leadership emerged from the inter-

---

[38] Montagne, *op. cit.* (n. 2), p. 286.
[39] E. Doutté, *op. cit.* (n. 23), pp. 400–402.

stices of a long and violent process of unification imposed from the top upon a relatively pluralistic society. In this context, a tribal chief could ascend through the sacrifice or violent integration of dissident tribes, including his own. In other instances, he played a Machiavellian game of courting the central power while presenting himself to the dissident tribes as the last rampart against a surrender to the state. In this position, he acted as either a partner or a counterpower. We can, ideally, measure the degree of power concentration and dispersion by combining some of the measures already suggested: (a) the ratio of agents appointed by the center; (b) the proportion of intermediary leadership; (c) the amount of tribes refusing taxation and maintaining their local assemblies as a sign of their independence from the central government. Although the available data do not lend themselves to a systematic response, we have enough evidence to present, in what follows, at least a schematic analysis of the particular constellation of power in each society; this provides us with a better foundation for the discussion of the different traditions in each state.

The central point from which the distinction between *Bled el-Makhzen* and *Bled es-Siba* emanated was Morocco, in which three groups continuously resisted state control. These three groups were the Rifains, Beraber, and the Chleuhs, and they were notorious for making their mountains inaccessible even to their own sultan. However, the real degree of state control remained obscure in past scholarship, which was satisfied with the official gross approximation that *Bled el-Makhzen* extended over a third of the country and to half of the population. This approximation, accepted by most French officers, is accurate only if *Bled el-Makhzen* is defined as the zones directly controlled by the monarchy. It is known, in fact, that in that area the monarchy tended to appoint its qaids to administer the small villages and the tribes; we also know that there were generally around three hundred qaids.[40] If this figure is com-

---

[40] There is a good description of this phenomenon in Erckmann, *Le Maroc moderne*, p. 122: "All the efforts of the sultan tend to substitute among the Berber tribes the qaid's authority for that of the *jema'a*, and in the Arab tribes to replace natural groups with artificial ones, in such a way as to augment the rate of taxation and to triumph more easily over local resistance. For this purpose, the sultan substitutes for the eighteen great *commandements* [military areas] which existed previously [throughout

pared to the global number of Moroccan tribes as estimated by colonial authorities, we find that direct control over the rural society did not extend over even half of the population.

But this is not the whole story. The most important feature of the power structure in nineteenth-century Morocco was that the political system was no longer composed of two protagonists, state and dissidents, but rather of three. The thread of antistate tradition was twice broken: on the one hand, by the expansion of the Makhzen; and, on the other, by the emergence of intermediary chiefs, Amghar-s, Chikh-s, and later the great Berber qaids. To a great extent, the constitution of these small rulerships, which were formed fifty years prior to the colonial takeover and which reached their highest point between 1897 and 1916, represented a genuine political revolution in the distribution of power. Why, however, did the tribal leaderships of the nineteenth century, unlike those of medieval times, forgo state conquest and limit their ambitions to state approval of their acquired powers in local areas? The answer to this question is twofold: first, the political stabilization of the state as it tightened control over the tribes (facilitated by the acquisition of firearms); and second, the religious monopoly achieved by the sultan.

If Evans-Pritchard's Nuer were still able to produce prophets in time of external threat, the tribal chiefs in Morocco were not. They ceased to manipulate the symbol of the sacré as their ancestors—*les hommes fétiches*—had done. As we shall see later, the sultan along with the saints and the nobility (*shorfa*) who were dependent upon the sultan succeeded in appropriating the religious forces and symbols and finally came to embody and manipulate them. For this reason, the vocation of the tribal leadership came to be primarily political, and chiefs like the Anflous, Mtouggi, Goundagi, Glawi, and Layyadi became the focal point of the most decisive political transactions concerning the whole Moroccan empire. From the amghar who imposed his domination upon a peripheral tribe to the grand regional chief whose strength called for his appointment

---

all the empire] a considerable number of small subdivisions—around 330—placing at the head of each a qaid. The new qaids are petty personages who would not think of resisting orders they receive; the cohesion of the tribes is being destroyed, and the taxes collected more easily."

as qaid, a complex confrontation was developing along all levels of the political hierarchy.

In the race for institutionalization of power, each chief, whatever his strength, made a career out of presenting himself to the state as the integrator of anarchical tribes and to the tribes as the last rampart against a fatal submission. This scramble for power weakened dissidence and rendered the chiefs powerful enough almost to share in a partnership with the monarchy, even though the whole process reflected a greater political unification of the empire. That the intermediary chiefs, more than the monarchy and, later, France, played a paradoxically major role in political unification can be seen from the way the Glawa brought a great confederation to submission, a fact well documented by Robert Montagne:

> It took the chiefs of Telwet four long years to reduce the great confederation. In the beginning, around 1890, the whole country resisted, without distinction as to leff-s, the penetration. The resistance was such that only a few cantons were won over . . . but when the amghar Zanifi's revolt came in 1906, aided by the amghars of Azilal, the Telwet policy succeeded then in gaining the two leff-s of Ait Tawiya, the Ait Oubial, and the Inmarakht, destroying the coalition. Finally, after the great *siba* of 1910 and 1913, the Glawa, solidly armed, conquered the valleys and put an end to the violent quarrel among amghars. . . .
>
> Because they were tired of the successive revolts in the country, the Glawa, beginning in 1913, undertook to organize it in such a way as to break any form of resistance. Their first effort was to destroy, in their armed passage, all the agadirs [storehouses of grain] existing in the valleys of Tifnout, Azilal, and Zagmouzen. Later, any pretext was used to ruin the collective fortresses of the small republics of the mountain. The most powerful amghars disappeared; they were replaced by small sheikhs, often without real influence, who, under the order of the Khalifats, became simple tax collectors. . . . The Ait Arb'in [the Assembly of the Forty] persisted as an intermediary to apply the customary law solely according to the whim of the qaid representative.[41]

The Berber chiefs' efforts at centralization, to the extent that the chiefs emerged from traditionally dissident areas, had two charac-

[41] Montagne, *op. cit.*, pp. 350–351.

teristics: In one sense, centralization proceeded everywhere by the elimination of local and more or less democratic institutions like the *I jma'an* and the *Ait Arb'in* and the substitution of a personal, despotic, and patrimonial form of government; but in another sense, although changes were justified in the name of the political and religious authority of the monarchy, sufficient autonomy was left to the intermediary leadership for the central power to regard its collaboration both as desirable and suspect. From this, the Moroccan monarchy drew some of its most significant features. Having emerged from an ethnically and culturally fragmented society and faced with multiple poles of power, the sultanate evolved a role of arbitration in which the classic style consisted of equilibration, mediation, and compromise.[42] To maintain the unity of the empire, the monarchy had to limit the arbitrariness of its notables and encourage intermediary chiefs to face dissident units, but it also had to check the power of the chiefs who might have become disloyal in time of crisis. In this function of reconciliation, the monarchy benefited most from its religious foundation of legitimacy.

To comprehend the crucial role played by the Moroccan monarchy, we need some knowledge of the traditions of political legitimacy in Islam and of the way in which Morocco's sultan came to represent almost the unique legitimate Moslem ruler. Islam possesses two relatively opposite political traditions which, following Clifford Geertz, we shall call the intrinsic and contractual forms of legitimacy. The first perceives authority as the emanation of individual charisma, tending to concentrate loyalty upon the descendants of the prophet. The second tradition tends rather to conceive of authority as based upon community approval and plebiscite; the foundation of authority rests in the election of a ruler and the recognition that the ruler owes his power to citizen-believers.

The Moroccan political system has been the only one, among the maghribi and Moslem societies in general, to combine both of these political traditions. The result was not simply an institution legitimate by default or justifiable on the grounds that, after all, order

---

[42] This idea is brilliantly analyzed by Clifford Geertz, *op. cit.* (n. 6), pp. 74–82, and by Ernest Gellner, "The Great Patron: A Reinterpretation of Tribal Rebellions," *Archives Européennes de Sociologie*, X:1 (1969), 61–69.

is preferable to anarchy, but one which truly captivated the imagination of the masses and the loyalty of the elite. Because of his mastery of the supernatural and the religious nobility of his ancestry, the sultan was able to meet the aspirations of rural Moslems who sought primarily the miraculous qualities intrinsic to the king's personal charisma. He also gained urban legitimation and acceptance by virtue of the fact that no investiture was actually carried out without the notables and the religious scholars' (*Ulama*) assent and that this binding arrangement (*bai'a*) was made in the name of the community. In summary, the critical achievement of the Alawites was that their sultanate "put together what, in most other parts of the Muslim world, were directly antithetical principles of political and religious organization: the principle that the ruler is ruler because he is supernaturally qualified to be so; and the principle that the ruler is ruler because the competent spokesmen of the Community have collectively agreed that he is." [43]

This religious legitimation extended even to marginal populations, which were officially in situations of political dissidence. History books are filled with cases in which the rural dissenters, having defeated the king's army and killed some of his bureaucrats, carefully led the emir of the believers to a more protected area. But, clearly, the monarchical power was above the pluralistic and diverse social forces and sustained the unity of the whole society through arbitration and religious transcendence. Throughout the last few centuries up until today, the Moroccan monarchy has been the alpha and omega of the entire society; in the contemporary situation, it has been impossible for the emerging elites to undertake any political change in the absence of the primordial context and obliged reference of the monarchy.

In Algeria, the dissident areas, or, at least, the zones not directly governed, were such that when the Turks agreed to the Convention of July 5, 1830, the only parts that were given over to the French, according to the historian Louis Rinn, were the city of Algiers, the Casbah, and the forts. It took France more than half a century to extend its control over the whole country. One of the anomalies which was, from the start, to weigh heavily upon the dynamic of the colonial system was that many communities which had never

---

[43] Geertz, *op. cit.*, p. 77.

recognized the Turkish state, and had even less reason to recognize that of the French, came to be perceived and summarily treated as rebellious and mutinous. "Neither the fiscal authority," writes Rinn, "nor the magistrate, nor the metropolitan administrations wanted to admit that certain groups of the Algerian population had remained, until 1830, independent from the dey and his lieutenants and had never submitted themselves to obligations like taxation which we [the French] intend to extend throughout and maintain for our own profit." [44]

Apart from the logic of conquest, some of the misunderstanding originates in the peculiar style of the Turkish government in Algeria. A penetrating examination of Turkish rule reveals that it governed Algeria without requiring the identification and loyalty of the society. It was as if the Turkish political system attempted to govern a fundamentally tribal society by exerting just enough power to levy taxes, without necessarily undertaking any effort at national unification. As a result of this policy, pursued for more than three centuries, and of the segmentary social structures, we find that the number of politically independent units and of semi-independent chiefs in nineteenth-century Algeria was sizable. Rinn's survey, summarizing most of the works by French officers and functionaries dealing with the Algerian territorial appropriation, yields some indirect evidence of power distribution in the pre-colonial period. Because this kind of inquiry is motivated primarily by territorial considerations, the results summarized in Table 2 concern rather heterogeneous entities ranging from military centers of the state (Makhzen) to independent tribal confederations.

Some caution is urged in interpreting this data; for the sake of simplicity, we did not include the territory occupied by each unit but preferred to concentrate upon the political components of each region. Suffice it to say that 516 units were classified in terms of direct or indirect occupation of 48 million hectares. The first advantage of the survey consists in showing the spatial universe of each major category. The 126 Makhzen groups and the 104 subject tribes controlled only 16 percent of the territory. A second group

[44] Louis Rinn,. "Le Royaume d'Alger sous le dernier Dey," *Revue Africaine* (1897), pp. 121–152, 331–350; (1898), pp. 5–21, 113–139, 289–309; (1899), pp. 105–141, 297–320; (Paris: Editions Jourdan, 1900) also presents the above in a special volume.

TABLE 2
ETHNOPOLITICAL UNITS OF PRECOLONIAL ALGERIA

Units	Regions				
	Algiers	Titri	Wahran	Qsantina	Total
Makhzen	19	14	46	47	126
Subject tribes	11	23	56	14	104
Semi-independent chiefs	20	12	29	25	86
Independent tribes	23	13	26	138	200
					516

composed of 86 grand chiefs and their confederations occupied nearly the same amount of territory—15 percent. The remaining territory—69 percent—was left to independent tribal units or was without any known form of appropriation.

The second advantage of the table is political: the table gains in classificatory coherence as we proceed from top to bottom—in other words, from the areas submitted to direct central control to the periphery. The last category includes 200 confederations and tribal units which were clearly autonomous; they refused to be taxed and were politically dissident. If we add the 86 semi-independent chiefs, we obtain a total which exceeds even that for Morocco; over half of the population was never brought under submission by the central power in Algeria. André Nouschi, who thoroughly canvassed the archives of the French Ministry of War concerning the region of Qsantina [Constantine], drew the same conclusion; he estimated that only one-third of the population was under the regular fiscal authority.[45]

In Algeria, the distinction between center and periphery assumed the name of *Bled et Turk* and *Bled el-Baroud*, or "land of the Turks" and "land of gunpowder" (the latter is sometimes called "land of abandonment," *Bled el-Khla*). In a way, neither of these areas was hospitable to the Algerians themselves because the government was in foreign hands and the marginal tribes could not be relied upon for cohesion and leadership in the society. As the contemporary political and intellectual elite of the Algerian society

[45] André Nouschi, *Enquête sur le Niveau de vie des populations rurales constantinoises* (Paris: Presses Universitaires de France, 1961), p. 99.

regard their past, it is solely in the intermediary *chefferies* that they find a link and a sense of continuity. This intermediary leadership antedates its Moroccan equivalents; some of them constituted a military nobility (*jawad*) which dominated the east of Algeria, and others were mainly religious chiefs who animated sects and were likely to influence the rest of the country. These forms of intermediary leadership seem to have gained strength in direct relation to the political absenteeism of the Turks and to the unwillingness to cultivate political and social unity in the country. While intermediary leaders were gaining esteem and distinction for the many services they rendered the tribal associations and, thus, developing autonomous power, the Turks strenuously tried to win their cooperation. The Turkish governors often found themselves overpowered by the heads of confederations, even though they did succeed in building alliances. The turks, however, were forced to avoid some chiefs, like the Awled Sidi Chikh and the chiefs of Jebel-Amour and Titri; communication was confined to a polite and distant exchange of gifts.

There are good reasons to believe that if they had been allied, the intermediary chiefs would have triumphed over the Turkish rule whose major defense was precisely the segmentation policy and the maintenance of divisions among them. As one might expect from the previous analysis, when the precarious equilibrium between the Turks and the Algerian leaders was upset in 1830 by the French conquest, it was not the Turks who stood the Algerian ground but one of the Algerian chiefs, Emir Abd-el-Kader. In the attempt to defend his country, Abd-el-Kader provided the first basis for national unification and for central authority. Even though it was short-lived and was stimulated by the colonial domination, Abd-el-Kader's enterprise deserves special discussion because of the emphasis we place upon the traditional legacy in nation building.

Colonial historians have distorted the meaning of the Algerian resistance by applying to it the convenient label of "Holy War." The contribution of the religious brotherhoods aside, there can be no understanding of Abd-el-Kader's social movement unless one gives necessary prominence to its political purpose of endowing Algeria with a national state comparable to those of Morocco and Tunisia. In a society that had always remained impervious to political unification, Abd-el-Kader's attempt to build cohesion into segmentary structures, to fill the political vacuum left by the Turkish administration, and to face the ferocious destructiveness of the French army marked him, for intellectuals and masses alike, as the symbol and legendary figure of national identity. He possessed the art of attracting to him the most significant Algerian elite, and when France later tried to recruit the best Algerian agents as intermediaries between its rule and the native population, it found, in the words of a high civil servant, that "the emir, with admirable foresight, had extracted Algeria's elite. We were then forced to address ourselves to second-rate men." [46]

For the purposes of our hypothesis, what is important to retain from this analysis is that there was not one but two political traditions in the precolonial history of Algeria: the Turkish rule, which was fragmentary, absenteeist, and utilitarian and which made no real attempt at societal unification or state building; and Abd-el-Kader's state which, though ephemeral and more valued for its potential than for its achievements, contained the possibilities of a unitary and legitimate political order.

Tocqueville's familiarity with North Africa was not surpassed by his expertise on France's *l'ancien régime* or on democracy in America. As a scholar and a politician, Tocqueville was struck by the contrast between the two political traditions in Algeria. He wrote, "The government of Abd-el-Kader is already more centralized, more agile, and stronger than that of the Turks had ever been." In his analysis of the Algerian resistance to the French conquest, Tocqueville could not have applied the appropriate concepts developed only later by anthropologists, but he did perceive in a markedly Khaldunian manner the kind of structural constraints which segmentary social structures tend to impose on societal cohesion. He showed how in a few years, Abd-el-Kader was able to build a modern army and to triumph over, if not neutralize, tribal division and dissidence:

> With his army, he raises taxes regularly which allowed him to supply and sustain it [the army] . . . and to build military stores, to gather resources, and to undertake long-range projects. With this permanent force, he is always ready either to prevent or to crush completely all resistance, whereas his opponents must go to the

[46] C. Rousset, *La conquête de l'Algérie* (Paris: 1841), I, 284.

trouble of gathering their forces and reaching an agreement in advance if they are to attack him successfully. Thus, he leads the majority through enthusiasm and the minority through fear. Such is the secret of his power, and it is not difficult to comprehend because what is motivating Abd-el-Kader is not new in the world. A social work is taking place in Africa today which is closely analogous to what happened at the close of the Middle Ages in Europe. Abd-el-Kader, who probably never heard of what took place in fifteenth-century France, is acting vis-à-vis the tribes precisely in the same way that our kings, and in particular Charles VII, have acted against feudality. . . . Without knowing the history of these princes, but obeying similar instincts, he disperses and destroys ancient and powerful families each day and replaces these with new ones who owe their authority to him and who have no ancient or well-established power with which to threaten him. He is making war not only with the French but also with the hereditary aristocracy of his own country.

With this, Tocqueville both registered his admiration for Abd-el-Kader and recommended his destruction:

One should not be overconfident to the point of believing that this power, after its brilliant moment, will disappear as have many others in the past. On the contrary, one should fear that Abd-el-Kader is in the process of building among the Algerians, who are surrounding us [the French army], a form of power more centralized, more agile, stronger, more experienced, and more ordered than any of its predecessors for centuries in this part of the world. It is, thus, necessary to try to prevent him from accomplishing this frightful work.[47]

The political traditions of Algeria had been historically weak, but had Abd-el-Kader succeeded, he would have provided precolonial Algeria with a state comparable to those of Morocco and Tunisia. Because all national political traditions were destroyed by France, especially at a time when an overall effort of centralization and unification was underway, Algeria's future was rendered more vulnerable. In facing the challenges ahead, the political elites would be unable to utilize any past residue of organization to buttress their sense of national identity.

[47] Alexis de Tocqueville, "Ecrits et discours politiques," Vol. III of *Oeuvres Complètes* (Paris: Gallimard, 1962), 222–224.

Tunisia, contrary to Morocco and Algeria, experienced far less political fragmentation; the classic territorial distinction between center and periphery was not decisive there. There was neither a Moroccan *siba* nor the "land of gunpowder" characteristic of precolonial Algeria. As Augustin Bernard noted, "There is something of a gradation across North Africa: In Morocco, there are enormous confederations like the Beraber; in Algeria, powerful tribes like the Larba and the Ouled-Nayl; and in Tunisia, only weak and miniscule tribes. Here the tribes had already dissolved before our arrival, and some of them, like those of the Sahel, have even lost their names." [48]

The governability of Tunisian society is confirmed not only by the absence of zones of organized dissidence but also by the absence of an autonomous *chefferie*. There tends to be a consensus among historians that the precolonial Tunisian state was by far the most centralized and most highly integrated of the maghribi states. Throughout the country, local institutions ranging from the *mi'ad* (local assembly) to the customary law were increasingly supplanted by supralocal institutions dealing with administration, education, justice, and economy. Without having undergone the whole process of modernization, the local life of the most isolated village had become intimately related and open to major decisions taken in the central cities. This is one reason why Tunisia failed to attract the ethnological studies on local communities that tended to blossom in Algeria and Morocco, where no retiring officer worth his salt would consider leaving office before writing his personal theory on the ineluctable conflict between Berbers and Arabs.

It is true, however, that ethnic solidarities persist and become visible in times of antifiscal crises; during these crises, for instance, it is not unusual for rural groups to reactivate traditional institutions against the abusive rise of taxation. What is different about

[48] Augustin Bernard, *L'Evolution du Nomadisme* (Algiers: Imprimerie Orientale, 1906), pp. 293–294; similar conclusions are found in Jean Ganiage, *Les origines du Protectorat français en Tunisie* (Paris: Presses Universitaires de France, 1959), pp. 161–176. Six centuries before, Ibn Khaldun remarked, "There are more traces of sedentary culture in Tunisia than in all the Maghrib; this is because the ancient dynasties have lasted longer in Tunisia, the customs and institutions are rather more similar to those of Egypt, and the great stream of exchange is intense between the two countries." Khaldun, *op. cit.* (n. 7), p. 764.

these ethnic solidarities in the Tunisian context is that they rarely took a primordial turn capable of undermining national unity. In 1736, a famous crisis of succession divided the country between two camps, the Bachi-s and the Husseini-s. A segmentary society would foster a division of, on the one hand, the state and the urban centers, and, on the other hand, the tribal dissidents who compose the bulk of the rural society. But, in Tunisia, included in each camp were significant allies representing all levels of society: the court, the cities, and the tribes. The same can be said of the dramatic insurrection of 1864. Originating from the monarchy's decision to double taxes, this generalized revolt engaged both the rural society and the urban coastal area of the Sahel.[49]

In other words, major social conflicts were channeled through the existing institutions and did not portend the usual threat of disintegration inherent in primordial movements. Revolts in nineteenth-century Tunisia appealed to the Ottoman authority, and concluded, no matter what degree of violence was entailed, with demands for participation in the hierarchy of power and the reduction of oppressive measures. This shows how deeply central authority had penetrated the fabric of the society and to what extent the political destiny of Tunisia remained in the hands of the men who happened to be in power.

Following a succession of beys and ministers who managed, through their vain imitations of Europe, to bring the country to financial bankruptcy, the appointment of Khayr-el-Din, writer and statesman of the highest caliber, was unanimously recognized as a sign of coming rejuvenation and reform.[50] The Tunisian population was not disappointed. Sweeping measures were employed to consolidate the administration of the country and to reorganize entirely the system of taxation. The modern college Es-Sadiqia which

[49] Bice Slama, *La Révolte de 1864 en Tunisie* (Tunis: Maison Tunisienne de l'Edition, 1967).

[50] The philosophy of Khayr-el-Din and his conception of the modern state are expressed in his book *Aqwam el-Masalik Li Ma'rifati Ahwal el-Mamalik* [The Surest Path to the Knowledge of the Conditions of Kingdoms], published in Tunis in 1867. See the English translation, "The Surest Path to Knowledge Concerning the Conditions of Countries," translated with introduction by Leon Carl Brown, Harvard Middle Eastern Monograph Series, 1967. For background on constitutional reforms prior to colonialism, see Mohieddine Mabrouk, "Regard sur l'histoire constitutionnelle tunisienne," *L'Action*, August 20, 1970.

still exists today, was designed to provide the state with well-trained civil servants. Thus, unlike the monarchy of Morocco, the Tunisian monarchy owed its acceptance by the people to these kinds of reforms, rather than religious sanctification.

The noteworthy allegiance of the Tunisian people to a monarchy sponsored by the Ottoman Empire can be illustrated in this colorful example. In 1854, the Awlad 'Aziz, deciding to take refuge in Libya because the taxes they had to pay were beyond their means, wrote a letter to the king. After enumerating their grievances concerning fiscal excess and expressing their intention to leave the territory in order to avoid opposition to the state through force, they added this astonishing formula: "We have been your subjects from father to son; and we want you to know now that escape in front of power is a form of obedience." [51]

Aside from the autonomy they achieved vis-à-vis the Ottoman Empire and their total commitment to the internal governance of the country, the rulers provided Tunisia with a legacy which would have long-range effect, namely, the participation of the local notability in the exercise of power. Under the pressure of the notability and of the emerging intelligentsia, the monarchy, in 1861, did concede to a constitution, which limited, to an extent, the absolutist form of power and aided in the expression of various political interests. Unfortunately, the constitution was later rescinded; paradoxically, the main agent of its elimination was France, whose constitutional interests happened to be better served by a despotic government. In the years to come, the constitution would be the unifying symbol and battle cry of the whole national elite as it tried to eliminate the monarchy and free Tunisia from colonial rule.

One of the objectives of Part I has been to clarify colonial and contemporary scholarship on maghribi societies. To justify past foreign domination and to support current theories of underdevelopment, many scholars have described the maghribi societies as

---

[51] Letter from the Miad, i.e., the full Assembly of the Awlad 'Aziz, addressed to the bey in 1854, *Archives of the Tunisian Government*, no. 18–205; as quoted by Mohammed Chérif in "Les Movements paysans dans la Tunisie du XIXe siècle," in *Mouvements Nationaux d'Indépendence* . . . , Paris: A. Colin, 1971.

constantly paralyzed by tribal struggles from the twelfth century on, as if these societies never possessed any political tradition or a sense of what Lévi-Strauss calls accumulation. Our analysis has focused upon the fundamental political and social transformations since medieval times and has demonstrated that nineteenth-century colonial domination did not take place in mere segmentary societies but among countries endowed with national political institutions and centuries of uninterrupted cultural identity. Through a comparative analysis of Morocco, Algeria, and Tunisia, we have shown how definite progress was achieved in terms of territorial sovereignty, administration, and legitimate use of force. We have assembled enough data to emphasize Burckhardt's idea according to which the state was established as a work of art.

One theoretical shortcoming of the approach to nation building is the twentieth-century criteria of established polities. A complete understanding of the subject requires great attention to the dramatic, difficult ways in which European nations were first founded; a reading of Burckhardt's description of the fourteenth- and fifteenth-century states would enlighten our contemporary theoreticians of modernization. In all the states Burckhardt studied, republican and despotic alike, he found that "the foundation of the system was and remained illegitimate and nothing could remove the curse which rested upon it." Closely related to the political illegitimacy of most fifteenth-century dynasties was "public indifference" and political instability:

> The conquests and usurpation which had hitherto taken place in the Middle Ages rested on real or pretended inheritance and other such claims. . . . Here the attempt was openly made to found a throne by wholesale murder and endless barbarities, by the adoption, in short, of any means with a view to nothing but the end pursued. . . .
>
> But, wherever this vicious tendency is overcome or in any way compensated, a new fact appears in history—the State as the outcome of reflection and calculation, the State as a work of art. This new life displays itself in a hundred forms, both in the republican and in the despotic States.[52]

[52] Jacob Burckhardt, *The Civilization of the Renaissance in Italy* (New York and Oxford: Phaidon, 1950), pp. 9–17.

Similarly, for the Maghrib, we have shown how state building and national unification was a violent enterprise taking centuries, destroying local institutions, and culminating in despotic forms of power. As in the European case, these steps have been the building blocks of today's national configurations, and in the history of nations, these processes seem rather to be the rule than the exception.

The intention of this work, however, is not to indulge the opposite extreme and write an ideological history of the Maghrib, because the established nineteenth-century states, as is clear from this study, were far from being polished works of art. Having considered our three political systems from the perspectives of cultural pluralism of the society, legitimacy of the political order, and degree of administrative centralization, we concluded, first, that national unification, although it was prematurely offset by colonialism, was an ongoing process far from being fully attained, and secondly, that the combination of these three dimensions placed Tunisia in the most fortuitous position for national integration and the development of political institutions. Although both Morocco and Algeria had little centralization and great ethnic pluralism, Morocco possessed a greater sense of cohesion than Algeria, owing to its strong religious foundation of legitimacy. For these reasons, the three societies had, from the beginning, unequal potentialities for national construction and state organization. To evaluate more fully the impact of these traditions on contemporary political systems, we must turn next to the influence of foreign domination on these traditions and on the maghribi societies as a whole.

Part II

COLONIAL DOMINATION:
SOCIAL CHANGE AND
UNDERDEVELOPMENT

All maghribi societies have been subjected to colonial domination, and, thus, none of their political traditions and institutions have been spared the tumult of assault, distortion, and ultimate redefinition. The changes and disorganization have been such that even today, long after decolonization, the impact endures and continues to shape the given social material and the major political choices. For this reason, one must acknowledge, at the outset, that European domination has not been a mere parenthesis in the evolution of these societies but a basic component of their history and of the structuring of their societies. We hasten to add, therefore, that European participation does not constitute an innocent and neutral part of the destiny of these countries but was and is part of the problem of decay and development in the area. Because particular outcomes depend, in each instance, on the interaction between patterns and forms of domination, on the one hand, and preexisting social structures, on the other, we must proceed from a definition of colonialism that includes its historical variations and its operative mechanisms.

We shall define modern colonialism as distinct from types of domination characteristic of historic empires described by Wolfram Eberhard in his *Conquerors and Rulers*[1] and from early mercantile colonialism in the style of the *l'ancien régime*. Modern colonialism is a European enterprise of expansion and domination spawned by the combined effects of rational bourgeois capitalism, demographic pressures, and power struggles among the nation-states of Europe. A detailed examination of such an expansion and its accompanying techniques makes more appropriate the word "imperialism." The motivations for imperialism are manifold: "A country may seek

[1] Wolfram Eberhard, *Conquerors and Rulers: Social Forces in Medieval China* (Leiden: E. J. Brill, 1952).

colonies in order to settle 'surplus populations,' that is, people who cannot readily be absorbed in various institutional orders. It may seek colonies in order to expand its politically guaranteed market area; or in order to win and establish a politically guaranteed monopoly over resources, raw materials, and labor, or it may merely wish to deny access to such resources to other powers. Again, and this is more modern, one power may seek to expand its military area of control by establishing naval and air bases abroad without assuming overt political responsibilities in the face of foreign political bodies. It may prefer other nations to adjust to whatever implications ensue from its establishment of such bases." [2]

Our main purpose in this part is to inquire into the differential impact of imperialism, which will hereafter be called degrees of colonization. It is obvious that one should not take the colonial project at its face value but should concentrate upon its actual practices and unintended consequences. At the same time, imperialism does not manifest itself everywhere in the same ways, contrary to the implications of its popular definition. One means of distinguishing different manifestations of imperialism is to divide the phenomenon into its key dimensions: economic, political, and cultural. Additional variables such as the duration and ideology of the colonization, the size of the settler population, and the institutional and organizational strength of the dominated society determine the specific configurations. If we assume that the objectives of colonialism are, in the broadest sense, economic, we can, in an introductory fashion, submit the following typology: (a) segmental colonialism, a form of domination that although motivated by limited economic purposes, does not undertake the destruction of the political and cultural order; (b) instrumental colonialism, a form of domination that is also exclusively economic but does not hesitate, when necessary, to intervene in other levels of the social structure; (c) total colonialism, an unrestrained domination of the whole society at all levels, based upon the negation of the social,

[2] Hans Gerth and C. Wright Mills, *Character and Social Structure: The Psychology of Social Institutions* (New York: Harcourt, Brace Harbinger Books, 1953), p. 205; see also J. S. Furnivall, *Colonial Policy and Practice: A Comparative Study of Burma and the Netherlands India* (New York: New York University Press, 1956), pp. 276–319; and Clark Kerr *et al.*, *Industrialism and Industrial Man* (Cambridge, Mass.: Harvard University Press, 1960), pp. 62–66.

cultural, and economic order of the colonized country. Although this typology seems generally applicable, it is most appropriate to North Africa, in which Morocco approximated the segmental model, Tunisia the instrumental, and Algeria the total.

This analysis does not overlook, need we emphasize, that imperial, especially French, administration tended to be exerted in a total manner and that transaction at one level of social reality never occurred to the exclusion of perturbations at other levels. The virtues of these ideal-typical constructions, however, will depend on their usefulness for analyzing the essential sociopolitical changes of the maghribi societies under the colonial impact. This part will treat directly the political and economic impacts of colonialism, and only secondarily the cultural changes; the total societal reacttions and constructive efforts at decolonization will be reserved for Part III.

Chapter 3

POLITICAL DOMINATION

The intensity of the colonial impact and, more specifically, the degree to which each maghribi society was politically subjugated depended upon a set of factors which, though tending to overlap, deserve to be kept analytically distinct. The most obvious factor is, of course, the length of time of colonial rule; whereas Algeria was invaded in 1831, and Tunisia in 1881, the French occupation in Morocco began much later—in 1912—and was officially instituted by 1934. Colonial duration was, hence, of 132 years in Algeria (until 1962), of 75 years in Tunisia, and of 44 years in Morocco (the latter two countries having become independent in 1956). More to the point are other factors: identification of the specific agents of colonialism, the prevailing administrative practices, and the status of the national state under foreign occupation.

The Agents of Colonial Domination

The beneficiaries of the colonial system were overwhelmingly European and only secondarily local notabilities. It is, however, important to distinguish the ruling categories that embodied colonial domination, instituted specific forms of government, and whose influence upon present political structures is still deeply felt. The military was the foremost agent of total colonialism in Algeria. Indeed, rarely has war as a means of domination, integration, and disintegration played such an important part as it has in this country. For a long time, Algeria was considered, not a colony, but a department in the Ministry of War which gave France most of its ministers of war, like Pelissier, Bourbaki, Mac-Mahon, and most of its Chiefs of Staff. There were three main reasons for the excessive militarization of the colonial enterprise: first, the multiple pressures of the most diverse European strata—businessmen, poor peasants, and political deportees who wanted land at any price; second, the pervasive unanimity of French society, from the left to the right and from the Saint-Simonians to the Church, as to the military occupation; third, the ardent struggle and resistance waged by Algerian society for more than forty years. These and other reasons contributed to the disproportionate weight of the military and of the elements of force and coercion in the French domination of Algeria.

Consequently, Algerian society was placed in "a state of war" every time it was deemed necessary; as Lieutenant General Bugeaud said, "in order to dominate it, modify it, and plunder it for the profit of a new people." Addressing the members of the National Assembly, Bugeaud added, "You will always have to be the stronger, either through a permanent army or by the nature and constitution of a dominating people." It took an army of one hundred thousand troops more than seven years to subdue the five to ten thousand men in the army of Emir Abd-el-Kader. To this end, everything imaginable was deployed: incineration of whole communities, destruction of villages, and burning of crops. The Algerian population which numbered 2,770,000 in 1861 had diminished through the ravages of war, famine, and cholera to 2,125,000 eleven years later.

As it accomplished this, the army appropriated to itself all domains of human activity, institutionalizing a reflex that could be satisfied only by total submission and total control, even to the point of consecrating violence as a permanent means of government. Because it operated in a predominantly rural society made up of scattered groups, most of which were openly resisting foreign aggression, the army tried its famous *regroupement* policy. This policy consisted in reassembling as much of the population as possible in areas similar to concentration camps; such a policy represents the essence of total domination. "We firmly believe," wrote a military theorist, "that the idea of these tent-cities in which we shall imprison the Arab population will ensure the peace of the country. It is necessary indeed to regroup these people who are everywhere and nowhere; it is essential to render them vulnerable to our seizure. When we capture them, we shall be able to do many of the things which are impossible today and which will, perhaps, permit us to take possession of their minds once we have secured their bodies." [3]

These ideologies and their practices were bound to contaminate

[3] Capitaine Chàrles Richard, *Etude sur l'insurrection du Dahra (1845–1846)*, pp. 190–192; as quoted by Mostefa Lacheraf in "Constantes politiques et militaires dans les guerres coloniales d'Algérie (1830–1960)," in his *L'Algérie Nation et Société* (Paris: Maspero, 1965), pp. 203–289.

the European population and the civil bureaucracy, which had already been exposed to and fashioned by the war psychosis. They precipitated mainly the disintegration of Algerian society, to the extent that acts of dispossession and segregation were not temporary and accidental measures but became permanent institutional procedures. These measures were so deep-seated in the Algerian historical context that 132 years after the beginning of colonial domination, they were still being used to resist the war for national liberation.

In Morocco, the agent of segmental and segmentalist domination was clearly not the military as such but the conqueror-ethnologist. Without overlooking the important role played by the army, one can argue that colonial ethnology provided the colonizer with a vision of Moroccan society which, though not scientifically accurate, was highly instrumental as a weapon for domination. The uses of ethnology for political ends can be best illustrated by a description of the strategic role of the famous officer-ethnologist Robert Montagne during the Rif resistance. In his last book, Montagne told the story of the dismantlement of this resistance:

> Supported by Marshal Lyautey, I had just passed two years in the western High Atlas studying the conflict between the grand qaids and the Berber republics of the high valleys when the events of the Rif abruptly took a tragic turn. I offered my services to study the dissident zone of the north through planned reconnaissance and intelligence reports. In a few months, it was possible to establish a provisional map of the whole massif, to study the tribes, including their ancient organization and their political life, and, finally, to assemble all the essential information pertaining to these events which would permit as exact a measurement as possible of both the power and the fragility of the movement.[4]

Montagne reached two conclusions at the end of the inquiry: that the head of the resistance, Abd-el-Krim, was powerful enough to make capture of his forces impossible; and that the use of a classic army against guerrilla resistance was ineffective. The lessons he drew from his research on the Berbers and the Makhzen and his political common sense led Montagne to suggest to the army a

[4] Robert Montagne, *Révolution au Maroc* (Paris: France Empire, 1953), pp. 162–165.

strategy of isolation and dismantlement of the ruling tribe and its leadership:

> The mountain roads reveal the existence of a sure and short passage in the north of Taza which could lead our troops as far as Targuist, geographical center of the war confederation of Abd-el-Krim. If we attempt it [a passage] in one quick leap, the arrival of our troops could easily and immediately lead to the disintegration of a movement which is more powerful in appearance than in reality. The prestige of Abd-el-Krim has been increasingly reinforced through his victories, but we may hope that by using force on the central nucleus of the coalition [of tribes], we can succeed in breaking it with one stroke.[5]

The army adopted his project recommendations and executed them successfully. Montagne's reward was a seat at the committee meeting for negotiation with Abd-el-Krim. "It was for an observer, like myself, a rare occasion to be able to judge the psychology and the personal values of a real statesman who appeared to embody the living symbol of the tribes' eternal resistance." [6]

Consequently, from the beginning, French colonialism in Morocco was oriented toward the study of the Moroccan culture—a study that was utilized as an instrument for domination by the privileged. The preparation of ethnographic maps and index cards containing information on tribes became the obligatory arsenal of each officer; for Gallieni, "Each officer who succeeds in drawing a sufficiently complete ethnographic map of the territory he commands is on the verge of obtaining its pacification." The ethos of the Moroccan political culture and attitudes of deference to local leadership became the working assumptions of French officers and administrators. In the documents of the Department of Political Affairs, one can find the following counsel to officers: "The rebel of old who submits to us is not guilty; he defended his land and his independence." As we shall discuss later, the manipulation of cultural and political loyalties in the rural society—a manipulation completely missing in Algeria—made of it a Moroccan stronghold for the new colonial regime. Somehow, cultural expertise proved more efficient than brute force and mere superior weaponry.

[5] *Ibid.*
[6] *Ibid.*

In Tunisia, the civil bureaucrat symbolized the agent of colonial domination. The predominance of the bureaucracy had several roots: the weak tribal segmentation of the society, the absence of any significant resistance to colonial occupation, the centralization of the national state, and, finally, Jules Ferry's preference for pursuing a purely economic form of domination. As noted by Brunschwig, the only way in which Jules Ferry could "succeed in Tunisia, as he wanted to, was to do the opposite of what failed in Algeria." A policy of colonization for the producers and by the producers did not require a central military presence. Even more, in order to implement his policy, "it was necessary to renounce the annexation of Tunisia which the military was insisting upon, thus rendering the protectorate not only civilian but, eventually, even antimilitarist." [7]

Administrative Practice: Regional and Local

The main trend of the colonial experience was the shifting of the basic structures of the society from tribal forms of solidarity to more differentiated social structures. From the vantage point of the new administration, the major achievement was to finish off the process begun in the past by incorporating tribal and marginal units into the administered society. The central government extended its control over the whole territory, fixing frontiers and bringing the most diverse elements in each society under a relatively coordinated, hierarchical apparatus. Because of its implication for later developments, the questions to be discussed in each instance are: What have been the modalities and practices of administrative unification? What have been the costs to the native society, and what shifts have occurred in the local distribution of power?

French administration did not usually display the criteria of universalism, impersonal neutrality, specificity, and achievement orientation that sociologists have been eager to ascribe to it.[8] Instead, the empirical facts of European administration reveal improvised formulas combining control techniques of maghribi and metropoli-

---

[7] Henri Brunschwig, *Le Colonisation Française* (Paris: Calman-Levy, Collection Liberté de l'Esprit, directed by Raymond Aron, 1949), pp. 55–56.

[8] For example, S. N. Eisenstadt, *Essays on Sociological Aspects of Political and Economic Developments* (Paris: Mouton, 1961).

tan origins; the manifest and latent functions of such control techniques were to induce, if not the subjugation, at least the neutralization of the dominated society. The debilitating and fundamentally coercive features of this administration did not escape Tocqueville, who remarked, "We did not bring to Africa our liberal institutions; instead, we dispossessed it of the only ones which resembled them." [9]

Although Algeria was considered an integral part of France and of the French administration, and received a lion's share of its military control, it was, paradoxically, characterized by a lack of real government and was, in fact, underadministered. This can be seen, first, in the policy pursued for the dismantlement of the social structure. The official principle of this policy was that "in terms of administration, the objective assigned is the disintegration of the tribe." For this, three measures were devised: cantoning the population, thrusting it back (*refoulement*), and segregating it. The *cantonnement* of the Algerian population, inaugurated in 1861, consisted of confining the tribes to limited territorial areas and denying them the right to leave their districts without the permission of the military. The Europeans, in their quest for land, were, however, permitted to travel through and settle in tribal territories until they grew dissatisfied with this one-way procedure. They then requested of and obtained from the authorities the further removal of the Algerian people. The *refoulement* operations were aimed at transplanting the Algerians to more distant land, mainly in the south. As we shall see in treating the economic impact of colonialism, confiscation was also a method of *refoulement;* and had it been completely carried out, it would have confined the entire native population to the desert, leaving the productive land of the Tell and of the coast to the French colonists.

The administrative practice was equally damaging in terms of dissolution of the social fabric, for, as René Maunier has written, "In deporting entire groups and dispersing them, no one troubled to reflect that by scattering them, their societies were broken up, their unity was destroyed, their traditions swamped, their customary law obliterated. From the social point of view, this type of segregation [the transplanting of the population] is a far more serious thing than *cantonnement* or *refoulement*, for it means the destruc-

[9] Alexis de Tocqueville, "Ecrits et discours politiques," *op. cit.,* p. 207.

tion of the tribal order, the dissolution of the ancestral group, which often forfeits even its name, even the memory of its past exploits." [10] In time, however, the military administration, organized along the lines of Arab *bureaux*, a replica of the Turkish administration, came under fire of the French settlers themselves, who complained out of their lust for more land and their desire for simple civilian rights.

When new administrative arrangements were substituted—departments and communes—they appeared to represent a civilian administration; but in reality, they represented a caste system based primarily on service to the Europeans and exclusion of the Algerians, whose presence in these bodies was deemed "an affront to the dignity of the French citizens." In the mixed communes, in particular, where 60 to 80 percent of the Algerian people were kept, the population was totally at the mercy of administrators whose function always remained military. Sporting military uniforms, promenading on horseback, and practicing praetorian justice (*chikaya*), these men represented an administration of the most patrimonial kind. In its content, it was highly repressive. From 1881 to 1930, it ruled by emergency powers: French administrators were given the powers which usually belong to officers in time of war. The Algerian population was thus subjected to exceptional penalties, ranging from administrative confinement to collective forfeiture and from arbitrary sequestration to the imposition of an internal travel permit which was required for any travel beyond one's district.

One enduring result of this form of total administration was the decay of urban and rural leaderships, a decay purposefully induced by the French in their struggle against what they called the Algerian feudality. Those tribal chiefs of second rank who were appointed as assistants (*Adjoint Indigène*) not only served the foreign domination but also lost all authority with Algerians, if they had ever had it in the first place. There was also a fundamental disjunction between the administrative apparatus and the Algerian people it was supposed to serve. In its drive for total control, dividing what was previously united among the Arab-speaking peoples and uniting what was previously divided among the Berber-speaking peoples, French colonialism found itself in the unenviable position of having

[10] René Maunier, *The Sociology of Colonies* (London: Routledge and Kegan Paul, 1949), II, 481.

official administrative assemblies not recognized by the people and subterranean popular assemblies not recognized by the authorities. This disjunction persisted for a long time without the realization of officials; only in 1954, the year of the Revolution, did an administrator of Kabylia acknowledge that throughout the colonial period there existed two local assemblies, one official and one subterranean, which entertained relationships of complementarity, ostracism, and conflict. There were generally two bodies, two cash boxes, and two sets of regulations; "It is apparent that in the daily life, the *Qanun-s* [customary law] were more often used than the Articles of the Penal Code." [11]

It is not difficult to understand that a society so politically and structurally eroded would develop for its survival the only defense mechanisms left to it—an avoidance of and refuge from the colonizer and a consequent utilization of practices and symbols that constituted his negation. In other words, the society adhered to a traditionalism of despair. Nor it is surprising that for all its excessive intervention, the French administration was both vain and crippling. Tocqueville described its effects:

> I am convinced that the civil power in Algiers is the most oppressive and the most evil. . . . It manifests itself everywhere, ceaselessly regulating, directing, modifying, touching, and retouching each day, each thing. We can easily comprehend the trouble and social malaise which it creates, if we imagine our French administration, with all the domineering, inquisitive, and bothersome instincts it inherited from the Empire and the red-tape habits it acquired from the Restoration, acting in a country where one has no right of appeal against it to opinion, civil tribunals, criminal courts, or even administrative tribunals. The truth of the matter is that there exists no society. There are men, but there is no social body.[12]

It was more practical for France, and less costly, to impose a form of indirect control in Tunisia. The administrative apparatus inherited from precolonial times was maintained, in its entirety, at the local and regional levels; even at the center, Tunisian ministers and council representatives were actively involved in the process of governing. The principal colonial innovations in ad-

[11] Jean Morizot, *L'Algérie Kabylisée* (Paris: J. Peyronnet, 1962), p. 117.
[12] Tocqueville, *op. cit.*, pp. 261–268.

ministrative practice were to facilitate the expression of bourgeois interests both through the Grand Conseil and the municipalities patterned after those of Tunis and to tighten administrative centralization by reducing the number of qaids from eighty to thirty-seven and the number of sheikhs from two thousand to six hundred. Aside from these changes, Tunisian administrative affairs remained in Tunisian hands. Although it is true that the nineteen *contrôleurs* discreetly supervised the body of qaids, they had no direct contact whatsoever with the Tunisian population; according to the law (Circular of July 22, 1887), "The *contrôleur civil* does not administer."

As things turned out, then, this pattern of administration not only alienated the Tunisian people from colonialism but also from their own administrative officials. Although administration by notables had checked colonial initiative and reduced the amount of social disintegration, Tunisians have never forgiven it its compromises and its opportunism. In contrast with many colonized societies, the Tunisian national movement demanded, from the beginning, not merely the end of colonial domination but also an end to the notables' rule.

The effectiveness of colonial domination in Tunisia also depended on the absence of tribal segmentation and dissent. It was for this reason, among others, that France settled for partial control. But the results in Tunisia were curious ones. Tribal dissidence led to severe military control in Algeria and Morocco, but it also fomented a grass-roots sentiment in favor of elected local assemblies and for revival of the old Berber republics. This vision of grass-roots democracy survives today. No similar visions were introduced in the Tunisian context, and it is ironic that France's major contribution was to reinforce the preexisting, highly centralized administration.

Morocco represents perhaps the most complicated administrative structure of the three societies. Neither directly administered by foreigners as in Algeria nor administered by nationals as in Tunisia, Morocco has been a country in which "the symbols of legitimacy, the loci of power, and the instruments of authority were rudely dissociated." [13] The complexity is revealed by the fact that although the monarchy was preserved (as will be discussed later), the admin-

[13] Clifford Geertz, *Islam Observed: Religious Development in Morocco and Indonesia, op. cit.,* p. 63.

istration of the society lay in the hands of European agents who acted in the name of the monarchy and through a body of qaids formally appointed by the sultan. The relevant question as to who governed is not difficult to answer. Unlike the *contrôleur civil* of Tunisia, who intervened only indirectly in daily life, the French officer in Morocco reduced most of the qaids to the rank of assistants and intervened directly in all branches of administration: the selection of assistants to local judges, collection of taxes, agricultural planning, and aid to settlers and tribes.

The most prominent qaids, however, conserved their power during the colonial administration. The policy of protecting and acting solicitous toward the Berber qaids, in particular, had fortunate results for the French, who later used these qaids and their tribal solidarities against both the sultan and the emerging national movement. To understand subsequent developments, it is important to remember that colonialism is not merely a synonym for administrative unification. Instead, it preserves the separation and divisions that it finds. As Frantz Fanon remarked, "Colonialism does not simply acknowledge the existence of tribes; it also reinforces and separates them. The colonial system encourages chieftaincies and keeps alive the old *Marabout* confraternities." [14] From these descriptions, it follows that the administration was far from homogeneous. Local variations and different configurations of power in each region resulted in an administration which was particularistic and scarringly heterogeneous. Consequently, each region eventually existed in an autonomous world of its own in which there was no reference to a national political framework. It is understandable that the combination of these factors resulted in the retardation of the movement for national consciousness and decolonization.

Status of the Autochthonous State

The distinction between direct and indirect administration so often used in literature on colonialism, although it has merit for purposes of generalization, has serious shortcomings. This was obvious in the previous case under discussion—Morocco. There, the situation is so complex that neither direct nor indirect administra-

[14] Frantz Fanon, *Les Damnés de la Terre* (Paris: Maspero, 1960), p. 51.

tion is a useful conceptual tool. In terms of our typology, the most appropriate description is that of a segmental form of domination. This description is appropriate because Morocco's political order has been maintained but is also segmentary and because the structure of authority and power is designed to provide the colonizer with an extensive area of manipulation in both administrative and ethnic affairs.

The distinction between direct and indirect administration has a second shortcoming: It emphasizes European forms of control and tends to treat indigenous political institutions as a residual category. One might forget that colonialism is a passing enterprise, a historical phenomenon, but the autochthonous state and its national institutions must eventually adapt to and live with colonial domination's permanent changes and transformations. For these reasons, the status of the national state during the time these structural transformations are taking place represents probably the most powerful element of prediction concerning future political development and decay in the societies. Thus, when significant changes are reshaping the structure of the society, it is important to understand the previous foundations of authority, power, and collective identity. Our analysis has continued to emphasize the state as the heart of political institutions and as the symbol of collective identity; therefore, whether a state is maintained, strengthened, or simply dismantled under colonial domination will have decisive effect upon the structuring of national elites and the pattern of political and economic development.

With the essential aspects of our typology of total colonialism in mind, one finds it consistent that the first act of the French army in Algeria was the systematic dismantlement of any existing formation of the political state, whether it was the ancient Turkish establishment or the emerging popular political organization of Abd-el-Kader. Tocqueville writes, "In place of the one [administration] that they destroyed to its roots, the French found it useful to substitute French administration. . . . From the previous [Algerian] government, the only things retained were articles used by the police—the *yatagan* [Turkish sword] and the baton. All the rest became French." [15] On the pretext of the need for assimilation,

---

[15] Tocqueville, *op. cit.*, pp. 142–143.

France devoted nearly a century and a half to the erasing of all existent signs of Algerian sovereignty. Nationality, culture, and local traditions were ultimately negated in the name of an ideology of integration. Not only did this policy destroy the state and force most of the urban bourgeois families to emigrate to the Middle East but it also took from the rural population its sense of identity and sentenced all Algerians to be pariahs in a caste society. In reality, integration meant that Algerians were sacrificed for and left out of the new French-administered economic system; the tragic result was that Algerians had no control whatsoever over the sweeping socioeconomic transformations of their own country.

By the end of the nineteenth century, total domination was acknowledged to be costly in many respects. In particular, the dispossession and exclusion of the local population combined with the collapse of the population's indigenous institutions made Algerian society into "a dust of individuals," totally ungovernable. A new policy, sponsored by Jules Ferry and Lyautey, was designed for Tunisia, Morocco, and Vietnam. Called the protectorate policy, it was based on the maintenance of autochthonous institutions and the superimposition of a parallel European administration designed to serve the interests of the settlers. As Lyautey said,

> Use the ancient ruling cadres instead of dissolving them. Govern with the mandarin, not against him. We must proceed from this: being and always destined to be a tiny minority, we cannot pretend to substitute ourselves for them, but at the most to direct and to control. Thus, we must not offend a tradition or change a single custom; we must say to ourselves that there is in each society a ruling class, born to rule, without which nothing can be done, and there is a class to be governed. We must use the ruling class in our interests.

Having remarked that this program was already succeeding in Tunisia, Lyautey added, "I have observed *de visu* in Algeria the absurdity of the inverse system . . . [which] failed everywhere and without exception in all our colonies, [which are] poor, diseased, sucked out, cataleptic, killed by direct administration." [16]

The protectorate policy permitted the Tunisian and Moroccan states to preserve their international individuality, their national

[16] Brunschwig, *op. cit.*, pp. 57–58.

territory (not to be confused with the French territory), their own nationality, and their national sovereignty, represented by the sultan in Morocco and the bey in Tunisia. Although these two sovereigns were compelled to make some reforms that the colonial authorities judged useful, they retained a substantial amount of power. Almost no law could be adopted or enacted without their signatures. Circumstances and the personalities of some of the rulers led them to use the veto frequently to influence French policy.

The cultural compositions and histories of the societies, however, caused a difference in the functional weights of the Moroccan and Tunisian sovereigns. The Moroccan monarchy had greater functional weight within the political system than did the Tunisian dynasty. As analyzed in detail in Part I, the Moroccan monarchy embodied political as well as religious legitimacy. Lyautey, who became the first Resident General of France in Morocco, not only realized what the sources of legitimacy were but was determined to reinforce them and, as he phrased it, "to restore the personal prestige of the sultan by reviving around him the ancient traditions and the old ceremonies of the court." [17] France also undertook the modernization of the sultan's administrative apparatus (Makhzen), which had been weakened in the years prior to occupation. In the end, the monarchy became the chief beneficiary of the colonial enterprise, because those tribes who for a long time had refused to submit to France were willing to surrender to the sultan's authority. It might seem paradoxical, but the unexpected consequence of the colonial experience in Morocco proved to be the unification of the society to the advantage of the monarchy. In no other place did the traditional forces of power have greater opportunity for survival.

The Tunisian dynasty, though kept in power, did not benefit from the new conditions as did the Moroccan monarchy. The long-standing system of succession resulted in rulers who came to power in their old age when their political awareness and interest had dimmed considerably. It became apparent that in Tunisia, a homogeneous society open to cosmopolitan influences, the beys who ruled but did not really govern would not be able to keep up with the pace of modernization. Among other things, the gradual debasement of the Tunisian dynasty accounted for the early emer-

[17] Vincent Monteil, "Les bureaux arabes dans le Maghrib (1833–1861)," *Esprit* (November, 1961), pp. 575–606.

gence of a political elite which, by the end of World War I, succeeded in becoming the major *porte-parole* of Tunisian society vis-à-vis the colonial system.

Before we conclude our treatment of political domination, it is important to note that the fate of the state and of political institutions during the colonial period was by no means distinct from the fate of the culture as a whole. The dismantlement of Algerian political structures was accompanied by the refusal to recognize Algeria both as a nation and as a specific culture. In a country in which religious tradition included no institutionalized clergy and in which nationalists were demanding the separation of religion and state, France preferred to create an Islamic clergy which it trained in a series of improvised schools. Although it professed to be secular, France tried, in fact, to base its rule on brotherhoods, or cults of saints, thereby trying to revive the most obscurantist and primitive forms of religious life.

The logic that suppressed the prerogatives of Algerian judges also permitted French policemen to apply, at will, French and Koranic laws and to limit and eventually close the existing schools of the country without attempting to replace them. The depth of this profound unlearning of culture (*déculturation*) can be gleaned from Tocqueville's judgment:

> There existed in its [Algeria's] midst a great number of pious foundations to help the needy and to provide for public instruction. Everywhere we have put our hands on their revenues. . . . We have ruined charitable institutions, dropped the schools, and dispersed the seminaries. Around us, the lights have been extinguished, and the recruitment of men of religion and of law has ceased. That is to say, we have rendered the Moslem society much more miserable, disorganized, ignorant, and barbaric than it was before knowing us.[18]

Unfortunately, it is beyond the scope of this work to treat in depth the repercussions of this *déculturation*, especially in view of the fact that the repercussions have been overlooked owing to the climate and emotions surrounding the national revolution of the last several years. Suffice it to say that rarely in history has any society suffered such cultural disintegration. We shall reserve discussion of

---

[18] Tocqueville, *op. cit.*, p. 323.

the impact of this disintegration upon the national political elites for the next part.

As far as the other maghribi societies are concerned, it is important to remember that whatever changes, cultural shocks, challenges, and reinterpretations were inherent in the colonial situation, their cultural institutions have, nevertheless, persisted. Therefore, the identity and fundamental structure of each society have been preserved. For instance, the universities of Qarawiyîn in Fez and Zitouna in Tunis continued throughout the colonial period to attract and socialize thousands of students from all over these countries. The universities, the trades, and the artisans all endured some crises, but none of them were fatal.[19] The learned strata of the old urban cities in Tunisia and Morocco continued to exert leadership and to command an overwhelming respect in the societies at large. In Algeria, however, except for the few Ulama and the literate bourgeoisie of Constantine, there were no leaders; the people had to seek leadership from other sectors of the society.

From another perspective, however, the forms of domination in each society are not so clear-cut. For example, having developed the Kabyle myth in Algeria, France continued to pursue the same Berber policy within Morocco. The Algerian Berbers were considered more assimilable than the Moroccan Berbers because they were assumed to be more "superficially Islamic." Because of this distinction, the French permitted them their local assemblies, their customs, and representation to the finance delegations; in turn, it liquidated all kinds of institutions (judges, Koranic schools, *sharî'a*) that embodied Islam. The whole policy was designed to prevent "the two peoples of Algeria from growing accustomed to contact with each other." Because the Kabyles were both rural and urban and because they were economically and educationally successful, the Berber policy in Algeria proved advantageous to them; it seemed to be a celebration of the urban capacities for adaptation to modern life in contrast with rural backwardness. The pro-Berber bias in Morocco took the opposite form and had, therefore, opposite re-

[19] Jacques Berque, "Dans le Maroc nouveau: Le rôle d'une Université islamique," *Annales, Histoire économique et sociale*, no. 51 (1937), pp. 193 ff.; M. Ferid Ghazi, "Le Milieu Zeitounien de 1920 à 1933," *Cahiers de Tunisie*, XXVIII (1959), 437–474.

sults; because the Berbers constituted the majority of the rural society, France acted out its bias by severing rural areas from the corruption of the towns. It thereby prevented any significant socio-economic changes that might have arisen in urban areas and spread to the rural world. Jacques Berque, once governor in Morocco and now a professor in the Collège de France, exposed the vanity of this policy, which was intended to create a Berberistan, by showing that it created, instead, nothing but Berber reservations.[20]

[20] Jacques Berque, *Le Maghreb entre les deux guerres* (Paris: Le Seuil, 1962).

Chapter 4:
ECONOMIC DOMINATION

It should be evident by now that the colonial situation never involved only acculturation. Theorists, however, still tend to ascribe to the European impact the universal attributes of urbanization, industrialization, secularization, literacy, and democracy, never specifying the mechanisms by which these processes took place, if they did, and overlooking entirely the vast *déculturation* and uprootedness which accompanied them. For one thing, France would not have been proficient at spreading industrialism until World War I; and some would argue that until recently France was primarily a rural society, at least in comparison with most advanced industrial ones.[21]

The impact France had upon North Africa was indeed significant, but it had nothing to do with industrialization. It can be best analyzed in relation to the different forms of colonial domination—total, segmental, and instrumental—because the economic impact will unfold within the structural limitations and constraints built into each political framework. For measurement of the differential degrees of colonization on the economic level, the most appropriate indicators are the percentage of Europeans in each society, its part in land appropriation and national income, and, finally, the policy pursued vis-à-vis the rural communities.

The initial purpose of colonialism was to reduce demographic

---

[21] Folke Dovring, "The Share of Agriculture in a Growing Population," *Monthly Bulletin of Agricultural Economics and Statistics*, VIII F.A.O., Rome (August–September, 1959), 1–11. As long as colonialism has grown up with capitalism, there is no sense in defining the colonial situation as the impact of an industrial society upon a backward one. France began colonizing in the beginning of the nineteenth century, but there is sufficient evidence that it did not begin to modernize in the industrial sense until the late nineteenth century. In fact, it has been argued that its economic structure remained highly traditional until the mid-twentieth century. See Alfred Cobban, *The Social Interpretation of the French Revolution* (Cambridge, England: Cambridge University Press, 1962); Alexander Gerschenkron, "Reflections on Economic Aspects of Revolution," in Harry Eckstein, ed., *Internal War* (New York: Free Press, 1964), pp. 180–204. The point is made even more clearly by Stanley Rothman, "Barrington Moore and the Dialectics of Revolution: An Essay Review," *APSR*, LXIV:1 (March, 1970), 61–82.

surplus in Europe; North Africa alone was to absorb more Europeans than all the thirty-odd colonies possessed by France. Although the aspiration to populate the areas always exceeded the real possibilities, the proportion of the European population grew to 10 percent in Algeria, 7 percent in Tunisia, and 3.5 percent in Morocco. As Table 3 shows, the differences in terms of absolute numbers are even more striking.

The intention was not, of course, to industrialize the Maghrib but to create another peasant France on the other side of the Mediterranean. From this comes the importance of the settler (*le colon*) and of what the literature calls not colonialism but colonization, that is, the appropriation and modernization of the land by European farmers. If, then, the settler came to symbolize the whole colonial enterprise within the Maghrib, it is mainly because of the fundamentally agrarian orientation and rural base of the colonial system. Although the functionaries, traders, and speculators played a passing role, the key basis of legitimacy and stability has remained centered in the settler as long as the system has lasted. For this reason, the acquisition and exploitation of land—and the repercussions of these policies—have become and remain today the central problem in the Maghrib.

In precolonial society, the modes of land appropriation were extremely complex. Apart from a limited portion of land recognized as private (*melk*), the patrimonial property of the sovereign (later called *Domaines*), and the inalienable property of religious institutions (Habous), most of the land was collectively owned and, as such, was of an indeterminate status. This structure reflected the predominance of group over individual rights; because the society was still structured along tribal lines, the majority of the land was

TABLE 3

COMPOSITION OF THE POPULATION, 1921 AND 1954–1955

	Nationals[a]		Europeans		Total	
	1921	*1954–1955*	*1921*	*1954–1955*	*1921*	*1954–1955*
Algeria	4,923,000	8,449,000	791,000	1,042,409	5,714,000	9,491,409
Tunisia	1,939,000	3,688,000	156,000	255,000	2,095,000	3,943,000
Morocco	5,140,000	10,120,000	85,000	350,000	5,225,000	10,470,000

[a] Of maghribi origin, i.e., Moslems and Jews.

simply called collective lands. The only operational distinctions made by jurisconsults and legislators were inspired by the Islamic notions of dead and rejuvenated lands. Dead lands produced nothing and were the property of no one, but the rejuvenated land developed by a given community and transmitted through generations was recognized as the collective property of that group by the rulers and the society at large. The ambiguity began with the notion of the sovereign's eminent right to grant to particular parties the privilege of rejuvenating lands. Although the sovereign's power to grant or to dispossess already acquired land was severely limited by the sanctity of tradition and by "the normative force of the actual," [22] the French abused the inherent ambiguity between the eminent right of the sovereign and the factual appropriation by collectivities.

In Algeria, there was a systematic attempt to dispossess the autochthonous population in favor of the European settlers. The newly instituted land laws were considered tools of war which broke up the previously indivisible land into individual properties; they reduced dissidence and resistance by dissolving tribal units and, thus, made land available for the European population. The initiators of the 1863 *Senatus Consulte* were quite explicit: The intention was to "provoke a general liquidation of the soil," to retain one part for the long-time Algerian property owners, not as a collective heritage but as "personally defined and divided," and to reserve the rest for "attracting and receiving European immigration." [23] This first *Senatus Consulte* was, at the outset, applied to the 372 tribes that were the most powerful and that traditionally occupied the best land of the Tell. Restricted to 667 hamlets, they were condemned to occupy only one part of their territory for the duration of colonialism. Another law entitled the *petit Senatus Consulte* was adopted in 1887; it fragmented 224 other tribes into 349 units. Although information for the extreme north and the extreme south is scarce, an estimation for the years 1887–1934 indicates that 337 tribes were broken down into 529 units. Ageron noted that by the end of 1934, only nineteen tribes remained unfragmented and that

[22] Georg Jellinek, *Das Recht des Modernen Staates* (Berlin: 1900); and N. S. Timasheff, *Introduction to the Sociology of Law* (Cambridge, Mass.: Harvard University Committee on Research in the Social Sciences, 1939).
[23] A. de Broglie, *Une Réforme administrative en Algérie* (Paris: 1860).

1,500,000 hectares were still to be reclassified and appropriated according to the new canons.[24] As it turned out, the operation proved to be an example of the art of total spoliation. The first *Senatus Consulte* applied to the 6,883,881 hectares possessed by the Tell communities; it left them with only 1,336,492 hectares, or 19.4 percent of their land. The second *Senatus* exploited even more the communities to which it was applied, leaving only 10 percent of their initial land.

Although the dispossession of land was effected according to the Napoleonic Code, certain clauses of the Islamic law were also employed for purposes of justification. The use of Islamic law was selective, of course: If the law favored appropriation, it was used; if it did not, it was ignored. The French used the eminent right of the sovereign to claim lands that the precolonial state had never claimed. Islamic principles were, however, quickly forgotten when it came to the expropriation of religiously inalienable land, the Habous.

For Europeans at least, this policy was undeniably successful; by the end of 1875, tribal insurrection had run its course, and the French became the dubious inheritors of the best land of the country. The final victory of the settlers was that for more than a century, their caste was to benefit from limitless governmental aid for creation of an economic infrastructure, an irrigation system, technical and financial assistance, and commercial protection. An estimation of budget appropriations for 1918 shows that Algerians paid 70 percent of the direct taxes and received only 3.1 percent of the allocations in the overall budget.[25] The settlers not only attempted to devour Algeria but they also succeeded in acquiring metropolitan markets. The landscape and the economy were restructured; the effects of this socioeconomic transformation will be discussed at the end of this part.

The excesses of governmental aid did not merely diminish the merit of the colonial project as a whole, but more importantly, they limited its capacity for adaptation to the local structure of the autochthonous society. To have an idea of the social costs of colonial policy in Algeria and to appreciate the degree of uprooted-

[24] Charles Robert Ageron, *Les Algériens musulmans et la France, 1871–1919* (Paris: Presses Universitaires de France, 1968), II, 740.
[25] *Ibid.*

ness which condemned the Algerian society to no more than a dust of isolated individuals, one should know what happened in the Mitidja as early as 1852:

> It has been estimated that in the Mitidja, the amount of ground held by the average family in 1830 was slightly less than 1 zuwija (about 10 hectares). In the west, it was probably somewhat more than 1 zuwija. The binding over of 364,000 hectares of arable land to colonization would appear to mean that approximately 36,000 families were displaced from the land. A few of these were cantoned. Where did the rest go? What new life did they take up? Did they emigrate to Morocco? die of cholera, hunger, acts of war? become laborers on the *fermes?* migrate to the cities? These families probably represented fully one-tenth of the Algerian population of the time.[26]

In Tunisia, the policy of populating land with settlers was much less sustained. The first wave of colonization was composed of anonymous companies involved in capital and land speculation; rarely did they show concern for directly exploiting the land. The initial intention was to respect formal agreements between the French and Tunisian state and to avoid transforming Tunisia's status from that of a protectorate into that of a colony. In 1886, State-Councillor Pascal declared,

> Tunisia is to be regenerated; it is not to be taken. We did not have to confiscate the territories of rebellious tribes; we did not have to take the possessions of the Domaine. [French policy would, then, consist of] the maintenance of a prince on his throne, and around him an autochthonous administration, directed by some of the best of the French elite. . . . If our government is not capable of restraining itself, if it transforms Tunisia into a fourth Algerian department, it would be only a source of expense and a warehouse for functionaries and speculators.[27]

---

[26] John Ruedy, *Land Policy in Colonial Algeria: The Origins of the Rural Public Domain* (Berkeley and Los Angeles: University of California Press, 1967), p. 104; see also H. Isnard, *La réorganisation de la propriété rurale dans la Mitidja* (Ordonnance royale du 21 juillet 1846 et Commission des Transactions et Partages, 1851–1867): Ses conséquences sur la vie indigène (Algiers: A. Joyeux, 1947).

[27] P.H.S., *La Politique Française en Tunisie* (Paris: 1891), p. 458. For a full treatment, see Jean Poncet, *La colonisation et l'agriculture européenne en Tunisie depuis 1881* (Paris: Mouton, 1961).

It was not long before land colonization forced itself on Tunisia despite attempts at restraint. The arrival of French peasants who were willing to substitute direct exploitation for mere speculation and the influence of settlers from Algeria who moved to Tunisia thirsty for more land and accustomed to other methods of intervention finally forced the hand of French authorities. The new orientation, emphasizing massive French settlement, was justified by the slogans of "the Italian peril," referring to Italian competitors, and "the demographic monster," referring to Tunisia's limited French population. This policy soon led to the liquidation of the lands of the Domaine and to a spoliation which, although it had less tragic results than did the policy followed in Algeria, was nevertheless substantial. Within the entire enterprise, however, local interests and institutions were taken into consideration. The matriculation system, under the control of a mixed tribunal, allowed European property to comprise 800,000 to 850,000 hectares, and at the same time, permitted Tunisians to validate their own appropriations (about two million hectares) in terms of the new juridical system introduced by the French. The issue of the Habous land indicates how far the Tunisian notability went to prevent total disregard for local interests. Although some of the public Habous was lost to the French, a number of groups, including the Habous Association (*el jem'yia*), the aristocratic elite, and the dynasty, succeeded in stopping a project designed to reject the inalienability of all Habous land.

The map of European implantation in Tunisia reveals two things. First, traditionally sedentary regions such as the coastal Sahel and Djerba island remained, like Algerian Kabylia, entirely impenetrable to settler colonization. One of the consequences of this (which will be taken up later) is that the bulk of Tunisian and Algerian elites eventually came from these respective areas. Secondly, an appreciable part of the old urban bourgeoisie, possessing sizable private properties was able to convert to modern methods of agricultural production, to the point of competing with, though not overtaking, the Europeans.

In general, however, rural society, to a greater extent in Algeria and to a lesser extent in Tunisia, was abandoned to the principle of Ricardian economy. The operational provision was that "we [the French Republic] must establish laws conceived uniquely for the extension of the French colony and then let the Arabs do their best, with equal arms, in the struggle for life." [28] Only in Morocco did the colonial project have the dual purpose of instituting controlled colonization while maintaining traditional society in its integrity. This orientation toward Morocco can be accounted for by the fact that Morocco was the last country to be colonized and that officials were appalled by the spectacle of social disintegration in the rest of the Maghrib. Also contributing to this orientation was the aristocratic vision of Lyautey, who believed in "pacifying without embittering and reorganizing without breaking." The agricultural policy toward the rural society was devoted to the preservation and reconstitution of the tribal patrimony and to the protection of local communities against the abuses of anarchical colonization. The *dahir* of April 27, 1919, affirmed that "collective lands are imprescriptible, inalienable, and unseizable." Parallel to the consolidation of their rights, local community assemblies (*jema'a*) were promoted to the rank of official and recognized organizations, although they were required to discuss most of their decisions with a tutelary council. This arrangement was elaborate on the local level and actually worked in a more or less satisfactory fashion, permitting the colonial administration both to take land for its European protégés and to make sure that local communities still maintained sufficient land for their needs.

In order to accommodate the peasantry, European agriculture centered on the public domains and used primarily the lands belonging to tribes of a military vocation (Guish). On the whole, more than four thousand settlers acquired farms averaging 250 hectares each. In conformity with norms and planning established at the start, these farms formed agricultural complexes that pursued complementary agricultural vocations and that were much more highly concentrated than were the colonial farms of Algeria and Tunisia. The collective lands, however, did not remain untouched. The requisition of part of these lands required collaboration with the notables and the Moroccan Makhzen, and in gaining it, the colonial administration permitted the notables to profit in the venture. Using their privileged position as part of the administrative hierarchy, the notables and qaids extracted for themselves great

[28] Spoken by Prevost-Paradol, an influential French politician; as quoted in Ageron, *op. cit.*, p. 38.

portions of land and control over water sources and every facet of production that happened to be under their surveillance.

The firm *encadrement* of the rural society, despite the acts of settlers and notables alike, spared the Moroccan society systematic dispossession and the social trauma that tends to accompany it. Jacques Berque writes of this,

> We do not see reproduced in Morocco the sorrowful excesses of the first Algerian colonization nor the lamentable consequences of the law of 1873. Not even the spoliation of the Tunisian law on the Habous, 1898. . . . The advancement of European ownership of property and the retraction of the autochthonous ownership operate in a mature context, through legal procedures, almost as if these were hypocritical. Thus, if legislation and judiciary and administrative services conspire in favor of the settlers' expansion, there also exist crosscurrents, recourses, and, even here and there, some courageous champions of equity.[29]

Although local communities were spared rapid disintegration, their patrimony, tribal basis, and local institutions having been maintained, simple survival in a changing environment meant that the Moroccans would remain stationary while settlers greatly advanced their agricultural and technological methods of production. Mere survival would eventually mean archaism and decay. During the period we are focusing on, the influence of modern economy and new economic relationships produced in the midst of the local assembly (*jema'a*) a profound antagonism between the collective orientation of those members who wanted to preserve indivisible property and those rival families, notables, and deviants who preferred the fragmentation of the patrimony into individual portions.[30]

To recapitulate the previous analysis, let us say that the degree of colonization on the economic level varied according to whether the colonial system was total as it was in Algeria, instrumental as in Tunisia, or segmental as in Morocco. Table 4 summarizes and compares the available data on land appropriation and shows how the proportion of colonized land came to represent 40 percent of the cultivated land in Algeria, 18 percent in Tunisia, and 12 percent in Morocco.

[29] Jacques Berque, *Le Maghreb entre les deux guerres,* p. 41.
[30] Jean Le Coz, *Le Rharb: fellahs et colons* (Rabat: 1964), 2 vols.

TABLE 4
REPARTITION OF THE CULTIVATED LAND BY SOCIETY
(IN MILLIONS OF HECTARES[a])

	Algeria	*Tunisia*	*Morocco*
Mediterranean zone			
Colonized land	2.7	.7	1.0
Autochthonous land	2.0	2.1	6.6
Zone of the Steppes[b]			
Autochthonous land	2.0	1.2	.9
Total	6.7	4.0	8.5

[a] One hectare equals 2.471 acres.
[b] Of almost no arable value.

By now, it should be evident that the dominant minority represented a superstratification juxtaposed to the autochthonous society and that it enjoyed an exclusive or quasi-exclusive access to the centers of power, wealth, and legislation. Table 5, analyzing the repartition of revenues between Moslems and non-Moslems for 1955, shows that in Algeria, Europeans, who represented 10 percent of the total population, acquired 47 percent of the country's income; that in Tunisia, Europeans, who represented 7 percent of the population, acquired 43 percent of the income; and that in Morocco, the French, who constituted approximately 3.5 percent of the total population, acquired 33 percent of the country's income. Table 5 also illustrates the impact of colonialism upon the rural

TABLE 5
DISTRIBUTION OF NATIONAL INCOME, 1955
(POPULATION IN MILLIONS AND INCOME IN FRENCH BILLIONS)

	Algeria		*Tunisia*		*Morocco*	
	Population	*Income*	*Population*	*Income*	*Population*	*Income*
Non-Moslems	1.0	298	.3	90	.7	214
Moslems						
Agricultural	5.3	117	2.3	52	6.3	204
Nonagricultural	3.4	222	1.3	68	3.4	226
Total	9.7	637	3.9	210	10.4	644

SOURCE: Samir Amin, *L'Economie du Maghreb* (Paris: Paris Minuit, 1966), I, 119.

society: Although the rural society represented everywhere more than half of the population, it received only 18 percent of the income in Algeria, 25 percent in Tunisia, and 32 percent in Morocco. These differences were not caused simply by the inherent wealth of Morocco in comparison with the other countries, as suggested by Samir Amin, for example. These differences emanated, instead, from a different colonial approach—one which made a principle out of maintaining the Moroccan patrimony.

The most conspicuous effect of colonial domination has been the weakening of the tribal basis of each society and the undermining of its old integrative principle both at the local and national levels. With the erosion of tribal links and relationships and with the increasing differentiation and stratification of maghribi societies into groups and strata, the old mechanisms of arbitration and control have been superseded by national institutions. Although these national institutions are no longer dealing with tribes or classes, it is more and more evident that they are dealing with occupational, professional, and regional interests which are identified neither with primordial symbols nor entirely with class interests. The literature on social stratification is very thin, and we can gain only some indications from examining the existing official data concerning the rural society.

The Algerian agricultural census of 1951 is inadequate in many respects; it does not distinguish between the productive land along the Mediterranean and the semiarid land of the Steppes, or between modern and traditional farming, or among Algerians, except in terms of size of property. It does, however, afford some useful information.[31]

The first striking contrast we draw from Table 6 is that 22,037 European farmers actually controlled 2,726.7 million hectares; at the same time 630,732 Algerian farmers and peasants possessed only 7,349.8 million hectares. In other words, the average surface area per

[31] Consult mainly M. Isnard, "Structures de la colonisation agricole en Algérie à la veille de l'insurrection," *Bulletin de Géographie d'Aix-Marseille*, no. 4 (1958); see also "Structure de l'agriculture musulmane en Algérie," *Méditerranée*, no. 2–3 (April–September 1960), pp. 49–59. For most of the tables and statistical data used in this chapter, we have drawn freely from the excellent work of the Egyptian economist and UNESCO expert Samir Amin, *L'Economie du Maghreb* (Paris: Editions de Minuit, 1966), 2 vols.; and André Tiano, *Le Maghreb entre les Mythes* (Paris: Presses Universitaires de France, 1967).

TABLE 6
Land Distribution in Algeria, 1951

	Number of units		Surface area (in millions of hectares)	
	Europeans	Algerians	Europeans	Algerians
Less than 1 hectare	2,393	105,954	.8	37.2
1–10 hectares	5,039	332,529	21.8	1,341.2
10–50 hectares	5,585	167,170	135.3	3,185.8
50–100 hectares	2,635	16,580	186.9	1,096.8
More than 100 hectares	6,385	8,499	2,381.9	1,688.8
Total	22,037	630,732	2,726.7	7,349.8

French farmer is 120 hectares, but the average per Algerian is 11 hectares. If we examine the breakdown of land ownership in Algeria, we find that 69 percent of the landowners (438,483) actually possessed less than 10 hectares each and owned only 18 percent of the exploited land. With their 3.1-hectare average, this 69 percent clearly fell short of the indispensable minimum for the subsistence of a family.

However, an analysis of agricultural income (Table 7) provides us with a more precise idea of the internal differentiation of each society. Algerian rural society has comprised very few farmers who have owned large farms and who have converted to modern methods of production. On the whole, such farmers constituted only

TABLE 7
Distribution of Agricultural Income in Algeria, 1955

	Number of persons (per 1,000)	Total income (in milliards)	Per capita income (in 1,000 francs)
Workers			
Permanent	100	10	100
Temporary	500	24	40–60
Algerian landowners			
Small	210	13	60
Medium	210	42	200
Large	50	28	560
Colonized lands	—	93	—
Total	1,070	210	

Source: Samir Amin, *L'Economie du Maghreb*, p. 130.

5 percent of the rural population and received 13 percent of the agricultural income. The middle-sized farms represented 22 percent of the agricultural population and received more than 20 percent of the revenue. The structure of rural property, however, is in constant modification owing to the colonial impact and to detribalization. It has been estimated that between 1930 and 1954, the number of landowners diminished by 20 percent, whereas the number of agricultural workers increased to 29 percent. Indeed, colonization has permitted the emergence of a small working elite amounting to 10 percent of the rural population; this elite's standard of living and style of life have become objects of envy, especially to the small peasant. On the bottom of the scale, we find more than half a million people who regularly alternated between their small parcels, temporary work on the colonial farms, and unemployment. In all of North Africa today, there is an unemployed mass which has become detribalized without having become integrated into a new society and economy and which has become proletarianized although it is not part of a proletariat. This mass represents the most blatant failure of the colonial system.

Since the structural transformations of the Tunisian and Moroccan societies were identical with those in Algeria, we shall avoid useless repetition by limiting ourselves to an investigation of the essential differences. Because Tunisia was subjected to less land dispossession and suffered less from rural overpopulation, we find that the average income per family was higher than it was in Algeria (140,000 old francs in Tunisia in contrast with 110,000 old francs in Algeria), and that the proportion of people in poor strata was lower (60 percent of the total agricultural population in Tunisia in contrast with 75 percent in Algeria). (See Table 8.) On the other hand, we also find that Tunisia had a greater medium-sized peasantry than did Algeria (29 percent of the rural population in Tunisia in contrast with 22 percent in Algeria), and a greater proportion of rich farmers (12 percent of the Tunisian rural population in contrast with only 5 percent in Algeria, as indicated previously).

Knowing the pattern of colonial impact in Morocco, we are not surprised to learn that this society has been, on the whole, less differentiated and that its population has undergone less impoverishment than its neighbors' populations. The medium-sized strata are found to be more substantial (43 percent in Morocco in contrast with 29 percent in Tunisia and 22 percent in Algeria); finally, al-

TABLE 8

DISTRIBUTION OF AGRICULTURAL INCOME IN TUNISIA

	Number of families (per 1,000)	Total income (in milliards)	Per family income (in 1,000 francs)
Workers			
Permanent	25	3	120
Temporary	110	7	60–70
Tunisian landowners			
Small	80	7	90
Medium	105	15	150
Large	45	20	450
Colonized lands	—	16	—
Total	365	68	

SOURCE: Samir Amin, *L'Economie du Maghreb*, pp. 136, 141.

though rich landowners represented only 8 percent of the total rural population, Tables 7, 8, and 9 show that the 85,000 rich Moroccan families received an income twice that of their counterparts in Tunisia and Algeria.

Up to this point, the focus has been on the differential impact of colonialism upon the three maghribi societies. Later in this work, the preceding discussion will be related to the structuring of national elites and the different ways in which each political system deals with its colonial heritage. For now, some concluding thoughts are appropriate. One thought concerns a peculiar and durable product of colonial transformation, namely, *déracinement;* by this,

TABLE 9

DISTRIBUTION OF AGRICULTURAL INCOME IN MOROCCO

	Number of families (per 1,000)	Total income (in milliards)	Per family income (in 1,000 francs)
Workers and tenants	415	29	70
Moroccan landowners			
Small	100	11	110
Medium	450	87	200
Large	85	77	900
Colonized lands	—	21	—
Total	1,050	225	

SOURCE: Samir Amin, *L'Economie du Maghreb*, pp. 136, 141.

we mean not simply the uprootedness of a great number of people but also the destruction of roots which can never be restored. Such destruction takes place without any objective possibility for the *déracinés* to be incorporated elsewhere, for example, in an industrial economy.

Colonialism has unequally but surely transformed the maghribi societies. Increasing differentiation, tribal erosion, rural exodus, emigration of more than a million people to Europe—such are the incontestable indicators of the "passing of traditional society." If it is true that a tiny minority of maghribi farmers was converted to modern methods of production and that a small minority of workers was incorporated into industry and modern farming, it also remains true that the majority of the peasant community has been and is being proletarianized without being given any possibility of integration into the existing economies and societies. It is important to understand that the colonial impact in the Maghrib introduced not merely a bifurcation between modern and traditional agriculture but also a cultural bifurcation in terms of which traditional society has ceased to exist. One paradox will illustrate the point: In North Africa today, most peasants in the so-called predominantly traditional sectors, when interviewed, declare themselves to be unemployed.[32] For the majority of the society, which is made up of the peasantry, working the land has ceased to be a profession and has become a nonoccupation.

Whether colonial regimes were total or segmental, direct or indirect, they did not simply subject the Maghrib to laws of acculturation. Rare have been the instances in which European models and patterns were exercised with such immediacy and omniscience. The enveloping tissue of constraint, the effect of demonstration, and the shock of ideas and images have all caused an extraordinary contagion of needs and an elevated level of aspirations which have had no equal but the objective impossibility of satisfying these aspirations. The weakening of traditional ties and the imposition of a new frame of aspirational reference have resulted in the development of anomie in the traditional society—an anomie which has been reinforced by the absence of new integrative institutions. To the extent that European ruling groups have assumed each new

---

[32] Pierre Bourdieu and Abdelmalek Sayad, *Le Déracinement* (Paris: Editions de Minuit, 1964); and Pierre Bourdieu *et al.*, *Travail et travailleurs en Algérie* (Paris: Mouton, 1963).

position of functional importance as it appeared, maghribi societies have ceased to exist naturally, in the sense that they have not developed adaptive responses to their environments.

The symbolic product of their crises can be seen in the person of the *paysan dépaysanné*, who is neither the peasant of old, nor the industrial worker, but rather a hybrid and contradictory social being; he is a peasant who has ceased to be a peasant. "The break with the peasant condition and the disavowal of the peasant spirit are the result of a purely negative process that leads to the abandonment of the land and the escape to the city or to the resigned maintenance of a devalued and devaluating condition, rather than to the invention of a new type of relationship to the land and the work of the land." [33] *Déracinement* is far more serious when one considers that it has involved the majority of the rural population, and that it is a cultural phenomenon with a powerful potential for disintegration. Nowhere else—not in Japan, China, or Latin America—have the transformations of the economic structure and the impact of European society prevented the peasantry from being peasantry before industrialization has even taken place.

It is evident that the Maghrib has fulfilled definite functions in the world economy and in the world polity; it is important to stress, for explanatory purposes, that the Maghrib's development has been limited and conditioned by the needs of dominant societies. In contrast with current theories based on simplistic dichotomies of the tradition-modernity kind and with theories which ascribe a modernizing halo to the West, this part has shown that European impact and influence are far from uniform. In its most aggressive aspect, namely imperialism, European impact can lead to the deliberate destruction of political and economic institutions. In other instances, it condemns, by its mere presence, the local institutions to anachronism. Finally, the Western impact can be involved in an intentional effort of retraditionalization of the entire social fabric; according to Geertz, "Keeping the natives native becomes a full-time job." [34]

---

[33] Pierre Bourdieu, *Le Déracinement*, p. 31. See also Michel Launey, *Paysans Algériens: la terre, la vigne et les hommes* (Paris: Le Seuil, 1963); it lacks a theoretical framework but contains a good deal of relevant material.

[34] Clifford Geertz, *The Religion of Java* (New York and London: Free Press, 1960), p. 363.

Given these elements, it becomes impossible to explain the dynamics of economic, political, and social development and underdevelopment by merely taking into consideration the structure of the dominated society and assuming the European contribution to that development and underdevelopment is unquestionable:

> The relationship of estrangement between so-called underdeveloped societies and technological civilization consists mainly in the fact that within them [underdeveloped societies], technological civilization discovers its own product or, more precisely, the negative counterpart of the destructions it operated in their midst in order to establish its own reality. . . . Development cannot be conceived of, as Malinowski said, in terms of "the result of the impact of a higher, active culture upon a simpler, more passive one. . . ." Simplicity and passivity are not intrinsic properties of the cultures in question but the result of the actions carried out upon them by development at its beginnings: a situation created by brutality, pillage, and violence without which the historical conditions of this same development would not have been met. . . . In approaching problems of industrialization of underdeveloped countries, Occidental civilization first encountered the deformed image, fixed through centuries, of the destruction it had first to carry out in order to exist.[35]

[35] My own translation of the following original French text:
"Le rapport d'étrangeté entre les sociétés dites sous-développées, et la civilisation mécanique, consiste surtout dans le fait qu'en elles, cette civilisation mécanique retrouve son propre produit, ou, plus précisément, la contrepartie négative des destructions qu'elle a opérées dans leur sein pour instaurer sa réalité. . . . Le développement ne peut être considéré comme le faisait Malinowski: 'résultat d'un impact d'une culture plus haute et plus active sur une culture plus simple et plus passive.' . . . La 'simplicité' et la 'passivité' ne sont pas des propriétés intrinsèques des cultures en question, mais le résultat de l'action, sur elles, du développement à ses débuts: une situation créée par la brutalité, la rapine et la violence, sans lesquelles les conditions historiques de ce même développement n'eussent pas été réunies. . . . En s'attaquant aux problèmes de l'industrialisation des pays sous-développés, la civilisation occidentale y rencontre d'abord l'image déformée, et comme figée par les siècles, des destructions qu'il lui a fallu d'abord opérer pour exister." Claude Levi-Strauss, "Les Discontinuités culturelles et le développement économique et social," *Social Sciences Information*, II:2 (July, 1963), 7–15.

Part III

THE EMERGING LEADERSHIPS

The preceding analysis has spelled out the differential impact of colonial domination upon the maghribi societies and the incapacity of the colonial system to resolve the contradictions brought in its wake. In the ensuing confrontations, the positions usually assumed in the conflict between the defenders of tradition and the propagators of modernity had been completely reversed. That is to say, the European dominant society was increasingly committed to keeping the native society native; and the dominated society, through its emerging leadership, was increasingly organizing itself along the lines of modernity, sovereignty, and development. By the end of the colonial period, it became even more apparent that European society was the major obstacle to development. However, the content of the confrontations between national movements and colonial domination, the degree of maturation of each social revolution, and the postindependent capabilities for national development remained very much a function of the past institutional heritage and of the particular colonial context, and, most important for the present discussion, of the structuring of the national elites.

The emergence of the maghribi elites on the national level was a new historical phenomenon brought about by negative conditions. First, the rural notability was incapable of political innovation because of the disorganization of the tribal solidarities and the weakening of traditional hierarchy. Tribally based resistance movements, such as those of Mokrani and Abd-el-Krim, were not able to articulate a suitable ideology for the spirit of the times or to lay the foundation of a continuous political movement. The ultimate impotency of these movements meant the end of the grand movements of rural and primordial character and the definite displacement of the role of political innovation from the rural society to the city. Secondly, within the city itself, many factors favored the monopolization of political life by the intelligentsia: the subordination of the autochthonous state or its destruction by the colonial system, the traditional weaknesses of commercial and rural bourgeoisie, and, especially, the impossibility of any autonomous political life due to the colonial constraints. The combination of these factors enabled the intelligentsia to assume the primary role of national actors. About this, Edward Shils wrote, "The gestation, birth, and continuing life of the new states of Asia and Africa, through all their vicissitudes, are in large measure the work of intellectuals. In no state-formations in all of human history have intellectuals played such a role as they have in these events of the present century." [1]

Apart from the collecting of biographies and statistical data, it is not an easy task to comprehend the leadership of new nations. Because practically all politics in the colonial period consisted of root and branch opposition to the machinery of the colonial state, the personal and contextual characteristics of the leaders were overshadowed. To the extent that we wish to understand the dynamics of nation building and to specify the common and differential capabilities for national development, concepts such as national liberation movements, modernizing elites, and petty bourgeoisie in power, are not very useful. Often employed without reference to the societal context in which a given elite operates, these concepts leave us without any theoretical perspective. The simple statement of the existence of an elite, as is common to the literature on the Third World, hardly prepares us to give a diagnosis; it prepares us even less to formulate hypotheses concerning specific patterns of future developments. One step toward a more fruitful approach to maghribi elites would be to develop some analytical categories which would permit us to distinguish among elites and to classify them according to explicit criteria. For our present purposes, we shall project two major categories: on the one hand, the elites' orientations and, on the other, their organizational structures and functional weights within each political system.

Ideological Orientations of the Maghribi Elites

In the midst of profound changes, both internally and externally induced, one clearly expects to find more consensus among political

[1] Edward Shils, "The Intellectuals in the Political Development of the New States," in John H. Kautsky, ed., *Political Change in Underdeveloped Countries: Nationalism and Communism* (John Wiley & Sons, 1962), pp. 195–234.

elites than in the society at large. But even in the most homogeneous societies, elites have been divided as to the perception and interpretation of the colonial challenge, the structure of their peasant society, and the vision of its future potential. In fact, there have been three essential, competing definitions of political reality in every maghribi society, although they have tended to vary in importance and saliency, depending on the context.

The first orientation, which we describe as nationalitarian-scripturalist, came to characterize the Moroccan renaissance, the Algerian Ulama, and the Tunisian Ulama of the Destour Party. It is hardly surprising to find this orientation in the Maghrib, for it has appeared historically in societies throughout the Arab world, in China, and in India. All these societies, including the Maghrib, possessed an oral and a written tradition and an architectural heritage, and they participated in the world of universal religions. The nationalitarian-scripturalist movement has consisted precisely in the calling for and reaffirmation of national, cultural, and religious integrity in the face of a domination that has represented and incarnated the most serious encroachment upon these values. In this perspective, the colonial situation has been primarily, though not exclusively, defined as a spiritual and cultural conflict between antagonistic identities.

The proponents of this cultural *intégrisme* issued mainly from learned, scholarly, and urban families, which historically constituted a distinctive status group. In a society without formal church or clergy, this group has, throughout history, monopolized the interpretations of sacral texts and actually embodied religious authority. For these reasons, it was the first group during colonialism to advocate maintaining national personality, and it reacted mainly by intensifying the effort to purify religious life and institutions. In its attempt to reaffirm national identity, this group has stressed the use, revision, and celebration of the Islamic heritage (scripturalism), and it has stressed Arabism as a language, culture, and common history (nationalitarianism).

Men such as Allal al-Fassi of Morocco, Ben Badis of Algeria, and Thaalbi of Tunisia, all of whom belonged to aristocratic and literate families and were educated in the old universities of the Zitouna and Qarawiyîn, incontestably represented the orientation now under discussion. They all perceived imperialist aggression as an accidental accretion and as a temporary decay which could be fought only by returning to the principal sources of the religious and cultural heritage and by seeking profound endogenous forces. Because the confrontation was perceived as primarily cultural, the scripturalist orientation concentrated on discrediting religious forces that are superstitious and popular, such as the cult of saints and the brotherhoods, and which would, therefore, endanger a genuine national reawakening. With his distinctive perception, Clifford Geertz beautifully summarizes this phenomenon:

> If colonialism created the conditions in which an oppositional, identity-preserving, willed Islam could and did flourish, scripturalism —the turn toward the Koran, the Hadith, and the Sharia, together with various standard commentaries upon them, as the only acceptable bases of religious authority—provided the content of such an Islam. Western intrusion produced a reaction not only against Christianity (that aspect of the matter can easily be overemphasized) but against the classical religious traditions of the two countries themselves. It was not European beliefs and practices, whose impingement on either Moroccan or Indonesian spiritual life was tangential and indirect, toward which the doctrinal fire of the scripturalists was mainly directed; it was maraboutism and illuminationism. Externally stimulated, the upheaval was internal.[2]

The second orientation, liberal modernization, developed among the intelligentsia, who were exposed to the European experience; their purpose was to shape the reawakening of their societies along the lines of the Europe of the bourgeois revolutions. At least two important groups were associated with this orientation: the proponents of liberal constitutionalism and, later, the populists. The liberal constitutional trend was usually everywhere animated by lawyers, journalists, and by what Max Weber calls honoratiores; these privileged intellectuals, having almost no contact with the masses, have limited their political demands to participation in consultative, legislative, and budgetary institutions. They have pleaded their case in pamphlets, books, and newspapers, without ever questioning the legitimacy of the political system. Had these intellectuals succeeded, North Africa might have maximized its chances of establishing democracies patterned on the European model; but

[2] Clifford Geertz, *Islam Observed: Religious Development in Morocco and Indonesia*, p. 65.

owing to colonial repression and to the intellectuals' own isolation, this alternative has been closed off. European-centered scholars, who often lament the low democratic potential of the new nations, should recognize by now that for the most part, the lack of democracy reflects only the deformed image of long-standing European repression.

The populist trend within the movement for liberal modernization was epitomized by men like Bourguiba, Messali, and Ben Barka (in his first years). Later, the leaders of the Algerian revolution assumed the same vision of liberal modernization but oriented their action toward a complete and exclusive reappropriation of the state. Sharing a more popular background than the nationalitarian-scripturalists, a high level of education, and a cosmopolitan outlook, the populist elite grew frustrated by the previous generation's failure to effect legalism and parliamentarism. The populist elite's major step has been to appeal to the people for a total mobilization against the colonial system and to make out of oppositional politics to foreign domination the alpha and the omega of their existence.

Given this activism, which has been based on a secular and modernizing view of political change, the insistence upon immediate independence is only half the story; a deeper examination of the populist elite reveals that they have been fundamentally gradualist in their approach. On the one hand, they have been profoundly marked by the national ideology, because their ideas, socialization, and historical perspective were formed in the absence of, and probably the ignorance of, the socialist mainstream. On the other hand, although most of them spent their lives fighting the French and many died in the course of the battle, this maghribi elite has taken Europe as a model and reference for its own growth. As a Moroccan intellectual said, "For three-quarters of a century, the Arabs have raised one and the same question: 'Who is the other, and who am I?' In February, 1952, Salâma titled one of his papers, 'Why are *they* powerful?' 'They' did not have to be defined; it is always understood to be the *others*, who are always present around us and within us." [3]

This obsessive reference to the European model, if it testifies to the profundity of the interaction among Europeans and the populist

[3] Abdallah Laroui, *L'Idéologie arabe contemporaine* (Paris: Maspero, 1967), p. 15.

elite, and the resulting questioning of identity, exposes even more clearly the inherent contradictions within the populist elite. Having to fight the real colonial France, the populist elite invoked the ideals of the French Revolution, its political activism and mass mobilization, and took on a Jacobin posture. But the Jacobin rather quickly becomes reconciliatory and gradualist when he finds himself confronted with the tasks of mediating, integrating, and coordinating the new forces of a nation in the process of being rebuilt. All these men would have been brilliant politicians in the preceding Fourth Republic of France, and indeed some of them were, like Ferhat Abbas. But given the context from which they matured and emerged—absence of parliamentary life, less differentiated societies, a total, as opposed to a marginal, form of politics—this generation of politicians was encouraged to become authoritarian and patrimonial in style, populist in language, and gradualist in methods of government. The theory underlying this analysis is, obviously, that contexts shape men's careers and personalities, rather than the reverse.

There is little doubt that in the last decade the political and cultural stage has been dominated by these two orientations. Although the nationalitarian-scripturalist orientation represented the beginning of national consciousness, the liberal modernizing one, in its dual Jacobin and reconciliatory aspect, has definitely set the direction and content of today's political movements. For this reason and especially because of its capacity to incorporate new groups drawn mainly from a third orientation, we shall designate it the national elite.

The third orientation, the elite who called for mobilization, emanated basically from the radical intelligentsia and the workers. This orientation appeared late, and, even today, its influence is indirect, making its contours difficult to delineate. If we base our appraisal upon the writings of the best known spokesmen, Mohammed Harbi of Algeria, Ahmed Ben Salah of Tunisia, and the late Mehdi Ben Barka of Morocco, we find that all of them have tended to take the infrastructure of dependency of their societies much more seriously than did their predecessors. For them, the fundamental values of the maghribi societies—values of identity, independence, and modernization—are to be actualized neither by the restoration of cultural traditions nor by mere adaptation and borrowing from European society. On the international level, they have tended to adopt the notion of multiple modernities; that is, they have submitted the institutional accomplishments of advanced societies to a critical examination. Although they have been receptive to the use of cultural and technological instruments of development, they have not believed that industrial societies have exhausted all the possibilities of modernity. Thus, they have elaborated new schemes of social organization, such as self-management and cooperative organizations, and have felt that the horizon of human creation is not limited by established practices.

On the national level, the mobilizational elite has tended to be critical toward national movements and regimes for assuming independence from colonial powers as an end in itself. Having an affinity with socialist regimes, the mobilizational elite has felt that maghribi society must be entirely reconstructed and the structural precedents altered, and that the political institutions—party government—should be used as an organizational weapon to break traditions and resistance to penetrating socioeconomic changes.

These, then, are the three definitions of political reality that have marked the maghribi elites and have shaped their ideological and cognitive frameworks. One can argue that although they have developed parallel to one another, in symbiosis rather than rupture, they represent three historical moments in the process of national consciousness. The interpenetration among these orientations has been such that up to this day many ambiguities persist. To the extent that each national movement utilized the double cultural dimension, Arab and Islamic, to mobilize the population against the forces of occupation, each has, in fact, borrowed from a common cultural heritage. This can be seen from the fact that even today there exists no significant criteria for distinguishing culturally a Tunisian man from an Algerian or a Moroccan. Furthermore, long after the *déclassement* of the nationalitarian-scripturalist elite, there was no conscious effort to distinguish between the concept of *umma* (community of believers) and the concept of *watan* (modern nation); this represented an intentional effort not to alienate political Islam. Thus, beyond the boundaries inherited from colonialism, the only way to make sense of the concentric circles of belongingness is through identification with a given leadership.

The answer to the question, which orientation predominated in each country, cannot be given yet. Where the history of nations determined only by ideational orientations, we would be tempted to say that the scripturalist orientation has predominated in Morocco, the gradualist orientation in Tunisia, and the mobilizational has triumphed in Algeria. Other determinations come into play, however; the most significant is the structure of the political elite and its relationship to the state and the state's power structure.

Structure and Functional Weight

Since the beginning of the century, the three orientations outlined above have presented three projects for nation building. To know which orientation or combination of orientations has prevailed, one must consider the political collectivity and the elite structure that compose a given orientation. Political elites vary significantly in terms of power, authority, and organization within each political system. It should be evident that, all things being equal, a homogeneous and cohesive elite that attains power is more capable of orienting the society to its values than would be a heterogeneous elite torn by inner dissensions. However, an elite can be well organized and committed to structural change but never reach a position of power; in that case, it will be unable to implement its programs. In terms of our paradigm, we intend to show that the structure of a given elite and its capacity for building institutions depend on a number of factors, the most important of which are its relation to the state, the degree of social change in process, the process of socialization of the political elite itself, its capacity for incorporating social and ethnic groups, and, finally, its success or failure in mobilizing the peasantry during the national revolution. This list of variables, though by no means exhaustive, is sufficient for the objective of this work. The following analysis attempts to explain why one elite, rather than another, came to predominate in each maghribi society. Later, Part IV will address itself to the capabilities of each political system for national and economic development.

Before analyzing the emergence of particular elites, we can, by way of introduction, formulate certain predictions. Owing to the centrality of the Moroccan monarchy in precolonial times and its maintenance during a brief and segmental form of colonial occupation, the national elites were unable to play a primary role in the society. The weakness of national institutions in precolonial Algeria and the disintegration of the existing social structure due to a form of total colonial domination lead us to predict that it would have been immensely difficult for any political elite to restore or attain a cohesive form of authority and social control. Finally, in Tunisia, because of a fortuitous combination of favorable factors —a homogeneous society, a traditionally centralized state, and an instrumental form of colonial domination—minimal conditions were met for the emergence of a cohesive political elite.

Probably in no other country did the weight of the political past fall so heavily as it did upon the destiny of the Moroccan elites. They had first to contend with the sultanate, the significance and central functions of which have no equivalent in the other societies. They also had to contend with a form of colonialism which, though short, was highly manipulative and conservative. As a result, they found themselves to be marginal and more or less divided minorities. From the multiple and complex events that form the contours of the current configuration of the political system, we shall trace only two, the promulgation in 1930 of the Berber Dahir and the deposition and exile of the Sultan Mohammed V in 1953.

The Berber Dahir represented France's attempt to isolate the Berber rural society through the maintenance and restoration of the customary law; hence, the traditionally marginal portions of the population were isolated from Islamic and Arab developments in the rest of the country. The implementation of this policy was dependent on the abolition of the Islamic law, traditionally administered by Moroccan judges. Implementation was, in fact, accompanied by the institution of a system of penal and criminal justice inspired by French principles of law, in which the control of the monarchy was entirely ignored. This policy merely legalized the old dual conception of Morocco as "land of government" and "land of dissidence"; not only did it institutionalize divisions, thus becoming a self-fulfilling prophecy, but it structured divisions between Berbers and Arabs. Aside from the compartmentalization of the society and the intensification of existing differences by military officers, the dahir made a decisive break by officially assuming that the Berbers might not have been as deeply Moslem as the rest of the Moroccans and that the sultan no longer represented the spiritual leader of the whole society. As such, it was the major violation of the Treaty of Fez, in which the Sultan was assured of his total religious sovereignty.

Historians are unanimous in ascribing to the promulgation of the Berber Dahir the emergence of modern nationalism. Most of the young intellectuals of Fez and Rabat commenced their protest, organizing first the Bloc d'Action Nationale, then the Parti National, and, finally, by the end of World War II, the Istiqlal, or the Party of Independence. What is important for our purposes is to consider the structural conditions within which these movements were formed. Let us briefly enumerate the conditions before analyzing them in depth.

First, because it was a pluralistic society and had historically experienced only partial movements of unification, Morocco was structurally conducive to political segmentation among different social and political forces. Thus, it was possible for the colonial administration, which retained substantial political power and which established a system of *chefferies* and of tribal control, to oppose the tribes against the cities, the notables against the intellectuals, and the *bon bled* (the real and good country) against the corrupted bourgeois. As a result, national leaders of any standing who frequently expressed feelings of Moroccan nationalism could be confronted at any time with the dissolution of their attempted unification by colonial-sponsored artificial *siba* and by threats of tribal insurrection. Because of the segmentalist policy pursued by France and its intentional reactivation of primordial sentiments as opposed to a civic policy pursued by national elites, we should refer to Moroccan peasant movements, not as a rural mobilization, but rather as a countermobilization.

Second, if it is true that the promulgation of the dahir engendered an active and united front of intellectuals, it is also true that these men came from different spheres. The protest movement expressed the liberals' fear of a partition of their society, but it was championed mainly by politico-religious leaders. Religious scholars expressing wounded Islam and urban bourgeois families organized mass demonstrations and public prayers appropriate to times of stress (*latif*) during which the leader Allal al-Fassi harangued the masses in many of the northern mosques. Hence, the social movements, developing as a response to the colonial attempts at national division, were, from the outset, shaped by scripturalist orientations.

Third, the emergence of this nationalitarian-scripturalist elite, in the name of primordial Islam and the unity of the Moroccan society, clustered its energies around the restoration of integral power in the hands of the monarch as the sole embodiment of the empire's unity. At the same time, because the sultan retained a sufficient amount of power and stood to benefit from the new confrontation, this elite, with its exigencies and aspirations, eventually tried to circumscribe monarchical power by revising its foundations. In this sense, "the decisive phases of nationalism in Morocco [from 1930 to 1960] can almost be described as a contest between the scripturalists and the Sultan [and, of course, between both of them and the French] for the Sultanate, for the right to define, or better, redefine it—a contest the Sultan, not entirely through his own doing, rather definitively won." [4]

The crisis set off by the dahir led to its immediate withdrawal, but it had already brought to the forefront the social forces and the essential actors whose interaction ultimately determined the form and content of the present political system. As suggested above, the vulnerability of Morocco's political elites is to be understood first in relation to a conservative form of colonialism and to the minimal transformations the society had undergone. Indeed, according to the colonial theory of equal but separate development, Moroccans had limited access to the administrative apparatus of the state; it has been estimated that in 1945 Moroccans occupied only about 26 percent of the 20,492 public posts. Of this 26 percent, only 771 were not at the bottom of the scale.[5] Access to modern education was also extremely limited. Between 1912 and 1955, scarcely over 1,000 Moroccan youths pursued secondary schooling and obtained the two baccalaureats. Most of these youths, who later achieved national recognition, came from the same urban, bourgeois, commercial, literate families of Fez, Rabat, and Casablanca. These families shared many close interrelationships, and, as they became threatened by new competition from the international markets, they all tended to orient their offspring to the acquisition of a modern education—the best investment a North African family could make. An examination of the biographies of Moroccan political leaders reveals that they constituted an inner circle which, aside from its common family origins, perpetuated relationships of friendship and rivalry dating from their graduations from the colleges of Moulay Idriss at Fez and Moulay Youssef at Rabat. Not one among the 200 or so belonging to the urban leadership circle, from Ben Jelloun to Ben Barka, did not graduate from one of these schools.

[4] Geertz, *op. cit.*, pp. 78–79.
[5] *Plan de reformes* (Rabat: Publication par la Résidence Générale de la République Française au Maroc, 1945).

In the shadow of this inner urban circle lies the rural notability composed mainly of about 325 qaids. If we consider the narrowness of its intellectual and political horizons, this body bears no mark of an elite; however, it did dispute the leadership of the Istiqlal and succeed in imposing its weight upon national development, with negative results. France expected more from the notability's youths, and in building the Collège d'Azrou for Berber students, it intended to create a leadership more favorable to its rule. The college produced leadership but not in the direction France had intended, for people like Zemmour used it as a center for the spreading of national consciousness. By contrast, the military academy of Meknès fulfilled the French founders' intentions and oriented the rural notables' youth toward military careers. The officers corps were expected to permit France to govern Morocco through modern military rulers who were favorable to the French presence. As the colonial system came to a close, however, these officers joined the sultan; to this day, they continue to govern the rural society on his behalf. Thus, for a long time, the provincial rural notables of the first generation, along with many of their sons who sought a military and professional vocation, not only escaped control by the urban national elite but were disposed to play the role of a counterelite in order to prevent any massive national organization. The Association of the Alumni of Azrou, dynamically run by some of the most brilliant Berber intellectuals, was not able, despite all its efforts, to close the gap between rural and urban elites as independence approached.

It follows that political organization by the national elites could be carried out only in the big cities of Rabat, Casablanca, Fez, and, to an extent, Salé and Kenitra. Only a few party cells were established, and party organization remained weak until World War II. Although the Istiqlal was capable of organizing powerful demonstrations and of attracting mobs and sympathizers, it often lost control of these demonstrations, at which point there was excessive, undesired violence. This was caused by the paucity of secondary, disciplined cadres as well as by the predominantly intellectual bent of the founders of the Istiqlal, who were better versed in public oratory than in mass organization. There were thirteen founding fathers, eight of whom had studied at the ancient university of Qarawiyîn and who were of a fundamentally legalistic and religious frame of mind. Like many of the scripturalists throughout North Africa, these men conceived of things less in terms of action and praxis than in terms of eloquent expression. This group, however, gained strength, when the Manifesto of Independence, which it put forward in 1944, was approved by the sultan. Among the fifty-eight cosigners of the manifesto, one finds the names of Ben Barka and Bouabid, leaders of the growing populist trend. This encounter of the young Turks and the Old Guard, which elsewhere would have led to the *déclassement* of the old leadership, led, in the Moroccan context, to the formation of a coalition. As can be seen from Table 10, this coalition contained eighteen teachers, ten *Ulama*, eight lawyers and judges, six administrators of the Makhzen, and thirteen rich families.[6]

A small party called the Parti Démocratique de l'Independence (PDI) was established by Wazzani in the industrial city of Casablanca. It attracted some liberals and republicans, but it remained a minority in face of the pact concluded between the monarchy and the Istiqlal. In order to create new bases of solidarity and to accustom the masses to the idea of independence, the Istiqlal organized tours and public gatherings during which the sultan, for the first time, mingled with the population. When the promised gradual reforms failed to materialize, the sultan decided to refuse to sign any more prefabricated dahirs, and he succeeded in seriously paralyzing the state machinery of the protectorate. The confrontation was long and difficult, and most of the time the sultan had to fall back on his own resources. Simultaneously accused of capitulation by some nationalists and of obstruction by the French authorities, pressured by the needs of the struggle and the constraints of political reality, the character of Mohammed V matured and, with this, the monarchy as an institution gained strength. The sultan's break with Chief El Glawi, who reproached him for being the king only of the Istiqlal and thus of the urban society, pointed up the latent conflict between the rising national movement and the traditional representatives of rural society.

In societies like Morocco, which are pluralistic and in which there

[6] Robert Rézette, *Les Partis politiques Marocains* (Paris: Armand Colin, 1955), pp. 294–309. These pages cover essentially the organizational structure of the Istiqlal party. See also Douglas A. Ashford, *Political Change in Morocco* (Princeton, N.J.: Princeton University Press, 1961), pp. 57–92.

TABLE 10
Istiqlal Party Membership in 1944
(Signers of the Manifesto of Independence)

	No profession	Moslem teaching		Ulama	Judges and auxiliaries	Attorneys	Makhzen civil servants	Government employees	Businessmen	Journalists	Farmers	Landowners	Doctors	Total
		Primary	Secondary and university											
Members of the executive committee, former national party	1	1	1						1		1			5
Members of the superior council, former national party		3		4					1					8
Alumni association leaders		3	2			2	2		1		2			12
Boy Scout leaders						1								1
Others		8	1	5	4	1	2	2	5	1	1	1	1	32
Total	1	15	3	10	4	4	4	2	8	1	4	1	1	58

SOURCE: Adapted from R. Rézette, *Les Partis politiques Marocains* (Paris: Armand Colin, 1955), p. 301.

has been complex social evolution, control of the rural society has always constituted the key to real power. We have seen how the colonial administration, with its military officers and loyal *chefferies*, enveloped the rural society and isolated it and how it also prevented the disintegration of tribal grouping in an effort to preserve the rural community. Colonial administration adopted somewhat egalitarian methods in the sharing of the common patrimony and tried to make the collectivity participate in rural modernization. The policy had some merit in that it favored the local communities and counteracted the tendencies of the notables to privately appropriate the land for themselves. Projects such as the one proposed by

Les Secteurs de Modernisation du Paysannat (SMP) were generous to the point of being utopian; launching their program with the symbol of the *jema'a* (the local assembly) on the tractor, they hoped to transform, in one blow, tribal and agrarian groupings into modern forms of collectivism. The program was extremely ambitious, but it is, of course, difficult to erase decades of conservative rural policy in only a few years. A year after it was initiated, in 1953, the pressure of political events led to the abandonment of this project. At any rate, the long-standing policy of keeping the traditional society traditional reduced the chances of rural mobilization for national purposes and permitted colonial authorities to commence rural countermobilization against the rising national movement of the urban centers.

The alliance between the monarchy and the national elites was bound to produce counteralliances, the forms of which varied from the apparently civic to the fundamentally primordial. These counteralliances, however, always centered around the rural notability. The first occasion seized by the colonial administration was November 1, 1951, the day on which the Consultative Chamber was to be elected. To counteract the strengthening of urban opposition, the colonial strategy was to expand the electorate, to the special advantage of the rural areas. The total number of voters was increased from 8,000 to 220,000, of whom 125,000 were rural voters registered for the first time. The idea of ruralizing politics is neither new nor limited to the Third World. A century before, in 1861, Napoleon III advised the Prussian state to introduce universal suffrage "by means of which the conservative rural population could outvote the liberals in the cities." [7] By further limiting the Istiqlal to ten days for submitting a list of candidates and for undertaking their campaigns, the colonial administration of Morocco intended to put the Istiqlal, which already lacked strong rural support, in an insoluble dilemma. If the Istiqlal chose to participate in the election, the administration would be able to demonstrate, at a low cost and through the electoral process that the national party had lost the support of the rural masses. To prevent this outcome, the Istiqlal chose to boycott the elections, and if one judges from the election results, the rate of abstention was extremely high: 98.2

[7] As quoted in Seymour Martin Lipset, *Revolution and Counterrevolution* (New York: Basic Books, 1968), p. 181.

percent in Salé, 92.7 percent in Safi, 95.9 percent in Casablanca, and 93 percent in Port Lyautey.

The failure of this first procedural attempt at neutralizing the national elite led France to resort to its favorite precolonial method —the fabrication and sustenance of tribal dissidence against the Makhzen. Indeed, after the departure of Lyautey, the administration refused to define the political situation other than in nineteenth-century terms. The French conspiracy against Moroccan independence took two forms: the repression of the urban elite and the reactivation of the dissidence of the rural notability.

In the last years of the colonial period, the Istiqlal gained strength within the labor movement, and union organization was progressing under the leadership of Mahjoub ben Seddiq. This alliance surfaced mainly during the Casablanca demonstrations, between December 7 and December 13, 1952, set off by the assassination of the Tunisian labor leader Ferhat Hached by French minutemen. The colonial administration welcomed the opportunity for a systematic dismantlement of the political leadership; not only was the repression of the demonstration ferocious—200 were killed—but a majority of the political elite was arrested—400 members of Istiqlal, l'Union Générale des Syndicats (UGSCM), and the Communist party. Most of these men, especially the 112 top leaders, were imprisoned until independence. The Istiqlal was badly organized for a clandestine resistance, and, as things turned out, it found itself in a position which made it unable to affect the final distribution of power. As a student of Moroccan politics described it,

> Since the riots of 1952, the party of the Istiqlal is profoundly disorganized. Its clandestine armature, which was put into operation in 1953, might lead one to believe in an apparent reorganization of the party; in fact, its scope is very reduced. In reality, more than four-fifths of the members have ceased all their activities in favor of the party, either through fear of imprisonment or because the party itself had spontaneously suspended any contact with the less loyal members. At this stage of decomposition, . . . the structures of the party are merely empty frames.[8]

Having isolated the sultan by dismantling his elite and urban mass support, colonial administration gave the signal for the mobili-

[8] Rézette, *op. cit.*, p. 304.

zation of the rural qaids and the religious brotherhoods. Robert Montagne, alive and thriving in 1953, wrote his book *Révolution au Maroc* in which he gave an ideological justification for a conspiracy which led ultimately to the deposition and exile of the sultan. He reports,

> The religious movements hostile to the sultan, led by the noble Abd el Hai Kittani, have in the last four years ceaselessly assembled all the Moslem conservative forces. They were launched into the battle, and an alliance was concluded since then among the members of the brotherhoods, the Glawi, and the qaids of the plains and the mountains. The objective was to prepare for the deposition of the sultan, through the mobilization of the traditional Moroccan masses. Religious chiefs and qaids were to respond to the action of propaganda and regimentation of the urban masses, which the Istiqlal had led for ten years. The efficacy of this enterprise would turn out to be total.[9]

Montagne plays down the fact that no political initiative by the qaids would have been possible without the French sponsorship. The inquiry of Stephane Bernard, made among colonial French officers, leaves no doubt as to the initiation, conception, and execution of this policy by the French administration.[10] This strange combination of rural *chefferies*, French administration, and the supporters of an antediluvian Islam did not simply try to undermine the national movement, but they also did their best to make this countermobilization appear as a spontaneous revolt, led by the "real" forces of Morocco, against a heretic and partisan sultan. A petition signed by nine out of the 23 city pashas and three hundred and nine out of the 325 rural qaids was addressed to the French Resident, asking him to "deliver the people from the extremists of the Istiqlal party and from whoever helps them." Glawi, the pasha of Marrakech, who became the *porte-parole* of the coalition, stated that the movement was a sign of the awakening of the Moroccan people, who oppose a sultan "whose policy is dangerous to the country's higher interest, and whose conduct is contrary to the precepts of the Koran." He added that according to Moslem law, the community of the faithful, *umma*, is entitled to express its views on the capacity

[9] Robert Montagne, *Révolution au Maroc*, pp. 236–237.
[10] Stephane Bernard, *The Franco-Moroccan Conflict* (New Haven and London: Yale University Press, 1968).

of the *imam* without having to use the Ulama, who apparently sided with the monarchy.

The sultan remained firm, and the palace issued a statement denying that the pashas and qaids "vested by *Dahir* of the Sultan with the power to represent him in the towns and in the country, had any right to rebel against the central authority gravely contravening the most elementary rules of orderly government." The statement also refused to recognize "any capacity to express themselves concerning the general policy of His Majesty's Government, still less upon religious matters which have never been within their competence." It finally declared that pashas and qaids had no basis for "claiming to speak for those under them who had no part whatsoever at any stage in their appointment." [11]

But the decisions had already been taken, and tribal countermobilization succeeded in attracting thousands of horsemen who surrounded Rabat and Casablanca; the sultan, who refused to abdicate until the last moment, was finally, on August 20, 1953, deposed and condemned to exile. The *coup de grâce*, however, proved to be the beginning of the end of colonialism, for it triggered an unprecedented wave of rural and urban armed resistance. Nothing better might be imagined to bring together such diverse factions as the Marxists and the Ulama than the restoration of the monarch. But the new forces which came to the forefront did not have merely the interest of the Istiqlal in mind; they substituted the demand for the reestablishment of the sultan for the broader goals of independence. The armed resistance, especially from the rural area, which broke and then intensified when the direction of events leading to independence became clear was not sponsored by the Istiqlal, and many of its members intended to dispute the Istiqlal's leadership. In addition, groups hostile to the Istiqlal—religious personalities, hundreds of notables, and pashas and qaids personally attached to the monarchy—organized a popular campaign for the sultan's return. To his French negotiators, the monarch could show 380 letters of retraction by the notability that had previously signed the petition against him. Even Moulay Arafa, the sultan improvised by the French and by Glawi, ended by asking the population to rally around their legitimate leader, Mohammed V. Glawi, him-

[11] All the above quotations are from Bernard, *op. cit.*, pp. 150–151.

self, as Lacouture so magnificently describes, had no choice but to recognize the irreversible ascendance of the sultan.

> In an October afternoon, 1955, the trumpeters of the old chief swept into the passageways of Marrakech, crying out, "The palace is open, Haj Timi (Glawi) invites you to celebrate the coming return of our sovereign. . . ." And all the doors of the palace opened. . . . Those who pushed their way in first, viewed an unforgettable spectacle: in one of his large rooms, replete with victuals and candy, the old pasha, a kind of guitar in his hand, begins a little dance, sings a brief hymn, with an air of festivity before murmuring in a wounded tone, "Ghadruni" (they betrayed me). In this way, even before his journey to Saint Germain to kiss the king's feet, the old enemy brought his picturesque contribution to the legend of the man exiled.[12]

The corollary to the emergence of the monarchy as the major beneficiary of independence was the *déclassement* of the national elite which was forced in this context to a secondary role. Aside from past repression, colonialism systematically pursued a policy which ultimately deprived it of the fruits of independence, by exclusively negotiating with the sultan and his representatives, on the one hand, and with the minority party, PDI, on the other. From then on, the Istiqlal, which had long wanted to be a unitary party, found itself drowning in a morass of pluralistic tendencies.

In our analysis of Morocco, we have seen that the fate of the political elite was a result of the fact that as Geertz wrote, "there is probably no other liberated colony in which the struggle for independence so centered around the capture, revival, and renovation of a traditional institution." He keenly perceived the conflict between the scripturalists and the monarchy but tended, however, to provide an ideational explanation for the political outcomes of the conflict. He writes,

> In the end, that is to say, after independence, the scripturalists found themselves politically disinherited, progressively isolated from the by now rapidly expanding machinery of state power. The strategy of embracing the twentieth century by reincarnating the

---

[12] Jean and Simone Lacouture, *Le Maroc à l'épreuve* (Paris: Seuil, 1958), pp. 111–112.

seventh did not in the end work out very well. Men whose religious commitments were more traditional and whose political ones were less came to dominate the nationalist movements, and, when those movements succeeded, the nations they created.[13]

We contend, rather, that the Istiqlal did not lose because of the political or religious impotence of its ideas. Geertz forgets to mention that the scripturalists were not the only ones to lose to the monarchy; all elites and factions, liberal and populist alike, were forced to accept a marginal role. The line of reasoning we have pursued should make it clear that we must go beyond the religious idea of traditional societies as a convenient explanation for everything and look instead for structural conditions for the failure of political elites. In this instance, the conditions involved were the structural incapacity of the elite to undertake the rural mobilization, the functional weight of the monarchy within the political system, and, last but not least, the colonial policy of segmentation, traditionalism, and praetorianism..

[13] Geertz, *op. cit.* (n. 2), pp. 73–74, 78; Leon Carl Brown's critical review of *Islam Observed* in *Middle Eastern Studies*, no. 1 (January, 1970), pp. 96–100.

Chapter 6: TUNISIA:
THE COHESION OF A RULING ELITE

Tunisia had long been a unified country, possessing all the institutions of a viable society. It did not have to discover that it was a state; thus it could concentrate on the task of becoming a modern state.[14]

Rarely have political elites benefited from so favorable a combination of circumstances as did the emerging political elite of Tunisia. It was as if the legacies of the traditional state and of the colonial state had maximized the chances for success and for the final emergence of a homogeneous, unitary elite entirely committed to the principle of coherent and rapid modernization. From the traditional state, the elite retained the principles of institutional reform and of a constitution.

These principles were symbolized by the accomplishments of Pasha Khayr-el-Din, a man recognized by all, ranging from the nationalitarian to the populist, as the Father of the Renaissance. The college Es-Sadiqia, founded in 1875 by Khayr-el-Din, remains a remarkable symbol of cultural and spiritual continuity; in the past, it produced the best civil servants ever known to the country, and today, its alumni include most of the ruling elite. The history of the demand for a constitution was so central that today's dominant party has called itself the "constitutional party" since 1920—a time when the constitutional debate had neither rhyme nor reason. The evolution of the party's names—Destour (meaning "constitution") in 1920, Neo-Destour in 1934, and Parti Socialiste Destourien in 1964—does not reflect simply a willful determination for continuity; each semantic transformation indicates a step in the elite's development.

The attitude of the colonial authorities toward the first generation of intellectuals was one of tolerance as long as the intellectuals confined their activities to aristocratic and literary clubs in the capitol. The Jeune Tunisien, which existed between 1896 and 1912, was one of these aristocratic clubs that never attracted more than a

[14] Leon Carl Brown, "Stages in the Process of Change," in Charles A. Micaud, ed., *Tunisia: The Politics of Modernization* (Praeger, 1964), p. 6.

thousand members. Members of the circle belonged to traditionally ruling families, mostly of Turkish origin, whose status increasingly came into question under the colonial impact. Because the colonial administration perceived this group to be the *porte-parole* of modern values against traditional ones, it closed its eyes to the movement's activities. One of the group's most outspoken members, Zaouche, exclaimed, "How would it serve the twentieth-century Moslems to return to the civilization of their ancestors and remain strangers to scientific progress? Have the Italians simply restored Roman civilization, or have the Greeks contented themselves, as in the past, with indulging merely in arts and philosophy?" [15]

The Jeune Tunisien militants, having been nourished by the reformist ideals of Khayr-el-Din and Sheikh Kabadou, called for the expansion of education, participation in the colonial enterprise, and the struggle against religious brotherhoods. They believed in France and had a tendency to associate progress with the West, but their sphere of action and influence remained quite limited. The unique occurrence of a public speech occasioned by striking workers was enough for France to disband the entire movement and to decree martial law from 1912 until 1920.

It was primarily between the world wars that the configuration of the contemporary elite was shaped, and with it the political destiny of Tunisian society. In order to understand the logic of the Destour's formation in 1920 and its crucial reorganization in 1934, it is first necessary to examine the changes in social stratification brought about by colonialism. It should be assumed, for purposes of analysis, that power, prestige, and wealth have tended historically to be unequally distributed among the diverse strata of Tunisian society, with the ruling families at the top, the commercial and learned urban bourgeoisie (*beldi*) in the middle, and the provincial families (*afaqi*) of an essentially agricultural background

---

[15] *Le Tunisien*, February 25, 1909. The leaders of the group were Ali Bach Hamba, Mohammed No'mane, Mohamed Lasram, Abd el jelil Zaouche, Hassan Guellati, Chedly Dargouth, Mokhtar Kahia, Sadok Zmerli, and Chîkh Abd el 'Aziz Thaalbi. All of these men, except for the last, acquired a European education. For more historical details about this group, consult Chedly Khairallah, *Le Mouvement Jeune-Tunisien* (Tunis: Imprimerie Bonici, 1957); and *Le Mouvement Evolutioniste Tunisien*, 3 vols. (Tunis: 1935).

at the next level. We leave out, of course, the people at the bottom (*el 'Ammah*), whose contribution to elite formation has been practically nonexistent.

The point is that colonialism induced a real mutation in the social and political *encadrement* of the country. Although members of the aristocracy occupied, with the benediction of France, important positions in the legal, cultural, and administrative institutions, they were undergoing a constant decline. Because of their collaboration, they lost authority with the native population, and the few families who attempted to use colonial methods of land cultivation incurred prohibitive expenses for their equipment, and eventual ruin. The decline generated a process of interpenetration and alliances, mainly in the form of marriages between aristocratic and bourgeois families.

The urban bourgeoisie was weakened by the introduction of manufactured products, which seriously reduced the revenue it counted upon from commerce and crafts. It was not, however, as shaken in its land patrimony as the Makhzen aristocracy. On the whole, people in both these strata sought ways to build careers elsewhere, especially in the professions and administration. But temporarily, at least, the urban bourgeoisie displayed a greater capacity for adaptation, mainly by trying to acquire the majority of the administrative positions. Furthermore, it overwhelmingly controlled the party of its creation, the Destour. It remained problematic, however, whether the traditional bourgeoisie would be able to represent and interpret the new forces created by the socio-economic transformation which accompanied colonialism. These new forces were the elite of the interior, formed by the expansion of education; an urban and rural microproletariat, formed around ports, other centers of transportation, and farms; and, finally, a landless peasantry.

In 1924, there was a forewarning of what would become a conflict between the nationalitarian-scripturalist and the populist elites. Young militants who were impatient with the purely parliamentary methods of the Destour and who were influenced by twentieth-century European revolutions, started to organize unions and cooperatives to prepare for the general overhaul of the society. Later, a similar attempt was made by some participants in the Algerian Revolution; however, the effort made in 1924 represented the first attempt to establish a system of mobilization for both the liberation and development of the society. M'hammed 'Ali, who was influenced by the Turkish experiment and the Spartacist Movement in which he participated as a student at Humbolt University of Berlin, and Tahar el-Haddad, an intellectual and reformer, were undoubtedly the most noteworthy figures of this political trend. Their movement reflected the profound social changes underway in the society and represented an attempt to transcend the purely constitutional features of an elite of notables, often satisfied with verbal protest and the circulation of petitions. "The Destour," wrote el-Haddad, "has constituted the first step in the popular reawakening, but now the people are beginning to realize that political action alone cannot influence the state [the colonial one], and that it is necessary to orient ourselves to economic and technical construction." [16]

We have shown elsewhere how the 1924 movement was a total social movement; it was marked by political radicalization in the struggle for independence, but it simultaneously appealed to economic initiative, both private and collective. It distinguished itself through its campaign for women's emancipation and its criticism of cultural archaism. One might add that Tunisian literature owes to it many Promethean themes. Mahmoud Messadi, who represented the spirit of the movement even though he wrote after its peak, was devastating in his ironic criticism of Oriental cultures: ". . . the pyramids of the pharaohs, the patience of Buddha, the beliefs of prophets, and even the quietude of the Tunisian who is not disturbed in a world completely upturned by wars and revolutions." [17]

It was to be expected, then, that the movement of 1924 would attempt to mobilize the workers and the popular masses in general. Increasing differentiation of the society, which weakened the tra-

[16] Tahar el-Haddad, *Al 'Ummal al Tunisyun wa Dhuhur al Haraka al-Naqabiya* [Tunisian Workers and the Appearance of the Labor Movement], Tunis: 1927, p. 10.

[17] Mahmoud Messadi, *Essud* [The dam] (Tunis: 1955). For an overview of this movement, consult Tahar el-Haddad, *op. cit.*, and his *Imra'touna fi al-Shari 'a wal-Mujtama'* [Our Woman in the Shari 'a (Islamic Law) and in Society], Tunis: Imprimerie d'Art, 1930. This book is also summarized for the French public in *Revue d'Etudes Islamiques* (1935), IX, 201–230. A systematic analysis of the whole period can be found in Elbaki Hermassi, "Le Mouvement ouvrier en société coloniale: La Tunisie entre les deux guerres," (Ph.D. dissertation, Sorbonne, Paris, 1966).

ditional sectors of trade, crafts, and agriculture, released upon the market a growing mass of unemployed. The elite was particularly sensitive to the nascent microproletariat's incapacity for articulating its demands, and found this milieu and the tensions within it especially favorable for introducing its ideas.

One such tension originated because the socialist-inspired European unions, to the extent that they admitted Tunisian members, did so at the price of gross distortions of both the prevailing unionist ideology and of the principles of socialism. Membership was extended only to privileged workers; the union leadership and staff were monopolized by European cadres; and there was a general refusal among European members of the union to fight for equal salaries for equally qualified people. As a result, there was a general congruence between the union's policy and colonial discrimination based on race. When the dockworkers' strike began, the radical elite laid the foundation for a national union, Confédération Générale des Travailleurs Tunisiens (CGTT), which was open to all sectors of the laboring class, national and foreign alike. During the brief but intense confrontation between the national union and the European union (November, 1924 to November, 1925), the radical elite made significant gains and were stopped only by direct intervention of the colonial administration. In an attempt to isolate the burgeoning union, the colonial state entered into negotiations with the bourgeois representatives of the Destour, asking them to use whatever power they possessed to halt the organizers and promising them to send a commission for reform from Paris to give them constitutional concessions. The Destour succumbed to the temptation, and its fifteen-man leadership signed a statement condemning the labor movement and asking the Tunisian workers to join the European union. Immediately thereafter, the union was dismantled, and M'hammed 'Ali, Mokhtar Ayari, and the internationalist Jean Paul Finidori (who joined them, putting his newspaper *L'Avenir Social* at their service) were accused of conspiracy against the state and were exiled.

The fate of the first national union ever to appear in North Africa, and even in Africa itself, was to remain a symbol and a reference point for Tunisian leadership of succeeding generations. First, labor leadership became fully apprised of the vital importance of nationalism as an instrument of mobilization. The Union Générale des Travailleurs Tunisiens (UGTT), which would be successfully established after World War II, adopted the famous strategy of distinguishing between antagonistic contradictions (nationalism versus imperialism) and nonantagonistic contradictions (national employers and workers). That is to say, the quest for building a minimum of congruence between workers and the other national forces predisposed labor leadership to a greater collaboration with the more openly political generations to come. Secondly, by 1930, a new generation of intellectuals, of provincial origin and advanced European education, appeared on the political scene; the members of this political generation were first co-opted by the Destour in an attempt to add new blood to a decaying body, but the young intellectuals soon discovered that the so-called party was nothing but a coterie of aged notables. Their openness to popular issues and people of all strata, and their alienation from Byzantine politics, led them in 1934 to take over the direction of the Destour party and, hence, of the national movement. This juncture of the emerging populist political leadership and the nationalism of labor leaders, which appeared early in the history of the national movement, largely explains the cohesion we find among Tunisian elites today.

Our concentration upon national elites as the major political actors should not be surprising in view of the fact that the Tunisian monarchy, in contrast with the Moroccan, held a secondary role in the political system. The structuring of national elites, and the substitution of leadership which took place in 1934, was so central that it provided today's ruling elite. For an understanding of the elites' socialization, their value orientations, and their capacities for organization and incorporation of social groups, we gathered comparative information pertaining to those leaders of the old Destour who led the national movement up to 1934 and those of the neo-Destour who have led it ever since.[18]

[18] Since the data collected concerns all the leadership population, there is no need to run statistical tests. These data include all leaders of the first Destour and the thirty-nine most important men of the neo-Destour. Given the criteria of selection I have retained—i.e., only men who continuously held positions at high levels such as the Commission Exécutive, le Bureau Politique, and the Organisations Nationales—the list seems to be quite exhaustive. In addition, secondary leaders in Tunisia did not have the opportunity to effect great influence and did not participate in political decisions. Among those who personally assisted me in the reconstitution of individual

The schism of 1934, which we interpret as the triumph of the populist elite over the nationalitarian-scripturalist elites, reflected overall changes of significant importance to later political developments. One change concerned the extension of the basis for recruitment. The first leaders, as in the Jeune Tunisien movement, emanated from the most privileged strata, and as can be seen from Table 11, although leaders did not come from only urban areas, 90 percent of them did come from Tunis.

Members of the new generation, which composed the bulk of the neo-Destour party, tended to originate from the interior of the country; more particularly, they came from the coastal Sahel and the island of Djerba—paradoxically, the areas least subject to colonial penetration. Some of the parents of these leaders, like Bourguiba's father, served the precolonial state, but most of them were farmers or traders and entertained, on the whole, some genuine relations with the rural mass. For this reason, the sons flattered themselves that they had come from and therefore understood "the people"; this, though true to a certain extent, should not be exaggerated.

For the first time, however, men from the interior did have access to positions of national leadership, but this was qualified in two ways. Rural origin did not immediately translate into rural representation, and contrary to what has been often assumed by superficial analysts, not all the leaders of the neo-Destour came from rural areas. The Tunis region continued to contribute 35 percent of the people who held the most important positions in the political party. Indeed, an intergenerational change took place among the prestigious families of Tunis, which, like the Mehiri and the Mestiri, contributed leaders to both generations of politicians. Apart from their availability for new political alliances, the old aristocratic and bourgeois families continued to supply one-third of the prefectural body, 75 percent of the judges and lawyers, and more than

biographies, I wish to thank Dr. Ben Milad and Dr. Slimane Ben Slimane. Their information was even more revealing because of their positions in, respectively, the Commission Exécutive of the old Destour and the Political Bureau of the neo-Destour. These two men today occupy marginal political positions; thus their contributions are also those of observers and intrigued analysts.

TABLE 11
TUNISIAN LEADERSHIP: PLACE OF ORIGIN

	Tunis	Rest of the country
Destour party	20	2
neo-Destour party	14	25

half of the doctors and pharmacists. To this day, their capacity for adaptation is still very significant.

In addition to the extension of the social base, a second change took place: Notables no longer devoted only part of their time to politics. Instead, the new leadership committed itself entirely to a political vocation. Table 12 shows that half the top men of the first Destour maintained their commercial and agricultural businesses throughout their political careers; however, in the neo-Destour, composed mainly of lawyers and professors, the members not only had more time to give to politics but, as can be discerned from their biographies, almost all of them abandoned their professions for a total commitment to political life.

It is true that in the beginning the Destour tried to address itself to Tunisia's major social problems. For example, in his book published in 1920, *La Tunisie martyre*, Thaalbi devoted a third of the work to illustrating the hardships suffered by farmers and peasants under colonial rule. The criticisms, however, were made in terms of an idyllic precolonial Tunisia which never corresponded to reality. The vehement tone of political discourse characteristic of the Destour was never matched in its daily political behavior which remained segmental, compromising, and purely symbolic. Having undermined, in 1925, the labor organization, the leadership lost not merely the support of the urban proletariat but it also lost what Marx called "the moral power of the shop"—organized craftsmen

TABLE 12
TUNISIAN LEADERSHIP: OCCUPATIONS

	Liberal professions	Traders and farmers	Administrative employees
Destour party	10	11	1
neo-Destour party	31	1	7

and small traders—who began to seek political guidance elsewhere. Thus, it was mainly among these dissatisfied strata that the young populist leadership of the thirties found its major basis of support.

Another change in the evolution of the national leadership concerns the *déclassement* of parochial leaders and the emergence of increasingly cosmopolitan elites. As one might expect, this development is very much a function of education. As late as 1934, two-thirds of the national leaders were graduates of the century-old Zitouna University. Without overlooking the important role played by this institution in the preservation of national identity and personality, one may say that the instruction at this university-mosque grew more and more at odds with the ongoing changes in the society. Zitouna University continued to transmit a medieval and theological culture and to produce men of religious and legal sophistication who had no expertise whatsoever in modern economy or politics. The sizable new intelligentsia, educated at the College Es-Sadiqia and at the European universities instead of at Zitouna, created what can only be called a cultural schism. The Zitounian membership of the first Destour pushed for a nationalitarian-scripturalist orientation, despite the reluctance of some of its more enlightened men.

The party that began with the intention of obtaining a constitutional monarchy and eventual independence ended by orienting its energies merely to the defense and renovation of the culture and the religion. Sheikh Thaalbi attempted the renovation of the spirit of the Koran, and Klibi spent many years trying to remove Islamic brotherhoods from religious prominence. This orientation in Tunisia remained ambiguous and, in many respects, reactionary. When el-Haddad published his book in defense of women's emancipation, *Our Women in the Shari'a and in Society*, many old Destourians applauded the attempt by the council of Zitouna University to ban the book. From Dr. Ben Milad, I learned that Sheikh Ben Mrad, the man who most opposed el-Haddad's interpretation and who wrote the most virulent pamphlet on it (titled "The Veil of Mourning Worn by the Woman of el-Haddad's Book; or Refutation of the Errors, Blasphemies and Blame-Ridden Innovations Contained in It"), had not even read the book so maligned in his pamphlet. Despite the levity of this personal remembrance, el-Haddad so feared for his own safety at the end of his life that he always carried a gun, a fact only his old union friends of the CGTT seemed to have known.

Modern views came to predominate only with the ascendance of the neo-Destourian elite. The overwhelming majority of the new intelligentsia, as is evident from Table 13, pursued a modern education offered primarily by the College Es-Sadiqia, which was a training ground for civil servants, members of the professions, and political leaders. For the lower classes, College Es-Sadiqia became the major tool of social mobility, just as it had once been the privileged ground of great families. In 1939, of the eighty students who passed the competitive entrance examination, only fifteen belonged to the traditionally prestigious families; more than half the rest came from the coastal Sahel, and the remainder came from the interior. This and later graduating classes have formed a network of enduring relationships covering professional, familial, and political spheres, from which has emerged a genuine *esprit de corps*. This *esprit de corps* continues, today, to influence and weld together the political elites.

Most graduates of College Es-Sadiqia went on to postgraduate study in France and became active in left-wing organizations in French politics. Compared to other North African students in France, the number of Tunisians seems to have been by far the highest. It was estimated that in 1931–1932, among the 151 North African students in French universities, 119 were Tunisian, 21 Algerian, and 11 Moroccan.[19] Upon their return to their countries, these elites swamped all the political and public fields; this was especially true in Tunisia, where elite possibilities were significant. United by a common socialization and committed to an enlightened view of modernization, they began immediately to enact their perspectives through mass mobilization. In the face of the insularity, traditionalism, and parochial stance of the old Destour, the scission was ineluctable. The following personal account of one of the founders of the neo-Destour gives us insight into the unification of the political elites through common socialization and similar political experiences:

[19] *Bulletin Annuel de l'Aemna*, North African Muslim Students Association, 1932.

TABLE 13
TUNISIAN LEADERSHIP: TYPE OF EDUCATION

	College Es-Sadiqia (modern)	Zitouna (medieval)
Destour party	7	15
neo-Destour party	38	1

Basically, leaving aside our personal rancor and petty ambitions, when we examine the Tunisian movement in general, we observe that everything everywhere tends to bring us together, to unify us; and unconsciously, despite ourselves, and even so to speak against our will, there was a slow but sure evolution towards this unification. . . .

In my past, there have been two decisive moments, confluent and important: first, when I graduated from the lycée and had to choose between the positions of Assistant in the College Es-Sadiqia and the Directorship of the El Arfania school. These two positions were offered to me at the same time, and my decision was to condition the rest of my existence. The second moment, and second conflicting pressure, came at the time of the scission from the old Destourians. . . . In my life, there were other decisions but they were less important, and their bearing had much less gravity. . . .

I had always tried to reconcile my younger comrades of the party with the elders with whom I had previously collaborated; but the divorce was such that one had in the end to choose one or the other. . . . My thirst for independence rendered my past ties to my previous existence and old relationships odious to me, and all this led me to accept the scission. With the neo-Destour party, of which I was one of the founders, I was launched upon a new path, carried away at an increasing and vertiginous speed. . . . What followed was success, the daily newspaper *El Amal*, considerable political activity, intense propaganda, the fall of the archaic [des archéos] . . . and then the exile, the events of September, myself exiled in Zarzis, where in my solitude, I recall my memories and my impressions.[20]

From the previous considerations, it should be clear that the ways in which the neo-Destour took shape gave the new elite the status,

[20] Tahar Sfar, *Journal d'un Exilé: Zarzis 1935* (Tunis: Editions Bouslama, 1960), pp. 16, 80, 82.

not of an isolated minority, but of an avant-garde; it also gave them the structure, not of a voluntary association representing a particular clientele, but of an organizational weapon without equivalent in the Maghrib or the Arab world. First, the elite appropriated to itself the symbols of legitimacy, continuity, and tradition; instead of establishing a new, oppositional party with different slogans and base, it took over the ancient organization, maintained the local directions, and simply adopted the name neo-Destour, arguing that the same goals were to be achieved through more radical strategies.

Between the years 1934 and 1938 and thereafter, the members of the Political Bureau covered every inch of the different regions of the country in an attempt to discredit the previous orientation, to establish a personal contact with the dispersed militants, and to transform the party into an instrument of combat for the attainment of power. Colonial authorities, who enjoyed every prospect of division, tolerated briefly the development of the new forces. They, however, grew disenchanted with the scission because what appeared at first to be an isolated movement soon took on a larger dimension and involved the masses. The establishment and subsequent reinforcement of the new leadership hinged upon the new elite's capacity for incorporation of new groups, such as the petty bourgeoisie—"dorsal spine of the party," according to Bourguiba —the intellectuals, the workers, and the plebs. For the purposes of incorporation, the party had to display significant organizational capabilities.

Having confronted the old Destour and the colonial authorities and having demonstrated that the new party, more than any other group, embodied the determination for independence and change, the new elite commenced an inclusive program, using the French and Arab press, organizing meetings, establishing cells, and creating, in fact, the conditions for a political life parallel and oppositional to the colonial situation. A state within a state was in the making, and every militant became accountable in terms of discipline and solidarity.

Concerning contact with the masses, the public speech remained the anchor and fundamental tool which allowed the chief (*zaim*) to form, inform, and mobilize the population. The usage of the Tunisian dialect as a means of communication facilitated access to the masses and rendered the Tunisian nation much more tangible than would have been the case if French or classical Arabic had been used. Although exacerbating to the Tunisian Marxists, the new elite's populism was nevertheless deep and quite real, and has endured until today.

Youth organizations also played a primary role, notably the Jeunesses destouriennes and the Etoile Scout. The party trained young, enthusiastic, experienced militants, who were organized along lines of discipline characteristic of Communist and Fascist youth organizations: These youths wore insignias, shoulder straps, and, later, scarves; they were trained in the party cells and were transformed into deployable, efficient cadres. In an adverse colonial context, these young men ensured the party's command over the scattered militants by coordinating strikes and leading demonstrations. With this background, a sizable number of the Tunisian young gained significant prestige and were prepared to assume higher responsibilities in the ranks of the party organization. The unified leadership at the summit of the hierarchy, by initiating younger militants and controlling access to strategic positions of power, thus maintained the coherence of the institution and ensured the procedure for leadership succession.

In its relationship with France, the party felt free to combine attitudes of intransigence with those of compromise. Whether France was governed by the left or the right, the neo-Destour was able to shift from cooperation to systematic confrontation. It accorded, for example, the Popular Front a favorable prejudgment in 1936 but was ready to withdraw it when France refused to make any changes in the colonial situation. Although similar political alignments and attitudes were prevalent in Morocco and Algeria, only in Tunisia did the major political party become the recognized *porte-parole* of the nation, even prior to the final confrontation which led to independence. In the Tunisian context, this role was never disputed by the old Destour, the monarchy, or even France itself. The broad membership of the party attested to a steady following, whatever the political vicissitudes. Even in one of the most bloody confrontations, in April 1938, the list of the people prosecuted was further proof of the continuing loyalty of the most diverse elements to the party. Out of sixty-five people who were prosecuted, and whose files have been kept, the party members included two farmers, twenty-one merchants and craftsmen, twenty-seven intellectuals, students, and professionals, four specialized workers, and eleven *lumpenproletariat*.[21]

The labor contribution to the national movement was paramount in strengthening the political party. The incorporation of labor organizations within the political framework was adopted by the political elite as a strategic exigency for the survival of social movements, and the lesson drawn from the experience of 1924 became a principle of action as much during the colonial period as thereafter. Bourguiba assured the labor union of full party support: "If the Destour of 1925 sacrificed the CGTT of M'hammed Ali to the Cartel des Gauches, the neo-Destour will not sacrifice the CGTT of Gnaoui to the Popular Front." And later, in the fifties, he added, "The experience—I could say, the proof and the counterproof—has shown that each time the solidarity between the party and the union was broken through the fault of one or the other, it is a disaster for both and both conclude by succumbing." [22] The coordination became so organic that the UGTT, the central union after World War II, eventually contained 80 percent of the neo-Destour membership; when its General Secretary, Ferhat Hached, who was best known to the American AFL-CIO as the builder of African syndicalism, was assassinated by French fascists, the loss fell hardest upon the top national elite. The integration of labor within the political framework was, of course, enmeshed with attempted co-optation and, sometimes, coercion. (This story cannot be told in full here, though it has received extensive treatment elsewhere.[23]) In any case, the enduring collaboration between party and union has historically cemented their relations and greatly reduced the probabilities of intraelite conflicts.

In conformity with the logic of an institution building institu-

[21] For an analysis of the mass basis of the neo-Destour, see Mohammed Cherif, "L'Organisation des masses populaires par le neo-Destour en 1937 et au début de 1938," Tunis University, mimeographed; Lucette Valensi, "Mouvement ouvrier et mouvement national en Tunisie en 1936–1938," Centre National de la Recherche Scientifique, Paris, mimeographed.

[22] Habib Bourguiba, *La Tunisie et la France* (Paris: Julliard, 1954), p. 386.

[23] For a more detailed discussion of the relationship between labor and nationalism in the colonial context, see Elbaki Hermassi, *op. cit.*, and Georges Fisher, "Syndicats et décolonisation," *Présence Africaine*, nos. 34–35 (October, 1960–January, 1961), pp. 17–60.

tions, the party also tried to bring rural society into its sphere by aiding in the establishment of an agricultural union in 1949, Union Générale des Agriculteurs Tunisiens. The goals of this union were vague because it was to represent the interests of both agricultural workers and owners of medium-sized farms. The secondary nature of economic concerns during colonialism, the absence of any economic perspective, and the primacy of politics account for the minor role played by the union in rural mobilization. The rural mobilization that did take place was due to two other factors: first, the rural roots of many members of the neo-Destour and their familiarity with the small villages and *bourgades* of the country; and, secondly, beginning in 1950, the deliberate organization of an army of liberation composed of peasants. This army, though unimpressive in terms of sheer numbers—it was composed of only a few thousand guerrillas—was able to constitute a significant means of pressure by successfully harassing the colonial farms and the French army. Moreover, it depended entirely upon the Political Bureau, whose members continued to ensure its control, even when they were in prison. The political elite's control of the rural mobilization deserves special attention, for out of all the armed insurrections which appeared in the Maghrib prior to independence, the only insurrection controlled by the national elite was this one of the Tunisian peasantry.

Along with seeking to incorporate labor and peasantry, the neo-Destour constantly sought the support of the bourgeoisie, but because there exists not one study on this point, we shall simply advance an open hypothesis. The political elite, otherwise homogeneous and unitary, seems to have remained deeply divided over what type of relationship the party should entertain with the upper strata. This dilemma has reappeared time and again, becoming an Achilles heel for the party, up to this day. For example, in 1933, some bourgeois families traditionally supportive of French control in Tunisia were threatened with the dissolution of their bank credit and of the Chamber of Agriculture and Commerce. Under the pressure of the settlers, Bourguiba, paradoxically, seized the occasion to defend these institutions, for he wanted to attract this new group to the party. Many of his comrades, some of whom were later suspected of bourgeois sympathies, criticized his initiative. As Hédi Nouira wrote to him, "It is a delusion and great folly to pretend that our policy would attract the discontented bourgeois elements, and to found hopes on these elements, which have been the allies if not the basis of colonization; it is to display an absence of political sense and a total incomprehensibility of the very essence of our movement." [24] Many bourgeois families did rally to the national movement, however, and it might be surmised that one of the costs of their support was the increasingly gradualist and accommodationalist role which the neo-Destour would pursue in the future. The forty thousand members of the business union Union Tunisienne de l'Artisanat et du Commerce who brought their support to the party obviously had an impact upon it.

Once the negotiations with France commenced, the neo-Destour's legitimacy and representativeness were not in question. As to who would hold power after independence in Tunisia, the political dice had been thrown between the two world wars. A long time had passed since an informal political system, a countersystem, had emerged from the colonial situation. From the social and historical conditions that had shaped them, the political elites preserved the two most distinctive marks of their organizational character: the utilization of the party as a powerful means of mobilization and, perhaps with some incongruence, a gradualist and reconciliatory vision of the evolution of social forces, especially in relation to the modalities of social change.

[24] Letter from Hédi Nouira to Habib Bourguiba, June 1936, from the prosecution dossier presented February 6, 1939, On French Colonial Courts of Justice.

He who wishes to understand too much will die of anger.
ALGERIAN PROVERB

Armed insurrections played only a secondary role in the emergence of Morocco's and Tunisia's political systems, but in Algeria, armed revolution was the decisive component without which an independent Algerian state would have been impossible. The literature on this revolution has focused only upon the phenomenal aspect of violence or the aptitudes of certain social classes to implement it. Rarely, if ever, has the literature contained a discussion of the structural conditions and contextual situation of the revolution. Such a discussion would have revealed that the revolution had unique aspects, both from the perspectives of its strengths and its weaknesses.

It is in this vein that Frantz Fanon interpreted the Algerian Revolution to be, par excellence, characteristic of the peasantry of colonized societies. Fanon was profoundly shocked by the total and totalitarian aspects of colonialism in Algeria; as a sign of his new allegiance, he declared himself an Algerian citizen (which was still not a formal reality), abandoned his profession of psychotherapy for active political struggle, and was invited by the National Liberation Front of Algeria to take a leading role in the revolution. He was, then, well situated to analyze the movement for liberation and attempted in *The Wretched of the Earth* both to offer a theoretical reconstruction of the dynamics of the Algerian Revolution and to present an ideological accounting of how a Third World revolution should proceed and what it should be. Four propositions can be discerned from his work. First, nationalist parties and Westernized elites are incapable of achieving decolonization owing to their reformist and legalist methods; parties and unions are structurally limited by their urban members, composed of workers, petty bourgeoisie, civil servants, and traders, who constitute privileged strata and profit from the colonial situation. Secondly, among these urban organizations, only a revolutionary minority, most of whom are tracked down by the forces of oppression, are capable of transmitting and then generalizing the movement of liberation to the rest of the society and especially to the peasantry. Thirdly, in the colonial society, the peasantry, which is usually not the main pre-occupation of the urban elite, is the sole revolutionary class:

> In the colonial countries, the peasants alone are revolutionary, for they have nothing to lose and everything to gain. The starving peasant, outside the class system, is the first among the exploited to discover that only violence pays. For him, there is no compromise, no possible coming to terms; colonization and decolonization are simply a question of relative strength. . . . The peasantry experiences naked oppression, and to prevent itself from dying of hunger, nothing less is permissible than an explosion of all the structures.[25]

Fourth, a dialectical change occurs in the dynamics of the revolution when the liberation movement takes its cue and starting point from the rural areas and penetrates the cities through that part of the peasantry which lives on the urban periphery. "It is within this mass of humanity—this people of the shantytowns, at the core of the *lumpenproletariat*—that the rebellion will find its urban spearhead. For the *lumpenproletariat*, that horde of starving men uprooted from their tribe and from their clan, constitutes one of the most spontaneous and the most radically revolutionary forces of a colonized people." [26]

We find that the approach of Pierre Bourdieu's analysis is similar, in that it deals with the predispositions and the differential propensities of social classes to articulate a revolutionary attitude. However, after an inquiry in depth among Algerian workers and peasants, Bourdieu reached conclusions quite opposite to Fanon's. Instead of focusing his analysis upon the armed peasants, Bourdieu chose to consider the contradictions in the consciousness and attitudes of the popular classes of the Algerian society, which developed as a result of the colonial coercion. Because of long-standing unemployment, *déracinement*, and the total uncertainty of individual and collective life, Algerian society appeared, to this author, to be stricken in its conduct and ideologies by a systematic functional disintegration. Bourdieu hit upon the chief failing of Fanon's analysis: Fanon would have us believe that total alienation and oppression, of necessity, produce total revolution.

> One must ignore everything as to the condition of the agricultural workers and of the *paysans dépaysannés*—haunted by the incertitude

---

[25] Frantz Fanon, *Les Damnés de la terre* (Paris: Maspero, 1968), p. 25.
[26] *Ibid.*, p. 80.

of today and the prospect of tomorrow, prevented from finding in a world which crushes them a beginning of realization of their hopes, and having no other liberty but to express their revolt through a mock effort and through daily ruses that corrode, little by little, any sentiment of dignity—in order to give the slightest credence to the eschatalogical prophecies that find in the peasantry of the colonized country the only true revolutionary class.

Being a good Durkheimian and a brilliant sociologist of consciousness, Bourdieu found that the situation of domination, uprootedness, and oppression can lead to the revolt of the oppressed, but that in Algeria the conditions that could have provided the required distance and the total grasp of the system were not necessarily met. Such conditions are indispensable for revolution. In this sense, "Absolute alienation deprives [the alienated] even of awareness of their own alienation. . . . The peasantry and the *lumpenproletariat* of the cities, who can constitute a pressure for revolution, do not constitute a revolutionary force in the real sense." [27]

The limitations of this approach, which tries to account for revolution exclusively in terms of the attitudes of social classes, are evident. Whether the peasantry is a force for revolt, as advanced by Pierre Bourdieu, or a force for revolution, as was argued by Frantz Fanon, these perceptions of the problem do not permit us to predict the character, content, and exact orientation of social movements based upon the peasantry. Whatever the attitudes of the peasantry in Algeria, a revolution did take place in which the peasantry did play a significant part. The questions remain: Was this revolution a mere national liberation movement similar to those in Tunisia and Morocco, or a peasant revolution of the Chinese type, or something altogether different, and, if so, in what sense?

The presentation of a diagnostic and of theoretical propositions concerning the structure of the Algerian Revolution clearly demands that we go beyond the mere attitudes of the peasant base. According to our paradigm, it requires the consideration of the structural context of the revolution, the attitudes of the state apparatus (here, the posture of the colonial administration vis-à-vis the

---

[27] Pierre Bourdieu and Abd el-Malek Sayad, *Le Déracinement* (Paris: Editions de Minuit, 1964), p. 170. This analysis constitutes the principal theme of Pierre Bourdieu's *Travail et Travailleurs en Algérie* (Paris: Mouton, 1963), pp. 307–312, 359–360.

dynamics of this struggle), the institutional inheritance of Algerian political authorities and their impact upon the elite structure. In what follows, the focus will primarily be upon the political elites, and discussion will be devoted to the impact of the structural constraints upon the dynamics of the Algerian Revolution and the emerging political system.

To state the problem empirically, let us say that as independence movements were among the rest of the Maghrib, the Algerian Revolution was undoubtedly an example of national liberation. But in contrast with neighboring societies, Algeria's independence movement evolved in the context of a total colonial system, and once begun, the movement found itself in a situation of absolute repression, having to face the most powerful army ever involved in a colonial war (one million French soldiers). The war lasted eight years, leaving one million Algerians dead and two million Algerians imprisoned in concentration camps. Most analysts who recorded the extent of the massive rural mobilization were convinced they were recording a socialist peasant revolution and were confused when, in the end, the movement culminated in a quasi-military takeover. The methodological approach that would break through this confusion would go beyond social history and would concentrate upon the actions of the political elites themselves. We discover that of the maghribi elites, the Algerian elites have been historically the most divided in their orientations, the most heterogeneous in their composition, and the most given to dissensus. This being a fact of history, the revolution, which many leaders of Algeria believed would furnish unity, in reality only intensified the existing antagonisms and created a new basis for dissension. To this day, there have been no satisfactory explanations of this interelite conflict and of the social conditions within which it has thrived.[28]

---

[28] Serge Bromberger, *Les rebelles algériens* (Paris: Plan, 1958); see also David and Marina Ottaway, *Algeria: The Politics of a Socialist Revolution* (Berkeley and Los Angeles: University of California Press, 1970). These authors continue in the tradition of interpreting interelite conflict (and actually everything) in terms of primordial conflicts between Berbers and Arabs, as if the elite factions could be conceived of as tribal segments, and as if twentieth-century maghribi politics were merely a repetition of the medieval period. The Ottaways have even less excuse because they arrived late to an old world and its issues and simply relied on dated nineteenth-century colonial ideology.

Until the armed resistance, Algerian national aspirations found expression in multiple and often antagonistic organizations. We can schematically distinguish three orientations. The first, norm-oriented and reconciliatory, expressed the aspirations of the intellectuals and of the liberal bourgeoisie and had its best symbol in Ferhat Abbas. The second orientation was born in the labor milieu of Paris, under the leadership of Messali; having been transplanted to Algeria in 1937 under the name of Parti du Peuple Algérien, it succeeded in laying the foundation for modern nationalism, thanks to its populist methods and the courage of its militants. Finally, the traditional literate bourgeoisie—or what was left of it in the city of Constantine—along with its Ulama composed the nationalitarian orientation, which confined itself to the defense of cultural identity and launched the slogan, "Islam is our religion, Arabic our language, and Algeria our country," made popular by its greatest *alem* (religious scholar), Ben Badis.

Despite many attempts, these three orientations were never merged into a single, recognized national leadership. It was as if each elite pursued its own goals, and that all coexisted in separate societies. It would seem that the ability of the Istiqlal in Morocco and the Destour in Tunisia to develop a coherent national party was, in part, due to the visible continuity of national institutions and political traditions. In fact, one of our hypotheses concerning the roots of dissensus among Algerian elites is based on the profound discontinuity these elites have experienced vis-à-vis the symbols and institutions of national identity, and the complete obliteration of their political state by a total colonial system.

The destruction of the state was discussed in Part II; therefore, we shall add only a few remarks concerning France's intentional eviction and demotion of the traditional grand families and the aristocratic elites. Augustin Berque's inquiry in 1949 into the dossiers of the qaids revealed that out of this body of 721 members, who were traditionally great aristocratic chiefs, only 100 were still of aristocratic origin; 200 were fabricated clergy, and the rest, of modest origin and with no authority whatsoever, were simply asked to assume the function of surveillance.[29] The *déclassement* of the

[29] Augustin Berque, "Esquisse d'une histoire de la seigneurie Algérienne," *Revue de la Méditerranée*, no. 7 (1949), pp. 18–34, 168–180; see also "La bourgeoisie algérienne," *Hesperis*, XXXV (1948).

great families and the successive waves of literate and commercial bourgeoisie immigrants deprived Algeria, in contrast with its neighbors, of a vital component in the integration and continuity of the society. It is no surprise to find that in a society which survived a century and a half of colonization with concomitant impoverishment, atomization, and deculturation, the fundamental problem was one of solidarity and authority.

From the pen of one of Algeria's intellectuals, Mostefa Lacheraf, we learn that Algeria lost "the essential support and the impetus for any genuine collective evolution." As a result, the discontinuity of national traditions was such that an appreciable part of the elite, despite the excessive protestations of the Ulama, came ultimately to doubt the very historical existence of the Algerian nation. The attestation, in 1936, of Ferhat Abbas, a man who traveled through all the stages of Algerian nationalism and who today commands the respect of all factions, should not be taken lightly. He wrote, "I have interrogated history; I have interrogated the living and the dead; I have visited cemeteries—no one spoke to me of the Algerian nation." [30]

Consequently, the liberal elite most exposed to European influence became the most assimilationist and was constantly challenged by the Ulama, who, in turn, fell into fundamentalist intransigence, alienating many intellectuals. In addition, France's pursuit, throughout the colonial era, of a policy of systematic repression against any political organization of national character augmented the propensity for sectarianism. Because every political organization found it necessary to change its name at least four times following repressive dissolutions, all forms of organization sooner or later reached an impasse. On November 1, 1954, when Tunisia had obtained its autonomy from France, and Morocco was heading for independence, a segment of the Algerian elite made an appeal for armed resistance; it is important to note, however, that this initiative originated from outside the existing political structures.

The launching of an armed struggle represented an attempt to transcend the inner divisions within the political elite and to break out of the vicious circle of political impotence. Those men who

[30] Ferhat Abbas, *L'Entente* (February 23, 1936); as quoted by André Nouschi in *La Naissance du Nationalisme Algérien, 1914–1954* (Paris: Editions de Minuit, 1962), p. 89.

authored the initiative came from the populist mainstream and were exasperated with endless legal arguments and prefabricated elections—the only forms of political life tolerated by the colonial system. They had previously tried to establish a paramilitary organization, Organization Speciale, which was immediately discovered and dismantled. This time, the same group, composed of twenty-two men, decided to play the part of a catalyst by setting off a war that would necessitate the unification of the divided political factions—a goal they were unable to achieve in any other way. Organized first as the CRUA and then definitively as the Front de Libération Nationale (FLN), this emerging leadership called for unity of action on the part of everyone, without judgment, whatsoever, of past differences. The following account by one of the leaders gives us a precise idea of the situational constraints, the most important of which were the absence of a precedent for organizational framework, and absolute repression:

> Two solutions were offered to the group of twenty-two: organize first and attack later or attack first and organize later. . . . We were forced to choose the second solution, that is, to fire first in order to create a favorable psychological climate for the national population to support completely the revolution. The group also decided that there should be a meeting three months later to analyze the situation. This meeting never took place because those most responsible were not free to move about at that time. In effect, after the attack of November 1, the events forced the leaders to disperse. And it was impossible thereafter for them to meet, [but] they were surprised by the participation, en masse, of the people in the struggle.[31]

It is true that through conscientious and systematic effort, the FLN leadership succeeded in achieving the fullest rural mobilization in the Maghrib, and that the predominantly peasant Armée de Libération Nationale (ALN) in its resistance to imperialism has had very few equivalents in the Third World (perhaps only in Vietnam and China). However, when it became clear that the peasantry had collectively joined the struggle, the colonial system decided to concentrate its war in the rural areas. Thus, Algerian rural society faced a French countermobilization that pathologically precipitated cultural, social, and economic disintegration.

[31] As quoted by Amar Ouzegane in *Le Meilleur Combat* (Paris: René Julliard, 1962), p. 200.

Confronted with the emergence of several national liberation movements, France chose to agree to the independence of Tunisia, Morocco, and even parts of Africa that had not fought for it, comparatively speaking. At the same time, it concentrated all its military forces in a desperate and bitter attempt to keep its *Algérie française*. Following its failure in Dien Bien Phu, the French army—apparently fascinated by its Asiatic experience—intended to succeed in Algeria (which, moreover, was only a few hours from Paris) at that which had failed elsewhere. For this purpose, the method of *regroupement* of the population constituted the army's most efficient weapon. Some statistics will help us to comprehend how the constraints surrounding the revolution and the nature of the war led to the disintegration of Algerian society, in general, and of the rural society, in particular. In 1961, it was estimated that the number of individuals forced into centers of *regroupement* by the army reached 2,350,000, that is, 26.1 percent of the total population; for a rural population of 6,900,000, this meant that one out of three people was uprooted and regrouped. Table 14, established on the basis of numerical data from the Service de Statistique Générale de l'Algérie, shows the percentage of regrouped populations by *arrondissement*.

Although the three *arrondissements* of Algiers, Sétif, and Paul-Cazelles were spared the policy of *regroupement*, their populations were altered by the rural exodus to these areas. From 1954 to 1960, Algiers' population increased by 85 percent, and Sétif and Paul-Cazelles were enlarged by 60 percent each. This movement of social and cultural disintegration was mainly extended to the twenty administrative units situated in the mountains and frontier zones, which

TABLE 14

REGROUPMENT BY ADMINISTRATIVE UNIT

	Number of arrondissements										*Total*
	3	13	10	18	9	4	2	5	3	4	5	76
Percentage of population regrouped	0	10	20	30	40	50	60	70	80	90	100	

SOURCE: Michel Cornaton, *Les regroupements de la décolonisation en Algérie* (Paris: Editions Ouvrières, 1967), p. 124.

had, until that time, been protected from colonial forms of dispossession. If we add to those regrouped in camps the number of peasant families which were *recasés* (a favorite expression of the military, indicating the removal of populations to controlled villages and cities), we arrive at the figure of 3,525,000 persons displaced, that is, more than 50 percent of the rural population. Forced relocation and the flight of refugees entirely undermined the peasant society, or what remained of it, and, in the words of an anthropologist, "made of the peasant civilization a *tabula rasa;* one could speak only [of peasant civilization] as something of the past." [32]

The political elite was far from being spared colonial repression —a repression that was immediate, total, and mercilessly effective. Of the twenty-nine most active and instrumental leaders in starting the revolution (including the first group of twenty-two men and the seven members of the Comité Révolutionnaire d'Unité et d'Action), thirteen were killed either by assassination or in combat, and five members of the exterior delegation were kidnapped and imprisoned until independence in 1962. These men were Ben Bella, Boudiaf, Ait Ahmed, Khider, and Lacheraf. There is no doubt that at its inception the Algerian Revolution was in the process of creating a solid organization able to link permanently the rural and urban societies.

For the first time, a serious effort was in the making to establish structures of leadership and authority capable of coordinating political and military struggles and of providing the society with a vision for the future. Apart from obstacles inherent in the society (which have been analyzed) and distinctive inhibitions among the elite (which will be discussed later), it is undeniable that the colonial system was ingenious and relentless in preventing political maturation and institution building, and that its preferred weapon was the physical liquidation of the fine flower of leadership. In September, 1956, Germaine Tillon wrote in *Complementary Enemies,* "The army received the order to annihilate the politico-military cadres of the insurrection 'by any means necessary.' The

[32] Pierre Bourdieu, *Sociologie de l'Algérie* (Paris: Presses Universitaires de France, 1963), p. 125; *The Algerians* (Boston: Beacon Press, 1962), pp. 145–192; "Révolution dans la Révolution," *Esprit* (January, 1960). See also M. Lesne, "Une expérience de déplacement de population," *Annales de Géographie,* no. 388 (November–December 1962), pp. 567–603.

politico-military cadres meant, in fact, all the notables, all the elites of the cities, all the educated youth." [33] Most of the militants were condemned to death, tracked down by the police, and dispensed with as if they were bandits and terrorists.

In a context filled with violence, adversity, and constraint, the FLN adopted—willingly or not—tenuous, rapid, and improvised methods in order to survive. It was induced to move its headquarters to Tunisia, to bring into its organization old members of the UDMA and MTLD, and to recruit among the young generation a sizable number of military officers and intellectuals. Given the extermination of many of the top leaders, and thus the rapid turnover within their ranks, it was to be expected that these youths would easily make their way into positions of leadership, thereby weakening the authority structure of the FLN as an emerging institution. In view of the widening gap between Algerian forces of the interior and those of the exterior, the Congress of the Soummam held on August 2, 1956, tried to provide a minimum of centralization. The fifty delegates, the majority of whom belonged to the *wilaya-s* forces (administrative units established by the revolution) which represented the men actually in combat, agreed to a political platform and to the establishment of an embryonic government. The principles adopted and actually applied until 1958 included primacy of the interior over the exterior, primacy of the political over the military, and collegial decision making.

For one of the members of the elite, Mohammadi Saïd, the Congress of the Soummam "represented a second November 1; until then, I was scared to death, because in view of the past, the organization could fail. After 1956, I no longer had any fear because solid structures were established." In reality, the institutions produced by the Congress—the Conseil National de la Révolution Algérienne (CNRA) and the Comité de Coordination et d'Exécution (CCE), both intended to be the fundamental governing instruments of the FLN—remained theoretical. Not only did their members rarely meet, but the logic of the war and the division of tasks among the different sectors of the elite condemned these institutions to be merely symbolic. At the same time, power was given to those engaged in combat—those in the interior and in the

[33] Germaine Tillon, *Les Ennemis Complémentaires* (Paris: Editions de Minuit, 1960).

organized army stationed along the frontiers. With the creation of a provisional government, GPRA, the interelite conflict broadened. Parallel to the constant tensions between the Algerian leaders of the interior and exterior, a new conflict set in opposition the two exogenous bodies formed in the wake of the revolution. These two bodies were the governmental bureaucracy of the provisional government, composed of old politicians, diplomats, and new intellectuals, and the Chiefs of Staff of the army, recently established to wage the war against the French electrified barbed wire system that surrounded the whole of Algeria.

As we have pursued our line of explanation, we have continually assumed that the differential and discontinuous political socialization of the populists, liberals, Ulama, and revolutionaries has played a significant part in interelite conflict. Differential socialization of a group would lead it to react negatively to other groups, to perpetuate its autonomy, and to challenge other people's policies, which seem to it deficient. One could even argue that the FLN's incorporation of the different factions of the elite did not succeed in preventing each group from perceiving itself as the unique embodiment of the Algerian Revolution. The fact remains that the co-optation of new talents—military personnel, intellectuals, and students—only accentuated the heterogeneity of the elite, its aptitude for exclusion and dissensus, and its formation of alliances on bases other than the institutional. (See Table 15 for the social background of the Algerian elite.)

The hypothesis of differential political socialization, however, would not account for either the overall interelite conflict or for the new alignments. This hypothesis cannot explain, for example, the fact that during the confrontation between the provisional government and the National Army of Liberation, a man who was previously president of the GPRA and the most coherent liberal of the Maghrib, Ferhat Abbas, came to ally himself with the army.[34] Owing to a conjunction of contextual variables—war, total repression, and, mainly, the absence of authoritative leadership—a revolu-

[34] This is the major limitation of William B. Quandt's *Revolution and Political Leadership: Algeria, 1954–1968* (Cambridge, Mass.: M.I.T. Press, 1969), which is otherwise a good historical account. Explaining interelite conflict exclusively in terms of different socialization is simply begging the question, Why is the elite socialized differently in the first place?

TABLE 15

SOCIAL BACKGROUNDS OF THE ALGERIAN WARTIME ELITE

	Politicians[a]	Revolutionaries	Military	Intellectuals	Total elite	Percent of total Algerian Moslem population (1948)
Education						
University	11 (100%)	2 (8%)	2 (8%)	11 (69%)	26 (34%)	<.5
Secondary	—	19 (73%)	4 (17%)	3 (19%)	26 (34%)	1.5
Elementary	—	5 (19%)	5 (21%)	—	10 (13%)	11
Unknown	—	—	13 (54%)	2 (12%)	15 (19%)	
Region of birth						
Algiers	5 (45%)	3 (12%)	1 (4%)	4 (25%)	13 (17%)	23
Constantine	2 (18%)	13 (50%)	3 (12%)	6 (38%)	24 (31%)	22
Oran	1 (9%)	5 (19%)	2 (8%)	1 (6%)	9 (12%)	40
Kabylia	3 (28%)	5 (19%)	3 (12%)	1 (6%)	12 (16%)	15
Unknown	—	—	15 (64%)	4 (25%)	19 (24%)	
Size of birthplace						
100,000 and over	2 (18%)	2 (8%)	—	3 (19%)	7 (9%)	6
30,000–100,000	1 (9%)	2 (8%)	1 (4%)	—	4 (5%)	7
3,000–30,000	4 (37%)	10 (38%)	1 (4%)	5 (31%)	20 (26%)	25
Under 3,000	3 (27%)	10 (38%)	6 (25%)	3 (19%)	22 (29%)	62
Unknown	1 (9%)	2 (8%)	16 (67%)	5 (31%)	24 (31%)	
Average age in 1954	39	32	28	27	29	
Top political roles per individual	2.7	3.3	1.3	1.1	2.3	
Total	11	26	24	16	77	7,600,000

[a] An aggregate of liberals and radicals.

SOURCE: William Quandt, *Revolution and Political Leadership: Algeria, 1954–1968* (Cambridge, Mass.: M.I.T. Press, 1969), p. 151.

tionary situation was created and generalized within which what really mattered was not so much the individual likes and dislikes of the elite's members but the relative strength and ranking of the organizations to which they belonged. Under these conditions, whatever the method of socialization, the means of political conflict tended to become delimited.

In such a situation, the appearance of new quasi-autonomous institutions vis-à-vis the FLN introduced new and previously unknown men to the different hierarchies of command. Within Algeria, the war isolated the *wilaya-s* from one another and from external sources of support, curtailing their fighting capacities and reducing them, by the end, to the level of petty principalities at loggerheads with one another over resources, tactics, and strategy.[35] In the midst of unrestrained competition among organizations, elites, and military units, the only organization that was characterized by *esprit de corps* and that commanded the loyalty of its members was the external army, under the leadership of Hawari Boumediène (this is the commonly accepted name, which is in fact Abu Medien). It was growing in direct proportion to the decline of the FLN and the fragmentation of the internal guerrillas. Moreover, as the provisional government came to rely upon the external army to crush the increasing internal dissidence, the army became the nexus of power.

Organization theory can be very helpful in comprehending revolutions. Arthur Stinchcombe argues, "The lack of consensus on the ranks of organizations and how the ranks may legitimately be improved, and because of the quality of the biographies of the new leaders, the commitment of the leaders of organizations to the norms which rank organizations tends to be weak during a period of rapid structural differentiation (or during a revolutionary situation). In the language of sociology, we would say that organizational leaders in such a period tend to be 'anomic.'"[36] If by anomie, we understand a low degree of commitment of the elites to the norms governing interorganizational distribution of power, there is

[35] Eric R. Wolf, *Peasants' Revolts in the Twentieth Century* (New York: Harper & Row), 1969.

[36] Arthur L. Stinchcombe, "Social Structure and Organizations," in James G. March, ed., *Handbook of Organizations* (Chicago: Rand McNally, 1965), p. 175.

little doubt the Algerian elites were in a totally anomic situation as they approached independence. The access to various organizations—the interior *wilaya-s* forces, the governmental bureaucracy, and organizations outside the army—was not defined by regulated and accepted norms but rather in terms of alliances, clienteles, and ambitions. As former President Ben Khedda said, "A military and political bureaucracy was forged in exile which was characterized by the absence of interior life. Internal democracy, criticism and self-criticism, and serious criteria in the choice of leaders were all ignored, thus opening the door to *arrivisme* and flattery." [37]

As a result, political careers were meteoric, and the turnover beyond belief. Between 1954 and 1970, the eighty-seven-odd leaders who occupied roles of importance did so only for an average of two years, and it might be said that the men in power today were not even known less than ten years ago. The anticipation of independence, with its promise of power and related values, only intensified the competition among these anomic elites; what began as public recriminations among leaders, concerning which institution—the CNRA, GPRA, or ALN—represented the ultimate authority, or concerning whether Evian's agreements with France were satisfactory or not, was to conclude in an open struggle for power. Each group accused the other of violating the sacred rules of the revolution and used this apparent violation to justify its own rejection of these same rules. All this combined to produce the famous Summer of Shame. On the final day of triumph, the provisional government and the National Army of Liberation entered Algeria not as a unitary body but as fighting factions. Civil war was prevented only by the intervention of the Algerian people themselves who cried out, "Eight years, oh chiefs; *baraket* [that's enough]!"

The reader should be reminded that this war brought French society itself to the brink of civil war. It did, at any rate, cause the fall of the Fourth Republic, and through General de Gaulle, established the French military in power. Once more, the colonial dialectic is revealed to be not the simple impact of an active society upon a passive one but rather a profoundly mutual interaction. As to Algeria, by the day of independence, the legacy of in-

[37] Ben Khedda, "Contribution à l'histoire de FLN," mimeographed, April, 1964, Algiers.

stitutional decay was conspicuous to all in the form of the final disintegration of the political elites and institutions. It was keenly perceived by the militant and intellectual Mostefa Lacheraf:

> The FLN has ceased to exist since 1958 as a party in the usual sense. The political and national authority it represented, as a guide to the nation in wartime, has withered insensibly without any serious organic differentiation. This amalgamated authority was later reduced to two purely theoretical poles of action, to two institutions, the GPRA and the CNRA, having limited prerogatives, often symbolic in relation to the mass of organized militants and to the interior's combatants.
>
> The GPRA, official holder of national authority, internationally recognized, did nothing to make of its nominal and intermittent power a genuine and direct revolutionary power, imposing everywhere the primacy of the political over the military. . . . Its ability to control and arbitrate over the interior was reduced or effectively passed into the hands of the *wilaya-s,* and whatever anyone says, into the hands of an organism which, because of its affinity to the military power, was institutionally a function of the high command of the Armée de Libération Nationale.
>
> From this stems, so to speak, the irrational conflict between theoretical institutions and the actual reality of the army. This reality, good or bad for Algeria, meant that the country was deprived of a political authority extended to all.[38]

In the course of this confrontation, ideological orientations became secondary. While the Algerian peasantry quickly occupied the vacant land evacuated by the French settlers, the elite factions and the army were busy tending to the succession to power. But it was already all too clear which group would come to dominate the political system; and as the Algerian proverb goes, "He who wishes to understand too much will die of anger."

[38] Mostefa Lacheraf, *L'Algérie: Nation et société* (Paris: Maspero, 1965), pp. 291–293. The relationship of the *wilaya-s* and the classic army had its ups and downs, and at the time of independence, the *wilaya-s,* in their turn, were divided for and against the provisional government. The decisive factor for Lacheraf, however, remains that both of them represented military forces and were far from being controlled by central authority.

Chapter 8: THE COHERENCE
OF THE NATIONAL ELITE

Before assessing the capabilities of the newly independent maghribi regimes to meet the tasks which confront them, it is important to bear in mind the major trends of political change and their implications for the political community. The contextual analysis developed in the preceding chapters was intended to identify the new social forces and the key groups that have come to play strategic roles in the political process. The analysis of these political changes was conducted in terms of a paradigm that permits us to explain in what sense Morocco inherited a marginal elite, Algeria a heterogeneous elite, and Tunisia a homogeneous one. As we shall see later, the identification of these groups and their orientations will tell us a good deal about the national capacities of the regimes and the manner in which they act upon policy alternatives. At this stage, however, a key issue deserves some treatment: the question of whether or not we are discussing societies which are at last nationally integrated. One of the values of our approach is that it permits us to answer this question satisfactorily.

Independence and postindependence mean liberation from a foreign and arbitrary political control and encourage among the people enormous expectations of governmental responsiveness. In such transitional politics, the people are aware that fundamental changes are in the making, and that the conditions in which they are living—whether they are political, economic, or social—are precarious and ephemeral. This often leads to dramatic confrontations and, more particularly, to a political struggle, involving the people and the elites—a struggle that is directed toward fundamental objectives instead of marginal benefits. When these conflicts take place in a culturally pluralistic society, the risk of rupturing national integration always exists. As Geertz writes, "The very process of the formation of a sovereign civil state . . . stimulates sentiments of parochialism, communalism, racialism, and so on, because it introduces into society a valuable new prize over which to fight and a frightening new force with which to contend." [39]

Maghribi independence was marked by intensive rural conflicts, which provided ample opportunity for the revival of theories of segmentation. Some analysts have insisted upon judging the rural conflicts of postindependent Maghrib as a symbol of the old dissidence (*siba*) against the state (Makhzen), and perceiving this as a sign of national breakdown.[40] In societies in which national identity is no longer problematic and in which cultural units are included within a larger administrative and institutional framework, the insistence upon applying a theory of segmentation amounts to interpreting in traditional terms what is in essence modern political conflict. The following pages provide a discussion of the events surrounding the establishment of the new political systems of North Africa, in terms of two underlying assumptions. First, the rural rebellion in the bifurcated social structure of the Maghrib is not to be interpreted as an instance of primordial politics but as pressure upon the state to assume its welfare functions vis-à-vis the different groups that constitute the society. It is assumed that most communities in North Africa have internalized the values of modern societies, but that given the low structural differentiation, these communities lack the institutionalized means for articulating their demands. Because of the disjunction between internalized goals and the absence of institutionalized means, social groups have to assume traditional postures to press for modern demands.

Secondly, the central conflicts in transitional politics concern, instead, confrontations among the national elites themselves concerning who will control the state and determine its developmental goals. Societal integration is no longer at issue. Today, North African states are integrated, centralized, and patterned along the lines

[39] Clifford Geertz, "The Integrative Revolution: Primordial Sentiments and Civil Politics in the New States," in Clifford Geertz, ed., *Old Societies and New States: The Quest for Modernity in Asia and Africa* (New York: The Free Press, 1963), p. 120.

[40] See, for example, John Waterbury, *The Commander of the Faithful: The Moroccan Political Elite—A Study in Segmented Politics* (New York: Columbia University Press, 1970); Amal Vinogradov and John Waterbury, "Situations of Contested Legitimacy in Morocco: An Alternative Framework," *Comparative Studies in Society and History*, XIII:1 (January, 1971), pp. 32–59.

of contemporary Europe. Thus, the main problems are those of the efficacy and legitimacy of these regimes.

Ernest Gellner's analysis of independent Morocco is similar to the interpretation we offer here. Gellner is intrigued by certain features of the rural rebellions that have occurred from the first decade of Moroccan independent political life up to the present: These rebellions have tended to collapse quite easliy; their leaders have been treated with leniency; and the uprisings have been almost invariably connected with members of the ruling elite. In the author's words, they have not made sense, "Tribesmen who proclaim themselves supporters of X stage a rebellion—whilst X is in office as Prime Minister. Or again: a Y stages a rebellion—which is then suppressed by Y himself, whose supporter the rebels claim to be, and in whose very support the rebellion was made." [41]

It might be useful to recall that in our treatment of political elites the Moroccan rural resistance came only at the end when the direction of events leading to independence had become clear. With the monarch still in exile and the Istiqlal leaders still in prison, a situation of uncertainty prevailed as to who possessed the real power. France eliminated a large base of maneuver by choosing its *interlocuteur valable* from competing candidates. The chances for a seizure of the state apparatus by the monarchy, by what remained of the Istiqlal, or by other independent forces in the capital were ultimately dependent upon who controlled all or part of the resistance in the countryside. Even though members of the resistance ultimately laid down their arms at the order of the sultan, a precedent had been set for the exercise of influence upon the center by the interior reaches of the countryside.

One might say that the uprisings of 1957 and 1958–1959 were related to two significant points: (a) a conflict of interests arising from the control of the flow of patronage and administration; and (b) the attempt on behalf of the monarchy to sustain any group that might rival Istiqlal dominance, even if the result was rural rebellions. In this very context, the revolt led by Governor Addi Ou Bihi and supported by Minister of Interior Lyusi was an attempt to prevent

---

[41] Ernest Gellner, "Patterns of Rural Rebellion in Morocco: Tribes as Minorities," *Archives Européennes de Sociologie*, III (1962), 297. See also W. Lewis, "Feuding and Social Change in Morocco," *Journal of Conflict Resolution*, V (1961), 43–54.

the Istiqlal from centralizing, to its advantage, administrative power. Indeed, the extension of the national law and abrogation of the customary tribunals, championed by the Istiqlali minister of justice, meant that the national party was the sole force capable of making judicial appointments. The new judges assumed the legal power usually granted to local qaids, and they were eventually perceived as a challenge to the local administrative power of the governor and his retainers. Furthermore, the Istiqlalis, who had not undertaken rural mobilization prior to independence, began to infiltrate the interior, the police, the Department of Education, and the public works. The party used its political weight to expel the hundreds of local qaids who compromised themselves under colonialism. The newly appointed qaids became the equivalent of the French district officers; the major aspects of this sociopolitical change were the abolition of tribal intermediaries between the central power and the local population, the elimination of what the nationalists called feudal elements, and finally the achievement of centralization of power, to the advantage of the Istiqlal party.

The final blow came when Minister of Interior Lyusi was replaced by Driss M'hammedi in May, 1956. The clash between the national elite and locally based power was not far off. In January 1957, Lyusi aided Ou Bihi in his plan to arrest this threatening advance of the Istiqlal. After having received arms from the French officers, Ou Bihi closed down the Istiqlali cells and imprisoned almost all the officials in his region, including the police chief and the judge, justifying his revolt in the name of safeguarding the throne from the machinations of the Istiqlal. Before long, two battalions of the Royal Armed Forces were dispatched to the region, whereupon Ou Bihi surrendered with assurance of the *aman* (a traditional gesture insuring fair treatment). During the trial, it became clear that Ou Bihi's entire objective was to maintain his patronage system. Many qaids testified in his favor, but many Berbers testified against him for mistreatment and quasi-feudal behavior. The Istiqlal was then at the summit of its strength, and it used the trial to discredit its "feudal" opponents and to dissuade the palace from interfering directly in the determination of national politics.

The Rif rebellion that broke out between November and December, 1958 came as a blow to the national elite, provoked a governmental crisis, and revealed without doubt the intention of palace policy. Following Governor Ahardane's dismissal and arrest for having engaged in partisan activity, the armed dissidents gathered around Oulmes, Ahardane's home town. It is important to note that Ahardane's venture was not unrelated to the palace strategy in creating counterforces intended both to weaken the Istiqlal and afford the monarchy the final position of arbitration. The king and prince are known to have encouraged Ahardane in creating a political party (Le Mouvement Populaire), and without risking public involvement, they did provide him with substantial assistance, even though the existing Istiqlal majority made it very difficult to legalize the party. That rural rebellion in Morocco has been mainly a consequence of interelite conflict can be further confirmed by a political actor's own account. "The political leader, Ahardane," writes Ernest Gellner, "later Minister of War, and apparently a loyal royalist, claimed to me to have been connected with the Rif rising, without actually taking part in it, in as far as he was co-responsible for its termination with the then government, on terms which included the official recognition of his own political party, semi-clandestine up till then. The demand for such a recognition was, he claimed, part of the motive for the rising." [42] A region, however, has to be well organized in order to put its patronage at the disposal of a faction and thus gain the ability to exert pressure upon the central government.

Another precipitating factor in the emergence of rural rebellion seems to be the feeling of objective deprivation of the region and the degree of responsiveness that it expects from the government. The Rif tribesmen felt that they had contributed substantially to the struggle for independence, and, therefore, they held great expectations for schools, jobs, improved communications, and welfare in general. The list of complaints which they presented to the state on November 11 included the following: (a) underadministration and the feeling of abandonment; (b) unemployment; (c) fiscal injustice; (d) lack of hospitals, roads, schools, and agricultural credits; (e) administrative snarls. Although regional discontent can play into the hands of parochial and conservative leaders, it is geared toward regional sharing in the benefits of modernity. It should be

---

[42] Ernest Gellner, "Tribalism and Social Change in North Africa," in W. H. Lewis, ed., *French-Speaking Africa: The Search for Identity* (New York: Walker, 1965).

evident by now that Merton's paradigm[43] describing the disjunction between internalized values and institutional means applies perfectly to Moroccan politics. Indeed, when confronted with the alternative of the old traditions and the benefits of modernity, the Moroccan rural society chose modernity even if that meant resorting to traditional modes of pressure in order to attract the ruler's attention.

Gellner's interpretation of the outbreaks of dissidence in post-independent Morocco, in terms of rival, informal networks of authority and patronage that did not respect formal hierarchies, is subject to one limitation. It assumes that these various outbreaks were only "dress rehearsals, trial runs, for a serious and decisive showdown between the main claimants to Morocco's political inheritance." [44] I am afraid that, here, Gellner misconstrued a performance for a dress rehearsal. In fact, it was a major confrontation from which the monarchy emerged triumphant over all rival claimants to power, and its triumph seemed to determine the political, economic, and social future of the nation.

It should have been clear from the different strategies by which Mohammed V managed to assert his control over the resistance that he alone would govern. For example, in his major address to the leaders of the insurrection, he said, "We address to you our whole-hearted thanks, and in receiving you today we receive faithful and loyal subjects. Now that independence has been achieved . . . and all Moroccans aspire to order and stability . . . it has pleased your sovereign to receive you . . . on this blessed day on which you have come in answer to the call of your king, to listen to his words and to heed his counsel." [45]

Numerous efforts—even the pretense of representing all elements of society—were undertaken by the monarchy in order to ignore the Istiqlal party. After having given his tacit approval to rurally based parties and having revived the weak Democratic Party of Independence (PDI), the sultan proclaimed himself above all parties and called for a government of "national union." In the first govern-

[43] Robert Merton, *Social Theory and Social Structure* (New York: Free Press, 1957), pp. 131–194.

[44] Ernest Gellner, "The Great Patron: A Reinterpretation of Tribal Rebellions," *Archives Européennes de Sociologie*, X:1 (1969), 61–69.

[45] *Le Monde*, March 31, 1956; and *Le Monde*, April 1–2, 1956.

ment, there was simply a combination of heterogeneous elements: five independents, six members of PDI, and a representative of the Jewish community. The Istiqlalis, who had nine representatives, were obviously to be considered one force among many others. By trying to present itself as the symbol of national unity and by exercising the primary function of arbitration, the Moroccan monarchy succeeded in reviving the old style of politics, reminiscent of the precolonial state. It was, assuredly, a reinvigorated, bureaucratically based restoration of the old monarchy, but it was a monarchy that succeeded in appropriating independence for itself.

That rural rebellions are a manifestation of interelite conflicts is even more apparent in Algeria. There, the conflicts were of greater intensity, partly because of the profound social discontinuities that disturbed the systemic integration of the society, and, as a corollary, because of the absence of an authoritative instrument of social control. At a time when the tasks of nation building were more pressing than ever, the political party was collapsing and could not meet the expectations of the various militants and sympathizers with the Algerian Revolution. Visiting Algeria in 1962, Jean Lacouture commented, "The party does not exist. This is the sudden discovery one is forced to admit when visiting Algeria today: the FLN might have a prestigious past, it might have a great future, but in the present it literally does not exist." [46] In the absence of a "combat" party, the political vacuum created by a disordered independence was filled by a loose and unstable coalition of a fraction of the political elite, some guerrilla commanders, and the major staff of the exterior army. It is virtually impossible to make sense of the rural rebellions and the instability of the Algerian political system, as a whole, without taking into account the many ways in which various elites have, in their struggles for power, exacerbated the latent social tensions and the existing conflicts within the society.

Brought to power by the army, a segment of the political elite ignored institutions, like the CNRA, established prior to independence and intended to govern the country in the name of a five-man committee of the Political Bureau. This segment of the elite was, in fact, simply the result of a tactical alliance; an adventurer-

[46] As quoted by Jean Claude Douence in "La mise en place des institutions algériennes," *Fondation Nationale des Sciences Politiques: Etudes Maghrébines*, no. 2 (September, 1964), p. 44.

populist like Ben Bella, a parliamentary liberal like Ferhat Abbas, and a scripturalist-nationalitarian like Tewfik el-Midani had nothing in common. Although some measures were taken to legitimize the national power—for example, the organization of elections for the national assembly—there was no consensus whatsoever among Ben Bella and his allies as to the structure of the government and the distribution of positions of power. The head of the government, Ben Bella, favored a single-party system but viewed the party as an instrument in the service of his own power. Kidher, Secretary General of the FLN, wanted a single-party system in which the government and the assembly would play subordinate roles. Such was the issue, in theory; in practice, Kidher, who installed Ben Bella in the first place, was willing to permit him all resounding titles, but he contrived for himself the ultimate power. On the other hand, Ferhat Abbas, president of the National Assembly, sought to establish a parliamentary regime conducive to a multiparty system, thus rendering the assembly the most important institution. As this conflict proceeded, the bulk of the political elite, which sustained the GPRA, either began to withdraw from politics or was forced to oppose the government.

Late in September, 1963, the struggle centered upon the writing of the constitution. Although one-third of the 196 members of the National Assembly were guerrilla leaders with minimal education, some top members of the assembly, like Ferhat Abbas and Ait Ahmed, intended to compose the document and to exert control over the government. Since Ben Bella's government was making all the major decisions without consulting the assembly, a crisis was obviously about to surface. Ferhat Abbas resigned, and Ait Ahmed withdrew to his homeland in Kabylia and declared his rebellion against Ben Bella.

This conflict between political elites took place at the same time as a confrontation between the guerrilla leaders of the interior and the General Staff of the Army of National Liberation. The General Staff was not only trying to impose the authority of the Political Bureau but was also planning a reconversion of the ALN into a new Armée Nationale Populaire (ANP); the latter involved the merger of the *wilaya* forces with the troops previously stationed outside Algeria. The attempt at military centralization was perceived by the guerrilla chiefs as a means of eliminating them from the political scene; although some of them accepted a new military command, others, like Si Hassan and Mohand Ou el-Hadj, respectively commanders of *wilaya-s* 3 and 4, refused. When the Kabyle rebellion broke, Mohand Ou el-Hadj and a group of former officers joined in.

The Kabyle insurrection lasted for the duration of Ben Bella's government. Peasant discontent had something to do with it, even though the maghribi peasantry, in general, proved to be less revolutionary in the long run. The Algerian government had ignored the outbreaks in the Aurès Mountains because these represented distant pressures capable of being resolved by the mere co-optation of local leaders to the agencies of the state. Insurrections have been far more dangerous in Kabylia than in other areas for two reasons. First, having produced the greater portion of the central political elite, the Kabyle peasantry has had more vital a connection with the politico-administrative apparatus than any other region in Algeria. The point being, if the Kabyle peasantry has succeeded, it has not been merely because it engaged in rebellion but because insurrections have been organized by the urban political elite. Secondly, as Jeanne Favret has shown, the social structure of Kabylia has been one of the most diversified of the entire society.[47] It has had a strong tradition of immigration—18.3 percent of the population in Algiers is composed of Kabyles—and it has also represented a significant part of the industrial working class. Like the Sahel in Tunisia, this region was less exposed to military operations and colonial destruction, and its population has been well prepared to adapt itself both to the colonial economy and to the new political changes.

Partly because of this differentiation, Ait Ahmed and his party (Front des Forces Socialistes) received neither the backing of all Kabyle leaders nor of all the Kabyle people. The majority of the deputies from the region remained neutral, and at least four top officers of the Seventh Military Region Command refused to follow Colonel Mohand Ou el-Hadj. Furthermore, when invited to boycott the national elections for the constitution, 50 percent of the Kabyle voters simply ignored the boycott and participated in the elections, making clear their allegiance to the Political Bureau.

[47] Jeanne Favret, "Le traditionalisme par excès de modernité," *Archives Européennes de Sociologie*, VIII (1967), 71–93.

Despite this, the rebellion in Kabylia took on the dimensions of a national crisis. Ait Ahmed underscored the notion that what was at issue was a dissensus among national elites, and presented his attempt as one way of resolving the drama: "The avant-garde forces are polarized not by ideas but by men. These men should provide proof that they have no interest in prolonging the isolation and the division of forces. Right now, there exists no perspective for unification. Still, it is necessary to find a means of escaping stalemate." [48] In answer to some observers and newspapermen who remarked to him that his attempt might be interpreted as an act of secession, he said, "There is no question of secession. . . . Colonel Mohand Ou el-Hadj and his men have not mounted a *putsch* but have taken *a political position*. [The italics are mine.] In principle, we are not opposed to a dialogue with our adversaries." [49]

The response of the central power, which was to become a patterned, institutionalized response, was a mixture of concessions and counterchallenge. Ben Bella gave support to the legitimate demands of the Kabyle population and met privately with eleven Kabyle deputies. In order to appease the restive *wilaya* leaders, the government appointed Colonel Tahar Zbiri chief of the ANP General Staff. Finally, to Ait Ahmed, who claimed to be more genuinely socialist than Ben Bella, Ben Bella responded with the nationalization of more than one million hectares of colonized land. When at last the frontier conflict arose between Algeria and Morocco, Ben Bella's government succeeded in placing the Kabyle rebels in a position in which they faced abhorrent alternatives: they could either continue the armed struggle and risk the accusation of treason, or they could combine with the central power, which was, in this particular situation, a legitimation of Ben Bella's forces. In view of our framework, which stresses the existence of national integration in the maghribi societies, it is no surprise that the second alternative was chosen. Indeed, the Ait Ahmed party offered its services in defense of the homeland, and Colonel Mohand left for the frontier with a large contingent of Kabyle troops. During this conflict, the progressive Moroccan opposition (Union Nationale des Forces Populaires) sided with the Algerian regime, favoring its socialist

[48] H. Ait Ahmed, *La guerre et l'après-guerre* (Paris: Minuit, 1964), p. 152.

[49] *Le Monde*, October 1, 1963.

orientation, such as it was. The Moroccan monarchy, however, was less impressed by the Algerian regime's ideology as it was threatened by its political instability. One of the paradoxes of the situation, as noted by Mohammed Boudiaf, was that the frontier conflict gave both regimes, monarchical and socialist, the opportunity to crush their opposition.[50]

In the end, the conflict was settled in a way that decreased Ben Bella's dependence upon the army and created a basis for new alliances. The negotiations with Colonel Mohand, besides substantial advantages for the Kabyle region, concluded with amnesty for all army officers and civilians who wished to leave the rebellion, the release of all political prisoners, including Mohammed Boudiaf, and the promise of a party congress within five months in which all leaders of the revolution could participate. It is, thus, ironic, as will be analyzed later, that in the course of his efforts to achieve new political foundations for stability, Ben Bella was ousted by the army in June, 1965.

Not more than Morocco or Algeria, and in reality far less, was Tunisia subjected to an internal split within the state. Although it is overwhelmingly recognized that the bifurcation between rural and urban structures has been less deep here than in the other North African societies, some writers have ascribed to the Pan-Arab orientation of Salah Ben Youssef a potential for undermining the state in the name of a suprastate primordialism. These writers described Ben Youssef as a partisan of Nasser and cast them both, in Geertz's words, as "the new States' most accomplished virtuosos in the primordial arts, . . . absorbed in juggling Pan-Arabic, Pan-Islamic, Pan-African sentiments in the interests of Egyptian hegemony among the Bandung powers." [51] In light of this description, let us look more closely at the political environment in which the Youssefist affair emerged, in the first place.

In Tunisia, the political inheritance was transferred in the most orderly fashion, and this consecrated the neo-Destour party as the overwhelming ruler and winner of the political power. However, the Franco-Tunisian Convention, assuring the country of internal autonomy, was far from popular among the masses. It contained

[50] Mohammed Boudiaf, *Où va Algérie* (Paris: Libraire de l'Etoile, 1964), pp. 143–145.
[51] Clifford Geertz, "The Integrative Revolution," p. 116.

much that was unacceptable for the militants, especially in view of the fact that they had been involved in a national struggle which lasted more than three decades. For instance, it contained provisions that gave France control over external and internal security for ten years, and it gave the French high commissioner the power to influence domestic matters. Not only did many members of the workers' union (UGTT) oppose some of these provisions, but Ben Youssef himself—at that time, a very high official—denounced the convention. The Algerian FLN and the Istiqlal of Morocco, still battling for independence, opposed the convention and gave Ben Youssef a powerful argument for continuing the struggle, instead of abandoning his brothers in exchange for a semblance of autonomy.

This conflict over values and the symbols of independence was hardly the sole motivating force for the coming confrontation. The new shift in the distribution of power within the cosmos of party and society at large was, in fact, the primary motivating force. For more than twenty-six years, Salah Ben Youssef was, as secretary-general of the neo-Destour party, one of the most active leaders. The party owes him a great deal for having convinced the monarchy to join the national cause and for having helped to create institutions like the Agricultural Union (UGAT) and the Commerce Union (UTAC). Beyond all this, he was, in the words of a Tunisian journalist:

> A redoubtable polemicist, intelligent and passionate, primarily a political animal, he had an instinct for diatribe, for debate, for assertion, and for compromise. A prolific and skillful talker, he knew in conversation how to seduce in trying to convince. He also possessed the art—by his lucidity, sincerity, tricks, calculations, and skillful use of time—of electrifying a crowd by utilizing the resources of dialectic as well as the arsenal of passionate slogans.[52]

Having been exiled for two years, during which time he toured Middle Eastern societies and attended the Bandung Conference as representative of the whole Maghrib, he found it difficult, upon his return to Tunisia, to accept the convention, and even harder to

---

[52] *Afrique-Action* (August 19, 1961); as quoted in Clement Henry Moore, *Tunisia Since Independence: The Dynamics of One-Party Government* (Berkeley and Los Angeles: University of California Press, 1965), p. 62.

relate to a Political Bureau that no longer contained his own men. It would seem obvious, since the bulk of the party remained recalcitrant to his views, that Ben Youssef had to rely both on his patronage within the party and on outside forces. In the society at large, Ben Youssef could count on support from his home area, the island of Djerba. Many members of the elite interpreted the clash between Bourguiba and Ben Youssef in terms of the rival cultural and economic attitudes of the Sahel and Djerba. The people of the Sahel—community-oriented, better educated, and predominantly members of the bureaucracy—are more disposed to the practice of *étatisme*. The Djerbians, who are essentially a trading people and who control the major network of commerce in the entire country, are suspicious of government bureaucracy and government planning. As will be shown later in the analysis of developmental policies, their presentiments of doom were far from being chimerical.

While these differences in values and interests contributed to the imminence of the crisis, the Youssefist dissidents had no objective chances for success. With few exceptions, the core of the neo-Destour party remained unified. It received the backing of the Sahel, which was the stronghold of the national movement, of the professions, and of the majority of the students. By touring with Ben Salah, who at that time was the head of the labor union, in the mining area of the south and in promising substantial economic reforms, Bourguiba managed to obtain the support of the labor unions. Assured of the UGTT support (some 90,000 of its nearly 100,000 membership belonged to the party, whose total membership at this time was almost 180,000), Bourguiba took the initiative against his opponent before Ben Youssef had time to muster his forces. With a keen sense of timing, he had the Political Bureau dismiss Ben Youssef as secretary-general on the day after the latter had publicly denounced the party and government policy. In his stead, Bahi Ladgham took office. At the same time, a party congress was scheduled to be held, not in the Capitol where Ben Youssef was very popular, but in Sfax, the home district of Hached and Achour. Sfax was the stronghold of the labor union, and a city whose business tradition was strong enough to keep out the Djerbian merchants.

As it turned out, Ben Youssef's misfortune was that he was dependent upon support wherever he could find it. Because the progressive forces were clearly beyond his reach, he tried to appeal to the traditionalistic forces. This was, in fact, mere theatrics and demagogy, for he had the reputation of usually dispensing rather harshly with Arab-Islamic movements. Part of his theatrics was certainly the flamboyant speech he gave in the Zitouna Mosque, attempting to revive the old nationalitarian-scripturalist tendencies which were incipient within Tunisian society. Although he said that opposition did not mean that "one must take up the battle with sticks and scythe" but meant rather a political battle to be organized within the framework of his General Secretariat, there was sufficient polarization to lead to a few months of urban and rural terrorism. During these months, the neo-Destour acted as a "combat" party, containing the oppositional forces and neutralizing, as legitimately as possible, Ben Youssef's strength. The neo-Destour congress confirmed the success of the tactics; Ben Youssef's boycott failed, because only 54 out of 1,314 men were absent from the deliberations. The congress ratified the party decisions, and a few days later, the police launched a three-day operation during which 120 Youssefists were arrested. Ben Youssef alone was secretly informed and made his escape to Tripoli.

If the neo-Destour party emerged as victor, the labor union did not fail to secure some advantages for itself. Its economic report was adopted by the members of the congress, and the neo-Destour committed itself to a progressive social and economic policy. If it is true that this conflict illustrated the vulnerability of the masses for nationalitarian slogans, it is equally valid that the political elite demonstrated its capacities for preserving the integrity of the state and of national institutions. It may be part of the piper's price that the maintenance of unity would encourage overzealous defense mechanisms.

Part IV

ELITES, INSTITUTIONS, AND DEVELOPMENT

Chapter 9: INSTITUTIONS AND INSTITUTIONAL COMPETENCE

Up to this point, we have attended to the complex task of describing and explaining the institutional structures of maghribi societies as they evolved historically and as they stood at the moment of independence. We have been guided by the conviction that to penetrate more deeply the problems of the present, we must explore their roots in the past. In order to study the impact of political traditions upon the structures and orientations of present governments, there is no satisfactory alternative to historical analysis and to the models which may be derived from it. As we relate the pre-existing political and social orders to the tensions generated by modern economy and colonialism, our approach enables us to explain, for example, in what sense Moroccan institutional continuity favors a regime whose primary commitment is to system maintenance and traditionalized modes of legitimation. It enables us to account for the survival of many of the values of old Tunisian regimes and for the national elites' adoption of a secular orientation and a commitment to socioeconomic transformation.

For Algeria, our approach has documented the breakdown of the old social order and suggested why it is impossible for any political regime to be based exclusively upon former social structures and hierarchies. Once the roots of praetorian politics have been diagnosed, a further conclusion is that Algeria is peculiarly situated to benefit from its institutional discontinuity, if it seeks to do so. Unlike its neighbors, the Algerian regime has to contend only with weak vested interests, and we would expect it to pursue a policy that is more independent of various social classes. Therefore, there is little doubt that in all three maghribi countries, the pervasive ideologies and commitments, the different styles of interest articulation and aggregation, and the tempo of socioeconomic change bear the stamp of the initial formations of these political communities. Our next task of treating these issues in depth is greatly clarified now that we understand the integrative revolution that has taken place in North Africa, and know that recent conflicts and those which may ensue have had and will have no chance to undermine the fundamental unity of these societies, whatever changes they might bring to the regimes.

Here we wish to direct the reader's attention to a major shift in the focus of our analysis. In this part, our work will be not so much concerned with diachronic correlations as with the systematic analysis of governmental effectiveness in building lasting institutions and meeting societal demands for economic growth and equality. Having all along stressed the role of leadership and institutions, we do not mean to neglect the significance of factors largely beyond the leadership's control, such as natural resources, economic infrastructure, and market opportunities. To account for variations in national development, a genuine explanatory model requires the incorporation of these analytical distinctions. This problem will be discussed in the following pages, and our emphasis will shift from the *formation* of institutional structures to the question of how these institutional structures *work*. How do leaders, given their political traditions and their situational facilities, pursue certain policies, and at what costs to their regimes? In short, such a shift of outlook requires a mode of analysis that is less historical and more synchronic and structural.

First, we believe that if a regime is to remain in power and is to bring about economic development and equality of opportunities, it must develop a new kind of institutional competence. Not only must it meet internal demands for distribution of benefits and political participation but it must also reduce the internationally underprivileged status of its nation. If we take these exigencies literally, they amount to no less than the awesome political project of consciously and deliberately transforming the entire social structure. Secondly, the failure of the middle class in North Africa, as in other new nations, to provide economic entrepreneurship and to sustain democratic forms of government[1] means that political alternatives are worked out at the center and not at the periphery, and that the government comes to represent the only social unit

[1] José A. Silva Michelena, *The Illusion of Democracy in Dependent Nations.*

capable of utilizing national resources for societal purposes. Indeed, in order to end backwardness, dependency, and the propensity of privileged groups for hoarding and consumption, the government alone is able to divert the potential economic surplus and the flow of export income into productive purposes and welfare programs. This nationalization of economic life has been unmistakable in the developments of all late-comers to industrialization.[2]

Socioeconomic reorganization and sociopolitical reforms require primarily the concentration of power and the mobilization of resources for national goals, that is, the capacity to create new power. These processes usually run into opposition from the interests and ideologies that benefit from the existing distribution of power, status, and rewards. Governmental effectiveness, in this sense, is the ability of the government to modify the privileges of vested interest groups in the light of public policy.[3] The problem is, of course, that a society is run differently from a mere organization, and that the public interest is a debatable matter in terms of implementation, if not in essence. Even in politically structured societies (i.e., socialistic) as opposed to economically structured societies (i.e., capitalistic), a political system has to build support in order to define priorities and transform the society. The various reforms tend to engage the government in devising ways of both organizing interest groups and associations to effect national policy and setting standards by which the national agencies will intervene in local systems. This means the establishment of an organized cooperation among groups and the assimilation of new groups into the political community, and, thus, involves the strategic problem of expanding power.

Huntington noted that in the highly telescoped processes of change, regime effectiveness has been synonymous with capacities for concentration and expansion of power, and that these capacities have been affected directly by the nature of political institutions. In comparing a wide range of "modernizing societies," he concluded that one-party systems were more likely to produce faster

[2] Barrington Moore, Jr., *Social Organization of Dictatorship and Democracy: Lord and Peasant in the Modern World* (Boston: Beacon Press, 1966).

[3] Alexis de Tocqueville, *L'Ancien Régime et la révolution* (Paris: Gallimard, 1967); see also Arthur Stinchcombe, "Innovation in Industrial Bureaucracies," A Report of the Joint Center of Urban Studies for Harvard and M.I.T., to be published.

economic development, more effective national integration, and were more stable than the no-party or many-party systems.[4]

In this section, Huntington's hypothesis will be discussed in relation to the degree of congruence between institutional frameworks and the imperatives of societal transformation. The party in Tunisia, the army in Algeria, and the Moroccan monarchy will be compared in terms of scope of support, institutionalization, and functional weights in determining the directions of development in the societies. The second section of this part, "Policies of Economic Development," will present a specification of the economic effectiveness of government. The treatment of planning will also touch upon the issue of distributive equity. From the perspective of the existing political systems, then, what is finally important is to evaluate their capacities for institutionally shifting their commitments and their bases of stability in terms of national policy and public interest. We call this institutional competence. This competence is not randomly distributed. The study of its manifestation in the political and economic orders gives us a sense of how and where political actors are apt to be constrained by their history and society or are likely to act upon them.

The Single Party as a Political Institution

By 1970, the strain of major structural change was clearly being borne by the Tunisian political system, more than any of its neighboring systems, because Tunisia was the first to become independent and the first to begin social and economic reforms. Therefore, it will be almost impossible to make the political structures and their evolution intelligible without treating the relationship between these structures and problems of economic modernization.

Tunisia is the only North African political system in which a political party played the primary role. We have analyzed the historical conditions in which the Destour managed to become the embodiment of authority and legitimacy for the overwhelming majority of the society. Its high level of institutionalization is confirmed by its chronological age. It appeared in 1920 and is the oldest political party in Africa and the Arab world. Because the colonial administration was willing to contend with the Destour and

[4] Samuel P. Huntington, *Political Order in Changing Societies* (New Haven, Conn.: Yale University Press, 1968).

its many years of underground activities, the party was given the time and context to become the fundamental institution of the nation. It underwent major generational successions in 1934, 1949, and 1961, and although the party has been too dependent upon one man, Habib Bourguiba, it has displayed, as we shall see, a significant functional adaptability. Its viable situation is also demonstrated by the scope of its support: it has 380,000 members, representing 33 percent of the male population over twenty years of age. Furthermore women generally join the Union Nationale des Femmes Tunisiennes, an auxiliary organization of the party.

By creating and co-opting associations and national organizations of businessmen and craftsmen (UTAC) and of farmers (UGAT) and by delegating some of its cadres to help organize the labor union (UGTT), the political party has tried to adapt to the increasingly differentiated economy and, at the same time, maintain the required institutional integration among these different spheres. After the party came to power following the Ben Youssef crisis, this institutional integration received its real test. It was the labor union, of course, that tried to assume partial control of the new state. Under the leadership of Ahmed Ben Salah, the union considered independence merely a first step toward "the profound revolution of the economic structure." Its economic report called for the nationalization of the Habous land, the transformation of the collective land into cooperatives, and the establishment of a powerful planning agency.[5] The conflict between the party and the union was contained within the confines of the power elite, and the mode of resolution is indicative of the party defense mechanism. Like most one-party regimes, the Destour cannot tolerate autonomous centers of power that exist outside of it. It was in the light of this structural incapacity that the party interpreted the union's bid for power and called for Ben Salah's resignation from his position as head of the union. Meanwhile, the party adopted in its Congress of Sfax the major economic position of the union and appointed four labor leaders to ministerial posts.

There seems to be a consensus in identifying the Moroccan regime with conservative forces and the Algerian regime with what are called the popular classes—workers and peasants. It is not so

[5] "Rapport Economique" Sixth National Congress of the UGTT, September 20–23, 1956.

easy a task, however, to describe the Tunisian regime and to analyze the power elite's degree of autonomy from vested interests. In reality, one can argue both ways depending upon the perspective. Tunisia has been the sole society in North Africa in which the generation that achieved national independence continued to assume the tasks of nation building. A long tradition of leadership, combined with a liberal bent, has generated an approach that is fundamentally gradual and pragmatic. Finally, the flexibility of party recruitment has enabled men of varied political perspectives to come to power at the same time, giving Tunisia both a liberal elite of aristocratic and middle class origins and a group of civil servants, intellectuals, and labor leaders entirely committed to state intervention in the economy.

Our basic hypothesis concerning political development in Tunisia is that the political system has oscillated between reconciliatory and mobilizational methods.[6] David Apter defined a reconciliation system as a system that places "a high value on compromises between groups which express prevailing political objectives and views," and a mobilization system as one which "tries to rebuild society in such a way that both the instrumentalities of government and the values associated with change are remarkably altered."[7] In terms of this hypothesis, we can analyze the Tunisian system as reconciliatory until 1962, at which time it became mobilizative in an attempt to change the structural basis of the society; then, in 1969, it became reconciliatory once more. (These years should be remembered as turning points.) In the five years following independence, the Destour concentrated on building the state and Tunisifying the administration and left the task of economic modernization to private entrepreneurship. For the political elite, profoundly influenced by Ataturk's model of modernization, the measures necessary for adapting Tunisia to the international context of nations were the provision of free education and the initiation of symbolic reforms, such as the nationalization of Habous, the introduction of

[6] See my analysis of this hypothesis in "Elite et Société en Tunisie," *Revue Tunisienne des Sciences Sociales*, no. 6 (March, 1969), pp. 11–19; see also Raymond E. Germain, "Administration dans le système politique de la Tunisie," *Annuaire de l'Afrique du Nord*, VII (1968), 139–156.

[7] David E. Apter, "System, Process and Politics of Economic Development," Reprint No. 224, Institute of International Studies, University of California, Berkeley, 1964, pp. 147, 149.

mass media, and the expulsion of religion from the temple of politics. Bourguibism, with its long-standing hostility to doctrines, became a synonym for pragmatism and for the gradualist policy of bargaining. By 1960, this approach had not succeeded in either attracting private investment or preventing a collapse in the economy. It was then subjected to a fire of criticism from unionists, students, and civil servants, who felt that "in itself pragmatism is not bad . . . but it becomes dangerous when it is developed into a system of economic policy." [8]

The regime could not afford to ignore the growing discontent of the landless peasantry, nor could it remain indifferent to the socialistic stance of Algeria and Egypt. For these reasons, the regime abandoned its reconciliatory policy and shifted gears. By adopting systematic planning, the elite intended to encourage economic growth, to break up the rigidities of social stratification, to equalize opportunities, and to increase social mobility. It proceeded immediately to incorporate the mobilizational elite, who had called for planning in the first place; thus, Ben Salah became minister of planning and finance and was included in the Political Bureau. An attempt was made to convert the party functions into an agency for mobilization, and the Congress of Bizerte, in 1964, ratified the new "socialist" orientation of the system. It is important to see how the party readapted to its new challenges; as the head of the party said,

> For a fighting party, victory may indeed be a factor of disintegration and death . . . just as it may commit the party to dictatorship or the pursuit of wealth. We have to remind ourselves that as the center of gravity of the republican regime and the essential initiator of the organs of the state, the socialist Destourian party is based upon the popular masses. Its imperative is now to mobilize creative energies and construct the socialist community. [9]

To create some congruence between the apparatus of the party and the requisites of planning, the party dropped many of the first hour militants, who were parochial in their views and whose behavior was detrimental to the national plan. Because collective in-

---

[8] Moncef Guen, *La Tunisie indépendante face à son économie* (Paris: Presses Universitaires de France, 1961).

[9] Parti Socialiste Destourien, Seventh Congress, Bizerte, October 19–29, 1964.

stitutions for the representation of local and sectional interests were becoming indispensable to the elaboration and execution of the new policy, coordination committees were established in each region. Owing to the multiplicity of interests within the member-ship at the elite level, however, these committees could only be a compromise between the appointment of the regional representa-tive of planning, which Ben Salah had hoped to authorize, and the preservation of the authority of the party by preserving the governor's authority over the committee and over the region as a whole. From the start, entrenched interests in the party apparatus conflicted with the newly co-opted planning team.

This reorientation produced a younger generation of adminis-trators and technicians who had a complete grasp of the economic and political implications of planning and who held their positions because of expertise rather than political partisanship. The general secretary and most of the new governors of the coordination com-mittees were relatively young and had, more often than not, an academic background; although all of them had been socialized within the party, many newcomers emerged from student organi-zations.[10] There is little doubt that this experiment transformed the entire society during the last ten years and increased the system's capabilities for group assimilation and political participation.

> The single-party regime in Tunisia was the most successful in arousing popular interest and stimulating a national response to the plan. Although some allowance must be made for a country . . . already on the way toward political integration, the single-party regime was prepared to extract the maximum significance from planning and, indeed, was probably compelled to do this or else face the possibility of the plan's full implications being exploited by latent opposition groups. The Socialist Destour was accustomed to the methods of mass appeal, and Bourguiba argued the need for a popular mobilization in response to planning more energetically than the Moroccan monarch.[11]

[10] Lars Rudebeck, *Party and People: A Study of Political Change in Tunisia* (Stockholm: Almquist and Wiksell, 1967).

[11] Douglas E. Ashford, *National Development and Local Reforms: Politi-cal Development in Morocco, Tunisia, and Pakistan* (Princeton, N.J.: Princeton University Press, 1967), p. 169; see also Ashford, "Organization of Cooperatives and the Structure of Power in Tunisia," *Journal of Devel-oping Areas*, no. 1 (1967), pp. 317–332.

But the party's capability for absorbing new ideas and new social forces should not obscure the fact that it was a petty bourgeois organization, and that its opportunism and lack of consistency kept it vulnerable. For it to act as a genuine organizational weapon would have required the development of a coherent ideology, the creation and sustenance of elites, and the control over the social composition of its membership. The Destour, instead, clung fiercely to unanimity and national unity, and, hence, ended up with a membership whose interests have been conflictual and whose aspirations have often been contradictory. Its distaste for open conflict led it to reintegrate within the Destourian family all the elite members who had, at one time or another, left the party, and its commitment to planning and land reform was never powerful enough for it to loosen its ties with the large landowners who supported the party during national liberation.

As a matter of fact, the effort of economic development only augmented and made more costly these institutional deficiencies. The Destour is the only organized party in which there was a successful transfer of political leadership from one generation to another. In a context of economic backwardness and issues involved in the process of development, however, it certainly takes more than institutional competence to preserve institutions.

The Army as a Political Institution

From Janowitz[12] who emphasizes the difficulties of transferability of military skills to the civilian arena to Huntington who tends to see the army as the instrument of praetorianism, "incapable either of sustained concentration of power necessary for reform or the sustained expansion of power involved in the identification of new groups within the system," [13] political scientists have unanimously stressed the military's shortcomings in exercising political leadership and in building political institutions. Without underestimating the Algerian military's inability to expand the political infrastructure, we shall argue that it did, nevertheless, provide Algerian society

[12] Morris Janowitz, *The Military in the Political Development of New Nations: An Essay in Comparative Analysis* (Chicago and London: University of Chicago Press, 1964).

[13] Huntington, *op. cit.* (n. 4), p. 146.

with a homogeneous leadership—probably for the first time in its modern history.

Leadership cohesion came late to Algerian society, but it was the contribution of the military which was decisive. The Algerian army's intervention in domestic politics did not take the usual pattern of a military coup undermining a civic polity. First, the army was formed by the national liberation movement, and the officers have always been men of profound political involvement. Secondly, the first regime emerging from the revolutionary context lacked a minimum of consensus among the political elite and was unable to use the FLN party to contain and resolve the major political crisis. As the regime shifted alliances, using the army to eliminate political contenders, appealing to the party to undermine the authority of the national assembly, and, finally, mobilizing workers, students, and militia against an army that had brought it to power, the officers of the army acted both as a faction of the elite and as a cohesive body in a political context of which they were the focal part from the outset. The army did not have to disrupt viable political institutions but had simply to put an end to what the Marxist Mohammed Harbi called clan parliamentarism. Much coherence and stability were required in an administration in which 47 percent of those occupying positions that involved decision making and 77 percent of those holding managerial positions owed their appointments to the previous, colonial regime.[14] The regional administration, given to innumerable replacements, appointed more than two hundred new prefects in sixteen departments in little more than two years; this gave each department an average turnover of one prefect every two months.

As paradoxical as this might seem, the army, in the name of "the institutionalization of the revolution" (as coined by Colonel Boumediène), brought a greater degree of governmental stability and of consensus on the basic issues than had ever been known before. One device for consensus formation was the maintenance of the initial military nucleus and a total disregard of the rest of the political elite. Unlike the Tunisian regime, which has maximized unity at any price and has regularly reintegrated political

[14] Gérard Chaliand, *L'Algérie est-elle Socialiste?* (Paris: Maspero, 1964), p. 89.

opponents such as Ben Salah and Mestiri, the Algerian regime, although it has safeguarded the cohesion of the top command, has shown no interest whatsoever in a reconciliation with political leaders of the past. Leaders known for past political involvements and anyone who currently enters into the opposition are nearly certain of permanent exile from government.[15]

The severing of past political legacies would have been impossible without the homogeneity of a nucleus called the Oujda group, composed of Boumediène's colleagues from the revolutionary days, Ahmed Kaid, Cherif Belgasem, Ahmed Medeghri, and Abdelaziz Bouteflika, that displayed a remarkable sense of internal cohesion —an essential aspect of the military profession and of the revolutionary period. Another device consisted of eradicating the sources of the classic cleavage within the army between officers trained in regular warfare and those incorporated from guerrilla units. This eradication came in mid-December 1967, when an ex-guerrilla leader, Tahar Zbiri, fearful that the balance of power between the newly hired technicians and ministers managing the industrial sector and the fighters of the revolution would swing in favor of the former, led a rather pitiful attempt to overthrow the government. With the help of the professional army, Boumediène was able to crush it in but a few hours. In view of the deep parochial ties of the guerrilla fighters, especially of the Aurès region, and in order to prevent the fragmentation of power through countercoup, Boumediène's regime seized the opportunity to eliminate all guerrilla fighters from positions of responsibility.

Along with the elimination of the past political elite and the establishment of an internal cohesion within the army's structure of authority, the new Algerian regime strengthened its hold on the economy and the administration by recruiting civil servants and technicians in such a way that the congruence between military and managerial elites was maximized. The fifty-odd civilian bureaucrats hired to run the increasingly growing oil industry and public enterprises were mainly selected on the basis of their expertise, and they have been characterized by youth and a pristine political record as far as interelite conflict is concerned.

[15] William B. Quandt, "Algeria: The Revolution Turns Inward," *Middle-East–North Africa Review*, X:4 (August, 1970), 9–12.

Whenever there has been the opportunity to bring new people into the elite, they have been men whose background and experiences quite closely parallel those of the current rulers. Of the seven cabinet ministers who have been named since 1966—Mohammed Ben Yahia, Lamine Khene, Mohammed Mazouzi, Tayebi, Yaker, Boukjella, and Kassim—most if not all are relatively young university graduates, former activists in nationalist student movement, the UGEMA.[16]

The major policy goals of the new regime were the national goals of the Algerian revolution in general. They preserved the March decrees which instituted the nationalization of the French-owned land and the Charte d'Alger, the important political manifesto written by Marxist intellectuals and devoted to the question of nation building in favor of the popular classes. The sole difference was the new emphasis placed upon efficiency and technical considerations, as opposed to the improvisations which characterized the first years. This orientation meant that the new regime came increasingly to depend upon the administration to implement its policy goals. This, in turn, was bound to reinforce the prestige of the administration within the stratification of organizations and simultaneously devaluate the position of the party by circumscribing its sphere of action. Indeed, the new technicians that the military brought into the apparatus of government are becoming increasingly the centers of innovation and power. As ministers and high officials, they represent today a team of technocrats, and are endowed with far greater power than the Tunisian party or the Moroccan monarchy would conceivably permit its own technicians. The Algerian technicians continue to demonstrate a solid competence in conceiving and executing new economic policies—qualities rarely found either in the military or among members of the party. The bureaucracy succeeded also in attracting to itself the secondary and intermediary elites, leaving to the party those who are less skilled.

Despite Boumediène's efforts to sustain the life of the party, the tendency to oppose the FLN is so powerful that it begins in the Cabinet and reaches into the lowest echelons of the government. *Révolution Africaine*, journal of the party, complained severely

[16] *Ibid.*, pp. 10–11.

about the resistance of the civil service to the FLN and its absence of political commitment:

> Among the cadres of the state, for example, certain [persons] maintain that one can be engaged in the service of the economic and social revolution without needing to belong to a cell of the FLN. They believe that their submission to directives of a technical and administrative nature is sufficient in and of itself. The theoreticians call that disassociating political from technical roles.[17]

Even at the level of the commune, one finds the same tensions between administrative and political functions; in an effort to prevent absorption of the party by the administration, the communal code has prohibited the combination of the municipal mandate with a position of responsibility in the party. Here, too, the attempt has not been successful; once elected, the members of the Popular Assembly, most of whom have been party members, "establish the loosest link with the local representative of the party. Although one would expect here a serious relationship characterized by frequent work sessions and regular consultations . . . one finds instead something quite different: in many instances, a kind of reserve if not hostility—at any rate, an absence of coordination." [18]

This tension between the administration and political party will persist, institutionally, for some time to come, because it also receives reinforcement from the antipolitical attitude of Algeria's society and regime. The meaning of the coup on June 19, 1965, was, according to Hawari Boumediène, in essence, "neither leadership, nor message, nor prophet" and, "[the exclusion of] all professional politicians, self-styled prophets, and historic leaders." [19] Many studies report that Algerians, in general, have inherited a profound distrust for political organization and a hostility toward what are perceived as political games; their attitudes are summed up by the word *boulitik* (nonsense).[20] Undoubtedly, such distrust is the fruit of an acrimonious political past.

[17] *Révolution Africaine*, no. 286, November 8–14, 1968.

[18] *Révolution Africaine*, no. 260, as quoted by Jean Leca in "Parti et Etat en Algérie," *Annuaire de l'Afrique du Nord*, VII (1968), 35.

[19] Interview with Boumediène in the Egyptian daily *El Ahram*, October 8–10, 1965, and speech on March 6, 1966.

[20] Discussion of the political culture of Algeria may be found in Pierre Bourdieu, "The Sentiment of Honor in Kabyle Society," in J. G. Peristiany,

That Algerians today continue to be ruled by a nonelected president, a nonfunctioning revolutionary council, and the shadow of a party should not convey the impression that there is no concern for legitimate authority, but simply that in this instance, legitimacy depends on performance. In this respect, the political order proved able to command respect, and by requesting that it be judged in terms of results, it was able to secure confidence from its economic accomplishments (as will be shown later in the discussion). In economic tasks, the administration proved to be highly functional. Of course, as in Morocco and Tunisia, the Algerian administration supports the petty bourgeois elites in acquiring and maintaining their privileges in face of the masses, making of these privileges a legitimate patronage. This has been analyzed by the sociologist Pierre Bourdieu, who writes,

> The preference accorded to administration is inspired by the fact that capitalist enterprise has been discredited and is perceived as being inseparable from colonialism and from exploitation, and, above all, by the conviction that only a state bureaucracy can ensure the functioning of all the institutions which have been abandoned by colonization. . . . It is also because the modern petty bourgeoisie and the intellectual elite are the beneficiaries of the maintenance of an organization which is disproportionate to the needs and the means of the country: juridical formalism and bureaucratic rigidity constitute, in fact, the best protection of the privileges provided by education and the best rampart against the revolutionary impatience of the illiterate mass.[21]

On the other hand, because the state tended to be the major entrepreneur and the major employer in the different spheres of the economy, the administration, in turn, became the focus of all expectations. In an increasingly nationalized economy, the administration was perceived as an efficient authority, responsible for the nationalization and the maintenance of social and economic resources. To the educated, it offered a position of command; to the

---

ed., *Honor and Shame: The Values of Mediterranean Society* (Chicago: University of Chicago Press, 1966); Quandt, *op. cit.*, pp. 264–276; Jean Leca, "Ideologie et Politique," *Etudes* (May, 1970), pp. 672–693.

[21] Pierre Bourdieu, "Le Désenchantement du Monde: Travail et travailleurs en Algérie," Centre de Sociologie Européenne, Paris 1966, mimeographed, pp. 167–168.

worker, it offered job security; and to the peasant, it offered the possibility of acquiring land, finding employment, or acquiring a passport for emigration. The peasantry's pathetic dependence upon the state was even more conspicuous than the dependence of any other social strata. Knowing the degree to which the rural structures have been destroyed by the colonial system and by war and knowing the nature of collapse suffered by the peasant society, we would expect that the hundreds of thousands of men who have ceased to be peasants would request the same urban privileges other groups have requested. They do not regret that the state has become the main protagonist of economic activities but wish only that the state's influence might extend to the local economy as well. That more than 70 percent of the "peasants" interviewed declared themselves unemployed is not only a sign of the devaluation of traditional agriculture but also of the induced belief that the only worthwhile jobs are those of urban functionaries in the public sector. Any traditional form of work is considered merely a pastime in which one can conceal his misery.[22]

The precise extent to which these expectations are being met will be taken up later, but there is no doubt that the military regime has been able to capitalize on these expectations and to increase its legitimacy because of them. It has also attempted some minimal political response, such as the grass-roots elections at communal and departmental levels, but as stated by Colonel Boumediène, the building of central political institutions still rests with the future:

> A state cannot be built in three or four years. The history of France itself shows that it took her centuries to build institutions. And despite this, these institutions have been seriously destroyed in her war with Algeria. . . . Our concern is to build a decentralized state in order to ensure the sharing of responsibility at each echelon and to permit those elected in the communes and the regions to resolve, themselves, those problems that arise in the cities, villages, and *wilaya-s*. We have already achieved communal and departmental reforms, and the assemblies of these collectivities have been elected

[22] This is true even among rural workers of the socialist sector. In response to the question, "Would you want your son to pursue the same vocation as yourself?" 66.8 percent of the self-managed farm laborers said no. See C. Kostic, "Transformations des communautés rurales en Algérie et en Yougoslavie," *Cahiers Internationaux de Sociologie*, no. 2 (1967), pp. 109–122.

through universal suffrage. They were given a large scope of power in order to make our state as decentralized as possible. We are just beginning to look into the building of national institutions. The time is not very far away when they will be constructed on a democratic basis.[23]

The Monarchy as a Political Institution

The Moroccan monarchy proved too powerful to be weakened by the political parties and too entrenched to allow the expansion of the political system. According to Samuel Huntington,

[The institutional dilemma of monarchies in modern times involves basically] the relation between traditional and modern authority. Three possible strategies are open to the monarch. He could attempt to reduce or to end the role of monarchical authority and to promote movement toward a modern, constitutional monarchy in which authority was vested in the people, parties, and parliaments. Or a conscious effort might be made to combine monarchical and popular authority in the same political system. Or the monarchy could be maintained as the principal source of authority in the political system and efforts made to minimize the disruptive effects upon it of the broadening of political consciousness.[24]

In Morocco, the first strategy has always been out of the question; the second strategy was attempted during the first years. The national elite, predominantly Istiqlali, took an active part in government. Governmental changeover—four times in four years —and the introduction of a National Assembly composed of seventy-six members, including representatives from political parties, trade unions, youth, economic associations, and the Jewish community gave many observers the illusion not only of an intense political life but of a democratic one. But the reconciliation of the monarchical authority with the modern authority of political parties proved to be so difficult that the creation of a stable government accountable to both authorities became realistically impossible. The national elite devoted all its energies to the construction of a constitutional monarchy in which the prime minister would appoint his own ministers and be given full responsibility for the

---

[23] *Le Mois en Algérie*, no. 10 (January, 1970), pp. 14–15.
[24] Huntington, *op. cit.* (n. 4), p. 177.

executive range of government. It also desired a government that would address itself to the most pressing problems: a policy of full austerity, the complete liberation of the Moroccan economy from that of France, and state-sponsored industrial investments. But it ran into snarls even in attempting to reduce the number of French clubs and social organizations, which had reached a staggering five thousand. More importantly, the king reserved for himself control over the army and the police and placed the Ministry of Interior in the hands of a former head of his private cabinet. This dilemma was to manifest itself time and again until a permanent situation of stalemate was reached. William Zartman described the dilemma well:

> In the first two Councils of Ministers, Mohammed V tried to create a government of national unity under an independent leader. Both eventually fell because they ignored party claims as well as realities. Certain members in the third government, and all members of the Council which followed it, were chosen as nonparty technicians, as logically consistent with the quasi-vizierial system in force. Yet in a young country such as Morocco, everyone and everything is political, and there are no nonpartisan technicians. The government was torn between responsibility to the the king and responsibility to party groups, between its vizierial and ministerial nature. Therefore, it too fell, since it was not responsible before the political groups which could make its work impossible, and since these groups were not committed by the collective responsibility of the Council.
>
> Even had there been no catalytic pressure from the prince to increase his governing role, the government would naturally have tended to seek a stable position as a purely vizierial or a purely ministerial system, simply to be comfortable in its role. Against partisan tendencies naturally pushing towards the latter system, the king acted in the other direction; the last government under Mohammed V, its continuation, and then succeeding governments under Hassan II were vizierial governments, with their members separately designated and individually responsible to the king.[25]

[25] I. William Zartman, *Destiny of a Dynasty: The Search for Institutions in Morocco's Developing Society* (Columbia, S.C.: University of South Carolina Press, 1964), pp. 60–61; see also Octave Marais, "Les relations entre la Monarchie et la classe dirigeante au Maroc," *Publications de la Fondation Nationale des Sciences Politiques* (Paris: 1969), pp. 1172–1185.

Because of the newly created situation in which the king and his personal royal cabinet made major political decisions which would have been the jurisdiction of the government (the different political parties who provided the various ministers), extreme tension reverberated throughout the entire political system. The Istiqlal, historically a unitary party, became hopelessly divided over the issue of what line of action to pursue vis-à-vis the monarchy and the new power arrangements. On January 29, 1959, Mehdi Ben Barka, symbol of the mobilizational elite, openly broke from the Istiqlal and formed with the then Prime Minister Abdallah Ibrahim and Abderrahim Bouabid the National Union of Popular Forces (UNFP). They were joined by Mahjoub ben Seddiq, who brought with him the support of 600,000 worker members of the Union Marocaine du Travail (UMT), and by Fakih Basri, one of the Berbers' most prestigious leaders of the Resistance. Some supporters also came from the Parti Democratique Indépendent, which split right down the middle, its left wing joining Ben Barka and the rest remaining with the old Wazzani. The common denominator of all these men is that they began to chafe under the prudent methods of the old leadership with respect to the despotic and retrograde monarchy. They reproached their elders for too much drinking of mint tea and dispatching of grandiloquent telegrams while the critical present required vigilance and a radical approach to full decolonization.

The UNFP, however, underestimated the strength of the monarchy and the complexity of Moroccan society. In what began as a struggle for survival and concluded as an effort to obtain exclusive dominance over the political spectrum, the monarchy was to display a rich versatility of strategy designed to weaken and segment the political elites. One such strategy was to keep alive all groups that were rivals of the Istiqlal and the UNFP. This policy of segmentation was carried out in at least two ways.

The first, a kind of traditional pluralism, consisted of reactivating rural and local loyalties in order to embarrass the Istiqlali-headed government. It was because of this that the Movement Populaire, which was led by Mahjoub Ahardane and Abd-el-Krim Khatib and which espoused the rural Berber cause against the Istiqlali government, had the full support of the monarchy. The summoning up of counterelites had no primary purpose other than to prevent

Morocco from following a mobilizational course. A spokesman for the Movement Populaire expressed this fact clearly:

> The first thing is to prevent our people from turning toward materialism—Marxist or any other. We want to build up a state which, although modern, is rooted firmly in Islam. We don't believe that we can progress according to our innermost nature without religion. Islam must dictate the emancipation of our women, problems of land ownership and land division, and even [problems] of commerce and finance. I don't mean the deformed Islam of the last thousand years, but its original spirit in all its purity.[26]

The other way of preventing one-party dominance was to advocate the same pluralism but try to give it a liberal justification. Its chief exponent was Reda Guedira, the long-standing head of the cabinet and close friend of the king. This group theorized that the complexity of the Moroccan society necessitated competition among multiple groups for governmental power, and that one-party rule would endanger the fundamental stability of the government. One-party rule would undermine the essential function of arbitration, without which the monarchy would become obsolete. Furthermore, this group argued, given the multiplicity of political, social, and ethnic components of the society, one-party rule could only be sustained through coercion.

On the strength of these and similar arguments, Guedira's group and the monarchy created a coalition of the most diverse forces in an attempt to counterbalance the Istiqlal and the UNFP groups, which in their view, constituted the major threat of one-party rule and structural change. A constitution was promulgated in 1962, and most groups expected the election for parliament to be the key test of their strength. The monarchy hoped to win a working majority, but the monarchical forces, organized into the Front for the Defense of Constitutional Institutions (FDIC), obtained only sixty-nine seats out of one hundred and forty-four. Among the oppositional forces, the Istiqlal gained forty-one, the UNFP twenty-eight, and the independents only six. As a result, the government became stalemated, and with it the constitutional experiment. During the second session, the UNFP and the Istiqlal presented a motion

---

[26] As quoted by Rom Landeau in *Morocco Independent Under Mohammed the Fifth* (London: George Allen and Unwin, 1961), p. 115.

censuring the government economic policy, and the Movement Populaire, a discontented part of the monarchical coalition, threatened to bolt the FDIC on this issue. In June, 1965, Hassan II suspended the constitution, dismissed the parliament, and governed the country with his Ministry of Interior. Until 1970, the country was governed under a state of emergency.[27]

For five years, there was no political life, and the atmosphere was poisoned by rumors of conspiracy and by the arrest of hundreds of political opponents and officers. Finally, in the summer of 1970, a referendum was passed and a new assembly was elected. For the first time, however, all the political forces boycotted the election, and the front created by the UNFP, the Istiqlal, the labor union (UMT), and the student association (UGEM) reduced the assembly, as one of their leaders Ali Yata said, to nothing but "a parade of figureheads of the administration." [28] Indeed, for the first time, the marginality of the political elite vis-à-vis the political system was total—as total as was the isolation of the regime itself.[29]

[27] For a good account of political life up to 1965, see F. Chambergeat, "Bilan de l'expérience parlimentaire marocaine," *Annuaire de l'Afrique du Nord*, IV (1965), 101–106; for political life after 1965, see John Waterbury, *The Commander of the Faithful: The Moroccan Political Elite* (New York: Columbia University Press, 1970).

[28] "Le Referendum et les élections législatives au Maroc," *Maghreb*, no. 41 (1970), p. 12.

[29] A UNFP leader declared to a journalist, "In the name of the new experience of parliamentary monarchy, the political reality is in no way different from what it was during the last five years of continual states of emergency. The king exerts absolute power legalized somewhat by the new fundamental law. As far as we are concerned, we are, though this time at least with our complete will, outside political life." Philip Herreman, *Le Maroc: Terre de Paradoxe*; as quoted in *Le Monde*, December 17–19, 1970; see also "La Constitution Marocaine du 31 juillet, 1970," *Maghreb*, no. 41, Sept.–Oct. 1970, pp. 29–38.

Chapter 10: POLICIES OF
ECONOMIC DEVELOPMENT

Were we simply interested in what is commonly referred to in the literature as political development, this work would have concluded long ago, and the reader would have been left with ample evidence of Tunisia's political accomplishments, Morocco's pervasive stalemate, and revolutionary Algeria's political vacuum in terms of institutions. Things are, however, more complex. The study of governmental effectiveness in late-comer societies demands further theoretical effort. It is important to understand that governmental effectiveness and legitimacy are closely tied to economic performance, as well as to institution building. Surprisingly, the literature rarely addresses itself to the full significance of this. Political scientists have been committed mainly to a concept of politics as a balancing of the claims of powerful interest groups; the task of government is to secure some distribution of benefits, commonly understood as the challenges of equality and welfare, for the underprivileged masses.

But developing nations have little to distribute save austerity and deferred wants; their basic problem is one of creating an industrial economy. For these societies, the capacity to expand their investment processes under their own control and for their own specific purposes is the real test of national effectiveness. In the Maghrib, capital accumulation made little headway, and colonial economy maintained the region as predominantly agricultural and highly dependent on Europe. (Algerian oil is a recent discovery.) Thus, the question of economic performance is certainly more complex than the commonly held belief that it can be achieved peacefully through economic assistance, technical cooperation, and the mere willingness to "modernize." The economist Samir Amin has estimated that even if the Maghrib achieved and maintained a growth rate of 6 percent from 1970 to at least 1990 (which implies rapid industrialization, sweeping agricultural reforms, and a significant reduction in demographic growth rate), by the year 2000 per capita income would barely reach one-third of what it is in the industrial societies; this estimate does not take into account the ten million unemployed.[30] Seen in this light, governmental effectiveness becomes no less than a Promethean objective.

One fundamental dilemma for all these regimes emanates from the contradictory exigencies of rising productivity and the social demand for increasing employment. On the one hand, the maghribi masses, which have experienced intensive exposure to the European standard of living, have come to focus on goals of immediate consumption, and they look directly to the government as the primary provider of employment and welfare. But modern industry and modern agriculture, whatever the latter's flexibility, can proceed efficiently only by adopting a technology designed to save labor and raw materials. In the last twelve years, Algeria has chosen a capital intensive policy, while Tunisia has pursued a labor intensive formula. But in both countries, the contradiction resists resolution. There is little doubt that late-comers' productive systems will employ the energies of a smaller segment of the population than did the European, Japanese, and Soviet systems during industrialization.

Whatever the policies pursued in the face of this dilemma, different regimes are constrained by the resources of their countries. Algerian leadership, for example, operates in a country which has significant extractive resources and in which a long colonial experience has left a sizable economic infrastructure. On the other hand, Tunisia is poor in terms of extractive resources and fertile land, and whatever the commitment of its political leadership, it has the least economic viability. With its rich phosphates and highly productive land, Morocco stands between them. It follows that a rich underdeveloped country has the objective possibility of utilizing the opportunities traditionally monopolized by foreign capital, whereas a poor country must seek or attract foreign capital in order to complement its deficient investment capacities. As a result, a further contradiction is created between the need for foreign capital and the objective of autonomous development.

In order to confront these contradictory exigencies, governments tend to adopt planning. Planning, as such, does not indicate a uniform posture toward development. Thus, Algeria and Tunisia have achieved total land nationalization, but Morocco has not; on the

[30] See last chapter of Samir Amin, *Le Maghreb Moderne* (Paris: Minuit, 1970).

other hand, Morocco and Tunisia encourage private participation in the plan, but Algeria does not. Still, all three countries have adopted planning. The coherence of the plan and its implementation usually represent a good indication of the national capacity. From the study of political institutions and political orders, we have drawn the profiles of maghribi societal transformations. It is important now to indicate in what sense these profiles are further affected by the different opportunities for economic growth.

First, the differential in resource availability implies that some political systems, in order to develop economically, must pay higher political and social costs. Societies like Algeria and Venezuela can rely on their oil resources and have less need than Tunisia and Chile, for example, to make their populations bear the cost of capital accumulation.

Secondly, as a corollary, a regime without initial legitimacy is able to draw some support from its economic achievements, and, conversely, even the most civic and stable regime, such as England's, suffers in the long run from a lack of economic opportunities. These points will become clearer as we proceed to analyze the individual plans. Should some readers find the next pages somewhat technical, we take note here that the economic policies are related at all times to the existing political and social choices. In any case, a résumé of our argument is found in the concluding section following this study of economic planning.

The Moroccan Experience in Planning

In 1962, six years after independence and three years after the initiation of the four-year plan (1960–1964), the global investment of Morocco represented 60 percent of that for 1952. With an investment rate of about 12 to 13 percent and a GNP growth rate of only 2.3 percent, Morocco was facing a serious economic stagnation and structural crisis of investment. This was not caused by a lack of potential for capital accumulation. The economist Abdel Aziz Belal has calculated, on the basis of profit and net revenues of the agricultural and nonagricultural sectors, that there was an annual surplus of about 301 billion old francs ($602 million), and that had the government been determined to develop the country, the volume of investment could have exceeded three times what was actually undertaken.[31] Evidently, however, the mobilization of such sizable resources would have been possible only by breaking with the status quo policy.

Since 1956, Morocco has adopted many transitional plans, most of which were equipment budgets. We shall focus our analysis on the four-year plan, not merely because it was precise in its goals and encompassing in its breadth but because, as elaborated by technicians sympathetic to the UNFP, it represents the only attempt of government and the opposition to collaborate in ensuring for Morocco an effective economic developmental instrument.

The plan called for a GNP growth rate of 6.2 percent to be obtained through an intensification of the extractive industries, import substitution, and the improvement of agricultural production by land reform. Based on these policies along with policies that met the requirements for the extension of education, the creation of 200,000 nonagricultural jobs, and "the mobilization of the rural masses," it was predicted that there would be an increase in the investment rate from 11.2 percent in 1960 to 22.3 percent in 1965. The private sector was to be associated with the implementation of the plan through a participation of 80 percent in industrial investment. The rest of the funds were to be supplied by the creation of a more favorable context for investment; thus, an investment code, a national bank for development (BNDE), and other offices were established. The state was counted upon to ensure the coherence of these diverse projects.

It was not long before the gross discrepancy between the plan's target and its outcome became evident to everyone concerned. Only 25 percent of the predicted increase in investment was realized, and this allowed an annual growth rate of only 3.2 percent, half the predicted rate. For the period 1960–1964, as well as for the succeeding years, the variables accounting for failure were the refusal to effect structural reforms required by programed development, the low extractive capacities of the government, and the

---

[31] Abdel Aziz Belal, *L'Investissement au Maroc (1912–1964)* (Paris: Mouton, 1968), pp. 347–350. I benefited very much from this work, which represents a systematic economic analysis without equal in the other maghribi countries; it is certainly to Morocco's credit to have produced such a fine scholar.

failure to stimulate private entrepreneurship. We shall analyze each variable separately.

One must acknowledge, regardless of his ideological perspective, that in any maghribi society land reform is absolutely mandatory for the increase of agricultural production, the enlargement of the local market, and the extraction of a maximum surplus of capital from agriculture to industry. It is even more indispensable in Morocco, which has both the most complex land tenure system and the agricultural resources that afford the greatest potential in the Maghrib. Instead of devising means to reorient the rural sector, the government, during the last decade, consistently prevented the implementation of any minimal reform recommended by the plan.

Half of the French land was bought either by private Moroccans or passed into the hands of bureaucrats and members of the ruling families. The rest is still in French hands. The adoption of the plan included the institution of the Office National d'Irrigation (ONI), designed to develop modern agriculture through state investment. It attracted, in the beginning, a sizable number of engineers and agronomists and was provided with financial and technical assistance. As it progressed, it tried to impose some discipline on both rich farmers and small peasants to cooperate in the rational use of irrigation. Given the regime's commitment to the maintenance of equilibrium and the local administrators' reluctance to serve as executives, a conflict between the ONI team of experts and the local authorities seemed unavoidable. In 1962, Mohammed Tahiri, first head of the ONI, waged his campaign to diversify agricultural production by trying to convince the peasants in the west to cultivate sugar beets. The governor of that region openly opposed him. Later, in 1963, when the ONI engineers pressed the issues of colonized land and of land reform, the government, intransigent toward everything but technical improvements, interpreted the ONI's suggestions as political threats and dismissed Tahiri. After many hesitations, the government fused the ONI with the Office National de Modernisation Rurale and placed the entire operation within the Ministry of Interior. Consequently, the governors were given full power over the personnel involved in the economic project.

The second major attempt to deal with rural society was known as the Promotion Nationale. Because the rural traditional sector had a productivity of only one-sixth that of the modern sector but provided food for 74 percent of the population, and because it was assumed that the industrial sector could not absorb all the unemployed, the government tried to use unemployed rural workers in projects involving irrigation and the planting of trees. It did so mainly through American aid in wheat. Its intention was to prohibit the rural exodus to the urban areas, which amounted to a systematic effort of social control. Knowing that the surplus labor force was evaluated as 300 million days of work, one can see from Table 16 that the Promotion Nationale failed because it used only 4 percent of this potential. The total labor force seeking work in 1964 was estimated at 2,627,000. For this number of people, the Promotion Nationale provided only 35,000 permanent jobs since 1961.

Competent economists do not advise the extension of this program because it uses vital resources which could have been more rationally utilized in the industrial sector. The regime, however, dropped most of its technicians and came to rely on the bureaucracy and the military for execution of the program. The Promotion Nationale permitted the governors to enter into contact with the king for the first time, and the army assigned many of its officers to assist the governors in the administration of the rural society. By 1970, while the regime was justifying its policy in pointing to the million hectares irrigated, the opposition objected that the

TABLE 16

PROGRAMS OF FULL EMPLOYMENT IN THE MAGHRIB
(PER MILLION WORKDAYS)

Year	Algeria	Morocco	Tunisia
1959	—	—	29.6
1960	—	—	31
1961	—	7.4	55.5
1962	—	16.4	57.4
1963	10	10	55.4
1964	8	15	56.4
1965	—	14	31

SOURCE: André Tiano, *Le Maghreb entre les mythes* (Paris: Presses Universitaires de France, 1967), p. 64.

considerable expenditure for irrigation would only benefit the already privileged minority, given the land tenure system. In any event, in the four-year plan and the successive plans, the idea of land reform was dropped entirely.

One of Morocco's more striking contrasts with its neighbors is its poor performance in collecting taxes and drawing resources from its population. Thus, while the Tunisian state increased its tax revenue to 28 percent of the GNP, and the Algerian state to approximately 27 percent, Morocco has lagged behind at barely 15.3 percent during the sixties. As in Algeria, however, the rural society has been consistently spared resource extraction since 1961. Although the agricultural revenue is supposed to represent 30 percent of the national revenue, the agricultural contribution has been evaluated at 2.6 percent.[32] From this figure, it is clear that retaining the support of the traditional rural constituency and meeting requirements for capital accumulation are antithetical objectives. On the other hand, in the absence of economic decolonization, a significant portion of the high-income bracket continues to be composed of foreigners, who generally transfer one-third of their revenues outside the country. The liberal aspect of the transfer regulations has proved to be very costly for Morocco. It has been estimated that the flow of capital leaving the country, both authorized and unauthorized, has been 65 to 70 billion old francs (about $130 million) yearly, against an average of only 3.4 billion old francs ($16.8 million) entering the country.[33] Taking place in the context of a nonexpanding economy, this transfer to the outside is, at the very least, clearly an instance of disinvestment.

On the domestic plane, the Moroccan economic policy has operated on the assumption that it was possible to reorient the bourgeoisie toward industrialization. It is true that during World War II an industrial boom of a speculative nature permitted the merchants of Tangiers and Casablanca to establish fortunes, especially the families of the Alami, Sebti, and Bennani. After inde-

[32] André Tiano, *Le Maghreb entre les mythes*, p. 542.

[33] Belal, *op. cit.*, pp. 314–316. Despite both large inflows of foreign aid (including $587 million from America between 1956 and 1967, and $236 million from France between 1960 and 1966) and tourist revenues amounting to $26 million in 1966, the Moroccan official reserves of gold and foreign exchange dropped from $185 million in 1961 to $76 million at the end of 1967. Foreign debt was some $485 million at the end of 1967.

pendence, however, these families were reluctant to play a dynamic role in the industrial effort. The investment commission for 1960 showed that 50 percent of the total investment was still of foreign origin, including enterprises established under colonialism; that 25 percent was contributed by the state; and that the Moroccan bourgeoisie financed only the remaining quarter. It will be recalled that the bourgeoisie was to carry the greater part of the industrial investment, as prescribed in the four-year plan. In fact, it contributed merely 10 percent of its expected share. The Moroccan fortunes were attracted, rather, by the more profitable textile industry, where 35 billion francs ($70 million) were invested between 1956 and 1966 by land acquisition, trade, and property. Although the Algerian and Tunisian governments have tried to compensate for the failure of private initiative through state industrialization, Morocco has consistently postponed its crucial economic decisions.[34]

Because Morocco shrinks from the task of genuine decolonization and refuses to reorient the national economy through structural reform, planning has not been able to raise the investment rate from 12 percent to 13 percent. Between 1960 and 1966, the growth rate of the GNP was only 2.3 percent, and per capita income fell from about $205 in 1958 to $185 in 1967. Such a dismal profile, along with the neutralization of most technicians and intellectual workers, can only serve to compound the society's alienation from its government.

Tunisia: The Ten-Year Perspective of Development

For a long time, the Tunisian government shared with Morocco similar assumptions about development, and from 1956 to 1961, it practiced a liberal economic policy. Private investment and initiative, however, did not manifest themselves and were not forthcoming. In 1957, for example, the investment rate decreased from the 19.5 percent of 1953 to 7.7 percent. Despite a vigorous fiscal policy, the backing of the currency, the creation of national companies of import and export, and limited experiments in land modernization,

[34] The general orientation of Morocco's economic policy has remained unchanged to the present time. See T. Bencheikh, "Modèles de planification agricole au Maroc," and Abdel Aziz Belal, "Investissement et développement économique," *Bulletin Economique et Social du Maroc* (April–June, 1968), pp. 35–48 and pp. 49–70 respectively.

the economic situation continued to worsen. By 1961, President Bourguiba and his party dismissed the liberal minister who had failed, and called upon the planners, a group of unionists and administrators who had long preached the adoption of planning. The Perspectives Decennales (1962–1971), elaborated by a team of economists headed by Ahmed Ben Salah, who became Minister of Planning, Finance, and, later, Education, were essentially the extension of Ben Salah's former union program. Under Ben Salah's direction, the plan of development was more specifically a labor-oriented plan than an economic one. The objectives were to attain, by 1974, a minimum income of fifty dinars per capita for the most disadvantaged strata, to limit foreign aid to 50 percent of the new investment to be undertaken, to attain a savings rate of 26 percent of the GNP by the final year, 1971. Calculations indicated that a growth rate of 6 percent was necessary to ensure achievement of these goals.

Although not totally unrealistic, these objectives required a tremendous amount of investment—an amount that was, in fact, disproportionate to the real economic capability of the country. The 50-percent foreign participation in the ten-year perspective attests to the vulnerability and fragility of Tunisia's position in undertaking autonomous development. Furthermore, because the government had proved able to control wages since 1956, it was hesitant to disturb the vested interests of entrepreneurs and landowners. Indeed, the perspectives specify that income per capita other than salaries can increase up to 40 percent, which means that "entrepreneurs" can retain most of their productivity's net gains. The economist Samir Amin recognized the political and financial limitations of the perspectives, recommending forced saving as the only means to reach the plan's targets. He writes, "But forced saving requires a structural framework based on more collectivist orientations [than exist at present]; without this, there is only one palliative, however false it may be: foreign aid. But, then, it is the objective of economic independence which is lost." [35]

The following discussion will show how a government torn between the affirmation of economic independence and the need

---

[35] Samir Amin, *Appreciation Générale des Perspectives*, Ministry of Plan, Tunis, mimeographed; see also his *L'Economie du Maghreb*, Vol. II (Paris: Editions de Minuit, 1966).

to compensate for its lack of endogenous resources through foreign aid, and between the desire to win over the rural masses and its fear of alienating the landowners, managed to move the country ahead only to fail in establishing an adequate balance. The difficulties faced in the Tunisian experiment deserve particular attention, especially at a time when Morocco has not yet launched its developmental effort and Algeria is but beginning.

In the absence of industrial resources, except for low-quality phosphate and the fundamentally speculative and short-term proclivities of the Tunisian bourgeoisie, the planners made agriculture the major battleground and the basis for capital accumulation. It has been estimated by the FAO that in 1962 each of four thousand French families held 240 hectares of land and each of five thousand Tunisian families held 100 hectares. This means that 3 percent to 4 percent of all farmers possessed about half of the arable land. The planners had a great range of power, but in order to extract the maximum surplus of capital from agriculture to industry, they had to contend with a party whose historical support came mainly from the landed commercial petty bourgeoisie. For this reason, national landowners were at first spared expropriation, whereas European lands were more readily nationalized (on May 12, 1964). In the effort to prevent an outflow of capital from the urban to the agricultural sector, the planners tried to retain ownership of nationalized land, coveted by large landowners, by persuading the National Assembly to prohibit the sale of land acquired by the state. They then inaugurated a new agricultural policy known as the Cooperative System, geared primarily to the modernization of agriculture and the support of the poor peasantry.

In the absence of historical precedent and with only impressionistic references to the Scandinavian and Israeli schemes for rural development, the Tunisian system tried to utilize the colonial farm, not simply to exploit its land and increase per capita agricultural production, but as a base for the support of the surrounding traditional areas. A cooperative unit was to be composed, ideally, of the original farm—about 200 hectares—along with 300 hectares of surrounding parcels. Thirty families were to farm this unit, with priority given first to the previous workers of the unit under colonialism and then to the peasants. This scheme was adopted to make possible the full use of equipment, fertilizers, and crop rotation, and also to transcend the bifurcation between modern and traditional agriculture.

As to the economic aspect, various efforts at diversifying and intensifying production cost the state 70,000 dinars, or $140,000 per cooperative unit. An enormous investment such as this can only be carried by the state in the short run; it constituted a heavy drain on the future cooperative budget. Ben Salah's team was, despite this, optimistic in forecasting that the income of each family would be 250 dinars a year and that ultimately the budget could be balanced. Aside from the Coopératives de production, there were other forms of organization for land appropriation such as the Unités de polyculture, the Coopératives de service, and the Pre-coopératives. Suffice it to say that there are two types of *cooperateurs:* those who are integrated within a state supervised unit and who are supposed to exercise direct management of the land, and those who work on their own land and who are encouraged indirectly either to improve their management or to market their produce through state offices.

In all this reorientation of the rural economy, there was one fundamental drawback that arose from the nature of its inception: The reform had been handed down from above by the power elite and was never the object of a power struggle in which those who would be the beneficiaries could later appreciate its value and its cost. Also, at no time were the organizers able to arouse the enthusiasm of the rural masses, which was indispensable to the formula's success. Although the *cooperateurs* were represented on the administrative records, in reality, the Unités were managed through the state hierarchy of organizations and technicians. An official report noted, "The population installed there does not really participate in the improvement work, except perhaps as salaried persons." [36] At any rate, the regional organizations set up by the plan and the party militants launched a vast and tireless campaign to convert a major part of the best land into cooperatives. By the end of 1966, aided by the governmental technicians, the cadres had established a total of 779 cooperatives with a membership of 206,633, including about 12 percent of the active population. By May 1968, 30 percent of the nation's cultivated land was in Unités or in Pre-

[36] S.E.R.E.S.A., *Region 08: Steppes ouest-Gafsa*, Secretariat d'Etat à l'Agriculture (Tunis: 1960), p. 58.

coopératives, which held more than 750,000 people and represented 27 percent of the rural population. Table 17 indicates the growth of cooperatives up to 1967–1968.

Another 20 percent of the cultivated area was organized into Coopératives de services, including olive oil and wine cooperatives which were formed more or less through voluntary participation. With the reform of March 1968 regarding retail sales of vegetables and fruit, the majority of Tunisian farm produce reaching the market was sold through cooperative institutions and state offices.

On the industrial plane, the state assumed the burden of the national effort. Despite the reluctance of foreign experts and financiers, new industrial projects were undertaken either with foreign loans or national capital, which was collected through fiscal policy and by authoritarian methods such as the *regroupements obligatoires*. The shopkeepers, traditionally part of a sect from the island of Djerba, corresponded in every respect to the Weberian prototype of the Protestant ethic. These people were regrouped into commercial cooperatives and reduced to the position of simple managers, and their financial surplus was reinvested in the modern industrial sector. The agricultural cooperatives were also compelled, despite their shaky financial situation, to channel 142 million dinars into new textile, lumber, and paper industries. It has been argued, in fact, that this forced investment alone accounts for most of the deficit. Through public enterprises as well, the Tunisian state tried to create an industrial base. We find that in comparison to the 5 or 10 million dinars invested by the private sector mainly in tourist trade, public enterprises and parastate banks invested, between 1962 and 1969,

TABLE 17

THE GROWTH OF AGRICULTURAL PRODUCTION CO-OPS

Year	Number of co-ops	Membership	Area (per 1,000 hectares)
1963–1964	128	12,852	148
1964–1965	177	14,348	205
1965–1966	246	17,745	279
1966–1967	682	37,496	614

SOURCE: Figures provided by Les Services de Statistiques, Ministre de l'Agriculture, Tunis.

238.9 million dinars ($480 million) in mines, oil exploration and refineries, manufacturing, transportation, and communications. Although substantial, the role of the state in industrialization has been mainly one of stimulation.

In fact, no stone has been left unturned in an attempt to attract foreign investment, and inside the country, private companies and individuals who reinvested one-third of their profits were exempt from taxation. For example, in the twenty projects corresponding to the first three-year plan of an industrial nature (1962–1964), state financial participation reached only 13 percent. But the ten projects representing 75 percent of the net investment were the result of state initiative; another five were launched by parastate bank organizations, like La Société Tunisienne de Banque and La Banque Nationale Agricole; and the remaining five projects grew out of contracts between the state and the private sector. Today, Tunisia has seventy-seven public enterprises, some of which are offices and industries taken over from France, such as the phosphate mines, but most of which are new. Of these seventy-seven, fifty-nine enterprises are directly controlled by the state, nine indirectly controlled, and nine created with foreign participation. Many of the new projects are import substitution industries such as sugar, textiles, and mechanical industries. In the face of serious obstacles, the state did develop heavy industry. By 1964, oil exploration led to the discovery of reserves sufficient to satisfy local consumption. It is expected that by 1971 the gross sale of oil will reach $60 million. There was also an attempt to develop a chemical industry, but its realization would have required the contribution of the other maghribi countries. As it happened, Ahmed Ben Salah was ousted from power, and his hopes for maghribi collaboration in building a chemical complex, Industries Chimiques Maghribines, in the south of Tunisia never materialized.[37]

In any case, the major achievement of the last decade was the

[37] Useful information on Tunisia's industrialization effort can be found in M. P. Brugnes-Romieu, "Investissements industriels et développement en Tunisie," *Cahiers du Centre d'Etudes et de Recherches Economiques et Sociales* [hereinafter *CERES*] (Tunis University: 1966); Philippe Aydolot, "Essai sur les problèmes de la strategie de l'industrialisation en économie sous-développée: l'exemple tunisien," *Cahiers du CERES* (Tunis University: 1968); C. Bistolfi, "Structures économiques et décolonisation monetaire: le cas tunisien," unpublished thesis, mimeographed, Paris, 1964.

government's ability to underwrite an impressive investment in its effort to develop; it did this in spite of marked scarcity of resources and the lack of significant private participation. Between 1962 and 1968 alone, the period of the first three-year and four-year plans, 785 million dinars were invested in the economy. Over the entire decade, the government invested 1,200,000,000 dinars ($2,286,000,000), three times more than was invested in the previous decade. The political costs of this effort will be discussed later; we shall limit the following analysis to an examination of the major defects of Tunisia's economic policy, reminding the reader that there is, unfortunately, no equivalent data for the Algerian economic policy.

We find that regardless of this unprecedented effort of capital accumulation, which rose from 19 percent of the GNP in 1956 to 25 percent in 1968, agricultural and industrial enterprises failed by large margins to reach the level of production designated in the plan—allowing, of course, for the fact that most investments were infrastructure investments and that, as such, one would expect mainly long-term returns. The growth of output in the oil industry, mines, and tourism (the latter came to represent 25 percent of the export earnings) should not obscure the fact that, on the whole, production growth was increasing only at an average rate of 4 percent, instead of the predicted 6 percent. The major causes of the plan's failure to meet its predicted 6 percent can be identified as the glaring managerial and technical deficiencies in the cooperative system and the public enterprises as a whole, the inconsistency of the leadership vis-à-vis the privileged social spheres, and financial dependence upon an irregular and conditional foreign aid.

A glance at most of the new industries reveals that the implementation of the diverse projects was overhasty, and that, in general industrialization was undertaken impulsively. Although complex, the reasons for this headlong rush were fundamentally financial and political—financial in the sense that given Tunisia's paltry resources and the heavy squeeze on local consumption and forced saving, it could never have committed so much capital to productive investment without loans from international organizations. A measure of this dependence upon foreign capital is the foreign debt-service ratio (interest plus repayment as a percentage of export earnings). According to the International Bank for Reconstruction and Development, the ratio for Tunisia was 23 percent in 1967, 25 percent in 1968, and 27 percent in 1970. This places Tunisia among the countries of the highest indebtedness in the world. Only India and some Latin American countries seem to have a higher debt-service ratio.[38]

By virtue of this, Tunisia is vulnerable. The irony of its position can be gleaned from the fact that having lost French participation and investment because of its support of the Algerian revolution, Tunisia lost the bulk of French aid, which went to Algeria because of its oil. Having tried to replace French aid with American investment, Tunisia lost the support of Kuwait and found World Bank loans expensive and highly conditional. Tunisia yielded at least twice to international pressure: once by introducing a stabilization program and devaluating its currency, and a second time, by promising the World Bank that it would not extend land reform beyond the north of the country.

At the same time, it is important not to overlook the fact that the planners were given a blank check by the political party. In an effort to prove that they were capable of accomplishing what the former liberals were not able to achieve, and in order to legitimize their political position and to create conditions for growth, the planners made capital accumulation and investment growth their overriding priorities. The drive to locate capital and implement programs often proceeded at the price of improvised projects which, undertaken in the absence of cautious marketing studies and reliable contractors, jeopardized some of the goals of the public enterprises.

The World Bank study requested by Ben Salah indicated that in the drive to invest quickly, serious risks were taken as to the quality of preliminary studies and the insufficiency of initial local capital, and that this partly accounted for the low level of performance in some public enterprises: "It appears that if the justifications for investment were not sure and if there was a choice between, on the one hand, the immediate implementation of a project the economic justification of which was only plausible and not certain, and, on the

---

[38] International Bank for Reconstruction and Development, *Current Economic Position and Prospect for Tunisia*, Washington, D.C., 1968, mimeographed.

other hand, the postponement of this project for a few years in order to ground it more solidly, the chances were great that with conscious deliberation, priority would be given to rapid implementation rather than to the exploration of the justifications." [39] Although this study reported interruption of production due to absence of spare parts and poor maintenance of equipment (as in the case of the steel industry—El Fouladh, cellulose, and textiles), the major failing of industrial management was in the area of cost accounting. Accountants have been rare, and when available, they have had only secondary positions, in contrast with the president directeur général, who was either a political protégé or a technician in a sector in which management and financial expertise were essential.

Partly because most of these enterprises were state initiated, the government financially supported those enterprises which were in tight straits; for social reasons, it refrained from shutting them down, even when they operated at a loss, with the result that the management no longer felt responsible for the financial outcome. With respect to agriculture, the idea of surmounting the bifurcation between modern and traditional land by combining the traditional units and the settler plots was generous but utopian. The planners soon discovered that every plot of land useful for modernization was already utilized either by French or Tunisian farmers, and that what was conceived, in the minds of social scientists and economists, as the traditional rural sector of the economy proved to be nothing more than scraps, sand, and rocks. Furthermore, because the government has constantly been eager to have a base of rural support, it subsequently adopted a full employment policy, including such measures as the yearly creation of 13,000 nonindustrial jobs. There were too many workers for the available jobs, however, and because the option for mechanization was also adopted, the cooperatives were able to provide only 150 to 180 work days per individual.[40]

[39] International Bank for Reconstruction and Development, "Tunisian Public Enterprises," August 31, 1969, Report on EMA, 132, nonofficial translation, p. 11.

[40] The Centre d'Etudes de Recherches Economiques et Sociales of Tunis University followed the whole experiment and devoted many issues of its

In view of the weight borne by the cooperative system in modernizing agriculture, providing jobs, and furnishing surplus to industry, it was assumed that the modern private sector would adapt its methods of cultivation to the social and economic needs of the country. Instead, the private sector abandoned to the state and to the small peasantry, organized in the cooperative framework, the entire burden of the costly investment for the transformation of agriculture. In fact, the private sector invested less than the other sectors while it retained the lands most suitable for agricultural diversification. The farmers who joined service cooperatives for the coordination of purchases and sales were not willing to comply with the criteria of rational production, and, in the middle of the ten-year perspective, the planners had to seriously confront this obstacle:

> This system has not fulfilled the high hopes it aroused because it has not contributed effectively to the increase and diversification of production. The great landowners of the north, the coastal regions, and the south (Cap-Bon, Sahel, and Jérid Oasis), in joining the service cooperatives, have found an excellent excuse to conceal their inability to follow the stages of scientific progress now open to agriculturalists. The state and the party will no doubt reexamine the system in the course of the coming year.[41]

---

publications to it. The most important studies are Ezzedine Makhlouf, "Structures agraires et modernisation de l'agriculture dans les plaines du Kef," *Serie Geographie*, no. 1 (1968); Habib Attia, "L'évolution des structures agraires en Tunisie depuis 1962," *Revue Tunisienne des Sciences Sociales* [hereinafter cited as *RTSS*], no. 7 (November, 1966); Hafedh Sethom, "Modification des structures agraires et industrialisation," *RTSS*, no. 6 (June, 1966), pp. 43–68; Abdelkader Zghal, "Changement du système politique et réformes des structures agraires en Tunisie," *RTSS*, no. 12 (1968), pp. 9–32; a special issue devoted to the problem of *encadrement:* see mainly Elbaki Hermassi, "Elite et Société en Tunisie," and A. Zghal, "L'Elite administrative et la paysannerie," *RTSS*, no. 16 (March, 1969).

[41] "Rapport sur le mouvement coopératif en Tunisie," submitted to the Constitutional Congress of the new Union Nationale de la Coopération, Tunis, 1968, p. 11. For an account of these difficulties, see E. Makhlouf, "La modernisation de l'agriculture en Tunisie," *RTSS*, V:15 (December, 1968), 17–53; and Lars Rudebeck, "Developmental Pressure and Political Limits: The Tunisian Example," *The Journal of Modern African Studies*, VIII:2 (July, 1970), 137–198.

This reexamination led to the conclusion that land reform had to be completely generalized if the total output was to increase significantly enough to achieve the plan's goal. However, by this time, the overall society had paid too high a price—political, economic, and social—and the pressures exerted upon the political system were such that Ben Salah and his planners were removed.

If Morocco proved unwilling to mobilize a surplus potentially present in its economic system and Algeria preferred to use primarily the opportunities created by its foreign export sector, Tunisia, in view of the paucity of its resources and its determination to develop, had no choice but to compel its population to bear the weight of a heavy industrial effort and to call for foreign aid. Because its political system intended to retain the support of all social classes simultaneously, it was, in time, to offend them all equally, without having undertaken a full, rational use of its investment effort. Under conditions normally prevailing in a nonmobilized society, the failure of a given policy to reach fruition could hardly be considered a national tragedy. But in the face of Tunisia's enormous effort, the failure to attain the plan's productive target is to be interpreted as a sign of major breakdown. During 1969, the Tunisian leadership found itself confronting a difficult choice, somewhat analogous to the one before Lenin on the eve of the NEP's inauguration. To have continued on the present course would have meant to face further economic obstacles and rising political discontent, which would have altered the structure of the political elite. Instead, the regime preferred to jail the planners, to reinstitute coexistence of the private, cooperative, and public sectors (Table 18), and to adopt a NEP attitude encouraging profitable forms of business. It remains to be seen whether, in the years to come, rational economic calculations will be more successful than impulsive planning.

In the short term, at least, the shift in economic policy has proved beneficial. The overall redress of the economic and financial situations, and the attempt by Hédi Nouira's government to create a climate of trust and reconciliation, enabled the country, in 1971, to attain a growth rate slightly above 7 percent. Because most of the investments made in the sixties were long-term investments and because a greater degree of rationality has recently been introduced in economic management, most available evidence indicates that the

TABLE 18
Relative Size of Economic Sectors (Private, State, Cooperative) in Tunisia, 1964–1971

Date	Agriculture — Nondomain	Agriculture — Domain[a]	Industry — Large and medium	Craft	Trade — Wholesale	Trade — Retail	Tourism and banks
June, 1964	private	state farms and 20 cooperatives	50% public, 50% private	private	public	private	mainly private
December, 1967	private	state farms and 50 cooperatives	66% public, 34% private	private	public	cooperatives and private	mainly private
December, 1968	90% private, 10% cooperatives	state farms and 300 cooperatives	66% public, 34% private	private and cooperatives	public	mainly local cooperatives	mainly private
August, 1969	20% private, 80% cooperatives	state farms and 300 cooperatives	66% public, 34% private	private and cooperatives	public	mainly local cooperatives	mainly private
April, 1970	90% private, 10% cooperatives	state farms and 300 cooperatives	66% public, 34% private	private	public	local cooperatives and private	mainly private
March, 1971	Private	20% private, 56% cooperatives, 24% state farms	66% public, 34% private	private	semipublic	private	mainly private

[a] Domain: the 740,000 or so hectares which historically belonged to the state from precolonial times.

Source: Adapted from *Le Monde*, April 11-12, 1971 (special issue).

coming decade will bring at least a definitely higher level of economic growth.

Economic Development in Algeria

Algeria's first three-year plan began late in 1967 and was primarily a schedule for investment. This, and the lack of any reliable data, make it very difficult to evaluate in precise terms Algeria's developmental effort. Algeria's striking singularity is its wealth in terms of rich mineral deposits; it is third in world production of natural gas and tenth in world production of crude oil. Natural gas and crude oil provide one-third of its national income and most of its exchange earnings, and have become the major assets in providing necessary capital for economic development. The Algerian regime, however, is the child of a revolution fought predominantly by the peasantry. It is possible to interpret the last decade's economic policy as, first, an unsuccessful attempt at land reform (up to 1967) and, then, as a total shift in the strategy of development from preoccupation with agriculture to a definite commitment to industrialization centered on oil and gas.

Algeria was, in the beginning, less prepared than Morocco and Tunisia to redress its situation and to institutionalize economic policy. There was the policy—if one can call it a policy—of the "scorched fields" (*la terre brûlée*), in which French activists destroyed the archives and obliterated installations and machinery before making their exodus from the country. Among the 800,000 French who left within a period of six months were most of Algeria's entrepreneurs and technicians. While the conflict raged among the political elites at the top, the Algerian workers and peasants spontaneously occupied the vacant farms and organized self-management committees to continue production and reassert control over land they had always felt was their own. Mostefa Lacheraf described this as "properly the socialist choice from which no political regime, whatever it stands for, can escape. The efficiency and the seriousness (i.e., the essence) of this action would depend, in the final analysis, upon those who are in power and upon their degree of revolutionary consciousness and their ideological, rational, and disinterested proclivities." [42] Indeed, the succeeding

[42] Mostefa Lacheraf, *L'Algérie, nation et société* (Paris: Maspero, 1965), p. 27.

regimes, despite other differences, never once questioned the policy of collectivization of land.

Spectacular nationalization of the French land was accomplished by the Ben Bella regime. The March decree of 1963 involved 200,-000 hectares, and by October, the nationalization of all French-owned land had been completed. Thus, by October 2, 1963, the socialist sector included 2,650,000 hectares of previously colonized land which would be progressively organized into 2,151 domains. Table 19 gives the distribution by size of domain.

Given the context in which the land was collectivized, the management of the socialist sector had to face many difficulties. It was hard to maintain the level of production which, in 1963, following the war and transfer of power, diminished by 22 percent. Aside from specific problems of management, commercialization, and manpower, the socialist sector was subjected to much confusion and abuse. Many of those who joined the self-managed farms were actually interested in owning property and were involved in the enterprise to benefit themselves. Some of the guerrilla leaders wanted their booty from the war and opposed the attempt of the union (UGTA) and the FLN party to organize this sector. René Dumont noticed that without the rapid establishment of a governmental authority, "whether by the army or by the party, the agrarian development [and Algeria's development in general] will risk being gravely compromised." [43]

There was also a great deal of ideological and organizational confusion; by making self-management the official ideology, the March decrees provided legally for a democratic and grass-roots management by the workers of the farm themselves. But, besides this principle of worker participation, there was no consensus either among the Algerian elite or its foreign experts as to the practical means of administering such a huge mass of land. For Mohamed Harbi, director of the weekly *Révolution Africaine*, the Moroccan Mohammed Tahiri, and a group of European Trotskyists, one of whom was Michel Raptis, head of the Fourth International, the essential goal was to place the power directly in the workers' hands and to eschew

---

[43] René Dumont, "Des conditions de la réussite de la réforme agraire en Algérie," in François Perroux, ed., *Problèmes de l'Algérie Indépendante* (Paris: Presses Universitaires de France, Collection Tiers Monde, 1963), p. 123. This study was presented to the Algerian government at its request.

TABLE 19

THE SOCIALIST AGRICULTURAL SECTOR, 1964–1965
(BY UNITS, HECTARES, AND SURFACE AREA)

	Less than 100 hectares	100–500 hectares	500–1,000 hectares	1,000–2,000 hectares	2,000–5,000 hectares	More than 5,000 hectares
Number	67	686	620	510	286	22
Surface area in hectares	3,730	213,000	448,000	711,000	743,000	144,000

SOURCE: Enquête agricole, 1964–1965, Algiers; André Tiano, *Le Maghreb entre les mythes*, p. 228.

the bureaucratic entanglement. The state, however, contrary to its professed ideology, hastened to apply René Dumont's recommendations in appointing directors to the farms and in setting up an Office National de la Réforme Agraire (ONRA). From that point on, libertarian socialism fell sway to state socialism. The ONRA personnel became functionaries, assuming the financial, commercial, and technical operation of the whole socialist sector. They did so by creating other institutions such as the Coopératives de la Réforme Agraire (CORA) and the Office National Algérien de Commercialisation (ONACO). The state, in fact, procured almost total control over the details of self-management. In his thesis, Hamid Temmar estimated that 70 to 80 percent of the personnel of self-management ended by acting and perceiving themselves as the bosses.[44] In the long run, despite peasant resentment against interference in their activities, and despite the efforts of the intellectuals and the agricultural unions (FTT) to defend the integrity of the revolution's purposes, the grass-roots battle was lost to the central power. As Pierre Bourdieu so appropriately wrote, "Confronted with the test of reality, this system, inspired by populist ideology, paradoxically experienced metamorphosis into an authoritarian organization. Progressively and—logically—in place of self-management is substituted what Roman jurists called *neotiorum gestio:* the tutor, i.e., the state in the person of the director and the *chargé de*

[44] Hamid Temmar, "L'Autogestion et la problématique du Socialisme Algérien" (unpublished thesis, Paris, Sorbonne, 1966); and "Les problèmes de l'autogestion dans l'ouest algérien" Diplôme d'Etudes Supérieurs, Algiers, 1964.

gestion, acting on behalf of the pupil who is regarded still as a minor." [45]

Self-management was also affected by the political instability that characterized the Algerian regime up to 1965 and the successive regimes' efforts to establish a basis for stability. Although Ben Bella championed self-management in order to gain the support of workers, peasants, and intellectuals, the new military regime was more concerned with war veterans; it tried to organize them on new lands and sometimes on established self-managed farms. As a result, according to El Moujahid, self-management involved 1.9 million hectares in 1968, against the previously higher 2.6 million hectares in 1963. For this and other reasons, the rural socialist sector proved a liability, with only 10 to 20 percent of the farms making a profit. The proponents of this system argued that the decrease was not due to the lessening productive output but to external agencies in charge of transformation and commercialization.[46]

Algeria deserves to be blamed less for its state capitalist orientation than for its exclusive preoccupation with the modern farms and its total disregard for traditional agriculture. Though socialized, the modern sector is providing only a minority—one-tenth of the estimated employable adult rural population—of workers with high incomes and permanent employment, while the fundamental bifurcation of the economy abandons the rest of the rural society—one-half million people—to unemployment. Some of them have chosen to emigrate to France, an old pattern of mobility that has increased the number of Algerians in Europe to 700,000. Most of the rest are waiting for the state to make good on its promise to integrate traditional peasantry within the framework of the modern economy. Until now, the new regime promised land reform three times, and each time postponed it.

As the Tunisian experience has demonstrated, the most difficult area for planning is agriculture, especially in the semiarid lands of North Africa. With a surface area of 593,152,190 acres, Algeria has

[45] Pierre Bourdieu and Abdelmalek Sayad, *Le Déracinement,* p. 173.

[46] Grigori Lazarev, "Autogestion en Algérie," *Cahiers du Tiers Monde* (1965). For a complete account of self-management, containing historical, legal, and procedural material, see Michel Raptis, "Le Dossier de l'autogestion de l'Algérie," *Autogestion,* no. 3 (September, 1967); Thomas L. Blair, *The Land to Those Who Work It: Algeria's Experiment in Workers' Management* (New York: Doubleday Anchor Books, 1970).

only 22,240,000 acres under cultivation. The most ambitious estimate foresees an increase of only 2,471,054 acres by 1980. However, even this kind of estimate is still a game for technicians. With a demographic growth rate of 3.2 percent, the population has already increased by 2 million since independence; consequently, one-sixth of all Algeria's imports today are food products (out of $645.52 million spent on imports, $97.3 million is spent on food products). At this stage, Algerian agriculture—modern, socialist, and traditional—cannot sustain itself and even less generate capital for national development. Whether Algeria will meet its declared objective of self-sufficiency in basic foodstuffs by 1980 will depend on the type of relationships which are established between the rural sector and the growing industrial sector. For the time being, the adoption of the three-year plan indicates that agriculture has ceased to be a regime priority. Indeed, the amount of capital earmarked for agricultural development during this period, 1967–1970, amounts to about one-sixth of that budgeted for industrial products. In the overall economic policy, therefore, the peasant society is neither helped nor heavily taxed—it is simply abandoned.

The new pattern of development has shifted the focus from this agricultural experiment to a complete concentration on industrialization centered on the oil potential. This shift of emphasis, and the new oil agreement signed in July 1965, coincided with Boumediène's ascent to power. Up to that time, the French companies held a privileged position, paying royalties far below average to the Algerian government, which acted merely as tax collector. According to the new agreement, Algeria gained not only an increase in oil revenue but direct participation in the industry. The agreement was negotiated between the two governments and their respective companies—the Algerian Sonatrach and the French ERAP—and represented a fruitful attempt at genuine cooperation: (a) The two companies were to be equal partners in the exploration for oil and in the exploitation of 180 square kilometers; (b) the framework for a "cooperative association" included the equivalent of a $4 million aid program to help promote Algerian industrialization by financing the natural gas liquidation plant at Skikda, a chemical fertilizer complex, a pipeline, and other projects; (c) the agreement determined the fate of private companies subjected to the same system of taxation (reference price, $2.08 per barrel) and, more importantly, obligated them to deposit half the operating capital in Algeria.

The arrangement was hailed as a breakthrough in relationships between oil-importing and oil-producing countries. It permitted the Gaullist regime to secure its supply of low sulphur oil at a lesser freight cost and to pursue an independent policy. For Algeria, it promised not only greater profits but the possibility of mastering the financial flow created by oil activities and reorienting the investment to further economic development. The first three-year plan, though transitional, exemplified this new orientation by calling for a total investment of 5.4 billion dinars ($1.08 billion), half of which was earmarked for development of oil and gas industries and their subsidiaries, such as fertilizer and other petrochemical industries.[47]

The four-year plan for 1970–1973 calls for a total investment exceeding by five times that of the previous plan, 26.4 billion dinars, 48 percent of which goes to industry, and 15 percent to agriculture. The generation of this investment will depend mainly upon the resources of the oil industry. For this reason, the major conflict over capital accumulation has centered on the relationship between the Algerian government and its export sector. To evaluate the significance of the Algerian achievement, it is important to understand the structural features of the contemporary oil business, which contradict the requirements for rapid growth of the developing country. International companies and newcomers, like France, are motivated by profit maximization. They have a very short-term view of investment projects, and it has been estimated that an investment would have to yield 20 to 25 percent per year in order to be undertaken.[48] Latecomers have also discovered that a well diversified

[47] For the details of the three-year development plan, see *Révolution Africaine*, no. 256 (January 11–17, 1968), pp. 16–18.

[48] Michael Tanzer, *The Political Economy of International Oil and the Underdeveloped Countries* (Boston: Beacon Press, 1969). This analysis of the conflicts between international majors and newcomers, such as France and Italy, is somehow weakened when it comes to their interrelationships with the Third World. During the recent confrontation between oil companies and oil-exporting underdeveloped countries, post-Gaullist France's reaction has been to hurriedly throw in its lot with the cartel and to entrust the defense of its interests to these international companies.

supply of resources is the best guarantee in dealing with blockage of supply, whether threatened or actual.[49]

On the other hand, Algerians are convinced that aside from natural gas, oil is their major resource and the only one that will eventually enable them to emerge from underdevelopment. The determination of the Algerian state to use oil as its leading sector for rapid industrialization only intensified the defense strategies of the foreign companies and increased the capital outflow from the country. France, already importing two-thirds of the Algerian oil, started the exploration of the newly designated oil fields but did not progress very far. Its companies, CPF and ERAP, preferred to intensify exploration elsewhere, not only in the Middle East but in Canada, Australia, and West Africa. To their Algerian partner, this was clearly a violation of the agreement. The Algerians complained bitterly about the underexploitation of oil, arguing,

> The French have the means to undertake profitable exploration here. Haven't they, with the increasing production, drawn from Algeria in three years 3.5 billion cash flow (net profit plus amortization)? Cooperation does not consist only of maximizing profits and reducing the amount of investment to the minimum required by the agreement. It must take into consideration the prior interest of the partner, that is, the rapid development of its oil domain.[50]

They also reproached the French companies for selling oil to their own affiliates at prices 20 percent below those of the world market. Because the companies were required to remit half of the revenues from gross sales, the Algerian government considered it a maneuver to reduce to a minimum the amount of money brought back into the country for future investment.

In this situation, the Sonatrach has combined a firmness of attitude with a flexibility of strategies in strengthening its control over the industry. The Sonatrach has increased its participation in the operations and has taken opportunities either to impose more advantageous arrangements[51] or to nationalize portions of the network

[49] Raymond Vernon, "Foreign Enterprises and Developing Nations in the Raw Materials Industries," *American Economic Review* (May, 1969), pp. 122–126.

[50] As quoted by Alain Mercier in "Le pétrole entre l'Algérie et la France," *Le Monde*, March 21, 1969.

[51] After subjecting the companies to pressures to increase foreign reinvest-

when the benefits exceed the costs. By June 1968, the Sonatrach gained a monopoly on the sale of oil and gas products, and it did not miss the opportunity of nationalizing most French firms that manufactured such products as construction materials, fertilizers, machinery, electric supplies, textiles, and food. Pursuing its working principle of participating in every phase of the production process, from the fields to the gas stations, Algeria increased its oil pipelines by 70 percent in 1970; moreover, its production reached 28 percent of the total volume of crude oil extracted in 1970 (it reached 18 percent in 1969). With the exception of Mexico, Algeria's is certainly the first successful attempt by an oil-producing, developing country to gain control over its oil industry. In association with countries other than France, but also on its own, Algeria is undertaking an exploration program with downstream facilities purchased from the Soviet Union and the United States. Sonatrach

---

ment in Algeria, Boumediène's government finally decided to force them to reinvestment through revision of the reference price, which revision he imposed unilaterally during the summer of 1970, first as $2.85 and then as $3.24. This gave the French companies only a net benefit of 4 francs instead of the previous 20 francs per ton. Most observers noticed that with this amount of profit for Algeria, the companies were not able to refurbish their capital in new investments. It is not a novel argument which assumes that an excessive increase in the share of profit and control harms both the firm and the oil-exporting country. It was advanced by Thomas C. Schelling, who, alluding to the dated arrangement of the 50/50, wrote: "There is simply no heart left in the bargaining when it takes place under the shadow of some dramatic and conspicuous precedent." *The Strategy of Conflict* (Cambridge, Mass.: Harvard University Press, 1960), p. 68.

But the Algerian and Middle Eastern countries' counterargument is growing increasingly powerful. The experts, Abdallah Tariqui and O.P.E.C. (Organization of Petroleum Exporting Countries), have established that from each barrel of oil, the Arab oil-producing countries gain $0.70 to $0.80 (for Algeria, $0.72), the oil companies gain $1.00, and the European governments receive an average of $5.00 in fiscal revenue. Under these conditions, the industrial powers should forego some of their tax revenue to protect their companies and to transfer additional funds to the developing nations. From the Algerian viewpoint, "Each barrel of oil carries a profit six or seven times greater for the French government than for the producing countries, and five times greater than for the companies themselves. If the French government thinks it mandatory for its interest that its oil companies ensure their capital reproduction, then let that government do the financing itself: this will only cost it a few cents a gallon. . . . There is no reason for the Algerian people to pay instead." *Nouvel Observateur*, no. 299, August 3–9, 1970; reproduced by the *Algerian Revue de Presse*, no. 147, August, 1970.

has begun large-scale production of natural gas at Hassi R'Mel, where production exceeds two billion cubic meters per year.

Tactical considerations aside, what is apparent from present policy is that the Algerian government will not curb its efforts to obtain complete control of oil resources—including the right to regulate exploration and production (see Table 20). In fact, on February 24, 1971, Algeria took major control of all French oil interests in the country and nationalized all natural gas assets.

French attempts to restrict savings sent home by Algerian workers and to apply pressure through aid and industrial investments have not affected the ultimate objective. The tide has turned, and Algerians should now give the French some time to adjust their oil revenue policy. Many Frenchmen working in Algeria are beginning to wonder whether the Algerian solution imposed upon some American oil companies, among them Getty's, is not inevitable. The Algerian solution presumes that the French concerns will give up the principle of concessions—a principle made unacceptable by its colonial origin—and become operating companies for the Algerian government. As André Fontaine has put it, "This far-reaching decision is one which would obviously have a serious effect upon the world oil market; yet there is every reason to believe that any other policy would be condemned to instability." [52]

Although it is difficult, at this point, to evaluate the impact of oil policy upon overall economic development, we can present some indications concerning potential for growth.[53] Up to 1967, the gross national product was steadily decreasing; but the reorientation of the economy, beginning in 1967, has permitted an increase at an average rate of 5.3 percent per year. Per capita income, which fell more than 15 percent between 1958 and 1965 (to about $210 a year), began recovering slowly and reached the 1967 level of $230. The objective of the four-year plan for 1970–1973 is a growth rate of 8.2 percent, with an assumed 13.2-percent growth in industrial production and a 3-percent growth in agriculture. Though

[52] *Le Monde Weekly*, January 27, 1971.

[53] El-Aziz Kouadri, "Place et rôle du secteur petrolier dans le développement de l'économie algérienne," *Revue Tiers Monde*, X:39 (July–September, 1969), 629–658; G. de Beaurepaire, "Le plan algérien est-il réalisable?" *Jeune Afrique*, no. 477 (February 23, 1970); "Le Plan quadriennal algérien," *Maghreb*, no. 40 (July–August, 1970), pp. 33–40.

TABLE 20

EVOLUTION OF PARTICIPATION IN ALGERIA'S OIL INDUSTRY
SINCE INDEPENDENCE
(IN APPROXIMATE PERCENTAGES)

	Prospect permits		Production		Transporta-tion		Refining		Distribution	
	1962	*1969*	*1962*	*1969*	*1962*	*1969*	*1962*	*1969*	*1962*	*1969*
Algeria	5	56	10	18	9	52	10	56	0	100
French companies	67	38	70	70	75	34	32	20	50	0
Other companies	28	6	20	12	16	14	58	24	50	0
Total	100	100	100	100	100	100	100	100	100	100

SOURCE: *Le Monde*, March 20, 1969.

ambitious and *volontariste*, most of these goals are attainable, in practice. Indeed, with the $250 million annual revenues from oil and natural gas and the $200 million of Algerian labor's savings in Europe, Algeria was able to accumulate $400 million in foreign reserves and to convert $200 million into gold, a step which, according to Boumediène, "will not fail to strengthen our money, build confidence in our country, and reinforce the most complete independence from all external pressures for both our domestic and foreign policy." [54] More importantly, the Algerian rate of investment, without oil resources, would have been 13 percent of the GNP, but it had already risen to 25 percent in 1969. If all the projected investments are undertaken, it is presumed that this rate will rise to 33 percent in 1973.

The Algerian pattern of industrialization systematically attempts to avoid forms of economic development such as import substitution, which would simply maintain Algeria's financial and industrial dependence upon the industrialized economies. The 150 investment projects which are in progress are designed to increase production capacities in the petrochemical, steel, electric, and mechanical industries. The basic idea is to utilize the available natural resources to build large-scale enterprises capable of producing great

[54] *Revolution Africaine*, no. 255 (January 4–10, 1968).

quantities at internationally competitive prices. The manufacture of intermediary products, such as fertilizers, chemicals, energy, and plastic products, is designed to feed into the consumption industry and to provide a major stimulus to the agricultural and rural sector. Today Algerian companies are active on all fronts, building pipelines, refineries, petrochemical facilities, with the anticipation of achieving a societal industrial base by 1980. Although it is true that the three-year plan of 1967–1969 fell short of its objectives in many areas (with an average of around 82 percent achieved in all sectors), the shortcomings are to be expected and are freely admitted.

Today, the first problem confronting planners is that the rate of return on the huge investment involves a good deal of capital and capital equipment and, hence, a dependence upon the outside market during the entire four-year plan. Secondly, the selection of large-scale production units means that the local market will not be able to absorb the output, and that in the future Algeria will depend on the outside market not for capital equipment but for outlets for its exports. In recent years, Algeria has been able to sell some of its oil (500,000 tons per year) to the Soviet Union. Japan, a latecomer, has become the main customer for the cast iron produced at Annaba. And Algeria is in the process of becoming the first foreign supplier of natural gas to the United States, which has already contracted for fifteen billion cubic meters over the next twenty years. Were Algeria to face difficulties of access to the international market, however, the diffusion of its investment processes would be endangered because its planning agencies have not allowed for the development of opportunities for profitable expansion in the maghribi markets. This is one of the disappointing features of the Algerian project as a whole.

As might be expected, it will take some time for Algeria to supply its industrial sector with the required technical skills. Today, it lacks 4,000 engineers, 100,000 technicians, and 30,000 skilled workers, as estimated by the plan agency. Even by 1973, the last year of the plan, it is expected that there will be a lack of 14,000 people to fill top- and middle-level management positions. But because the country is determined to end the "rent out of ignorance," it is trying to attain skilled management and total control of its industry by investing in human resources, learning techniques from Soviet and American experts, and even postponing "Algerianization" in order to keep 15,000 foreign personnel working in the country.

Finally, because the investments undertaken today are capital intensive, they will only create 250,000 jobs. The planners show a total disregard for the problem of unemployment. One of them argues, "It is better to have an immediate elite of 300,000 skilled workers in strategic sectors than to lose our money making hammers and spoons." And another claims, "With the $70 million that this ammonia plant has cost us, we could have employed thousands of idle men, but what would be the real benefit for our country and its agriculture?" [55] There is little doubt that these options are realistic in the long run, because synthetic ammonia cannot be manufactured by enthusiastic peasants. Thus it is important to realize that what was initially a peasant revolution has culminated in a form of vigorous state capitalism, utilizing both modern large-scale techniques and small-scale local plants. This policy is, then, in sharp contrast with the Chinese policy of "walking on two legs." The fundamental price Algeria will have to pay is, of course, that by the plan's termination, it will have three-quarters of a million people unemployed, and that in the process of industrialization, the tragic bifurcation of the society into isolated poles of growth and stagnation will persist for a long time.

[55] Interviews in *l'Express*, November 2–8, 1970.

Chapter 11: CONCLUSION:
CONTRASTING STRATEGIES

The time has finally come to draw together evidence gained from the study of political institutions and economic policies and to evaluate the overall performance of maghribi regimes. It should be noted that we first analyzed the maghribi states' historical traditions, the differentiation of their political communities from those of the Arab-speaking world, and the manner in which these states shaped the configuration of present societies and resolved their problems of national integration. The unmistakable point which emerged from this analysis is that the maghribi societies, contrary to superficial observations, are presently equal in national cohesion to any European society. Regimes may stand or fall, depending on their performance, but the nations—established and secure—are here to stay.

We have also argued that in each society national unification bears the stamp of the institutions that shaped it, the unique events that marked its formation, and the social forces it brought to prominence. These institutions, social forces, and specific events were to influence the ways in which political systems would meet the social, political, cultural, and economic challenges of their time. In evaluating the regimes' strategies in meeting these challenges, we find the most telling contrast can be drawn between Morocco, on the one hand, and Tunisia and Algeria, on the other.

National unification of the Moroccan society had to overcome ethnic, cultural, and political fragmentation, out of which the unifying center cultivated the vocational practices of negotiation, arbitration, and compromise, rather than blunt initiative and reform. The complexities that were introduced by European domination, such as greater social differentiation and new elite formation, were maintained under the monarchy's control. Finally, the absence of rural mobilization during the national liberation movement and the inheritance of a strong bureaucratic apparatus from the former regime strengthened both the monarchical family and privileged groups. After independence, the transformation of the society was deliberately limited in order to maintain the existing relationships among groups and to safeguard the monarchy's position, which could have been threatened by changes, the effects of which it would have been unable to control.

Short-term stability has, thus, been obtained at the price of handing the modernization projects to the minister of interior, for whom political considerations override economic exigencies. Goals of reform have been set aside.[56] Problems are selected in reaction to outside pressures, and measures are taken simply to undercut the substance of the opposition's claim to power. "In such a political picture, perspective is lost, depth and vision are absent, and all problems are treated as short-range concerns." [57] The political system exhausts its energies in mediation and neutralization, rather than devoting them to mobilization and change. One of the ramifications of this stalemate is a corrupt administration and the disenchantment of most of the elite, including officials themselves. Ernest Gellner writes,

> One rural official observed to me in December 1967 that, after all there were only two honest ways of earning a living—agriculture and trade. This is a very Moroccan remark, if indeed it is not a saying. The implication was that administration and the occupancy of a power-post was *not* honest: he had accepted it only because of family pressure. The fact that this pressure was effective and that others are eager for such posts shows that there are compensations in holding such posts. The other interesting implication of the remark was one of which the speaker was quite unaware: industry was not mentioned as an alternative, not because it is less than honest, but because, on his social horizon, it simply did not exist.[58]

In Algeria as well as in Tunisia, national elites with cosmopolitan outlooks and popular orientations (such people were only marginal

---

[56] Analyzing Morocco's agrarian policy, an observer noted, "If the present action is pursued with the usual help of traditional notables, there is every chance these notables will confiscate the very fruit of the governmental policy." Octave Marais, "La politique agraire du Maroc, problèmes et perspectives," *Analyse et Prévision: Futuribles*, VII:5 (May, 1969), 295–306. I drew much insight from this keen observer of the Moroccan scene. See also Michel Rousset, "Le rôle du Ministère de l'intérieur et sa place au sein de l'administration Marocaine," *Annuaire de l'Afrique du Nord*, VII (1969), 91–106.

[57] I. William Zartman, *Morocco: Problems of New Power* (New York: Atherton Press, 1964), pp. 258–259.

[58] Ernest Gellner, "The Great Patron: A Reinterpretation of Tribal Rebellions," *Archives Européennes de Sociologie*, X:1 (1969), 67.

in Morocco) acceded to central power and brought with them a common determination for rapid economic development. They proceeded, however, from different starting points and in the midst of significantly different national contexts. Tunisia's ideological and cultural homogeneity, its early unification, and the continuous evolution of its political institutions contributed to the formation of a unified, pragmatic, and gradualist national elite. Algeria, on the other hand, historically has been much less integrated, and its national identity emerged from a profoundly felt segregation, which the Turks and the French tried equally hard to preserve. The lateness of its unification and the context in which it took place left a strong legacy of oppositional politics that eroded institutions and divided elites. Equally important is the fact that the Algerian regime initially had little legitimacy and significant economic potential, whereas the Tunisian regime inherited less economic opportunity but commanded significant political support.

A close examination of their developmental strategies reveals that these two governments seem to have made intuitive assessments of the costs and benefits of mobilizing different sectors[59] and of assigning to some groups the weight of the developmental effort. Thus, they have had to confront different forms of internal and external conflicts. Having wrested from foreign investors one of the best arrangements any oil-producing nation has had (except perhaps Venezuela), the Algerian government is able to make a tremendous investment effort without risking internal political costs. Up to now, at least, the Algerian population has been spared the price of capital accumulation. The government even drew national support during its confrontation with foreign governments and businesses. In Tunisia, by contrast, economic development can be realized only through the limited endogenous resources, and the polarization was, thus, purely internal. In an attempt to reorient the economy, this traditionally gradualist government went so far as to politicize the social and economic spheres. As national issues penetrated the most peripheral areas, a good deal of tension was generated. With land reform, the nationalization of most of the trade, the creation of new industry, and related measures such as the upgrading of women's

[59] Warren F. Ilchman and Norman Thomas Uphoff, *The Political Economy of Change* (Berkeley and Los Angeles: University of California Press, 1969).

status and birth control, the political system became more encompassing and, hence, more vulnerable.

In addition, the comparative analysis of planning has shown that the Tunisian political system was oriented excessively toward employment and welfare, and that the Algerian, by adopting a pattern of industrialization characterized by high capital intensity, failed to present any solution for its massive unemployment. By narrowing its economic involvement to the industrialization of only some sectors, the Algerian regime seems determined to condemn the rural society to slow death through attrition.

It is possible at this point to rank maghribi regimes, though schematically, in terms of political institutionalization, on the one hand, and economic productivity and welfare allocation, on the other (see the figure). It is clear from the evidence presented that the Tunisian political system has so far displayed the greatest effectiveness. This system's competence is a result of its leaders' statesmanship, the viability of its political institutions, and the political support it has managed to collect, despite the crises emanating from economic policies. If our hypothesis that legitimacy depends as much upon institutions as upon performance has any validity, we would expect the Moroccan monarchy, in view of its poor achievements in economic growth and welfare, to suffer diminishing legitimate authority. And we would expect that there would be increasing acceptance of the governmental authority of the Algerian regime.

The Moroccan monarchy is already racked by permanent crisis. The Moroccan political elite, having tried for an entire decade to

PROFILES OF GOVERNMENTAL EFFECTIVENESS

Ranking order	Political institutionalization	Productivity	Welfare
1			
2			
3			
4			

Algeria   – – – – –
Tunisia   ——————
Morocco   —·—·—·—

establish collaboration with the monarchy and having participated in different experiments that combined progressive and conservative lines of action in an attempt to break the existing stalemate, has completely withdrawn from the political system. After the dispersing of its ranks and the assassination of its leader, Mehdi Ben Barka, in 1965, the elite's immobility can be broken only if a segment of the elite and of the young officers decide to stop paying the high price of the status quo. Without discounting the external impact, one is struck by the precipitating factors of frequent student demonstrations, the reemergence of urban guerrillas, the peasant disaffection,[60] and repeated attempts to assassinate the king.

In sharp contrast, there is little doubt that public service and efficient management in Algeria have been successfully substituted for the mixture of improvement and "clan parliamentarism" that marked the first years of independence. Algerians with whom this author has spoken, both casually and officially, feel that the regime has ceased to be perceived as purely military. It has ended the instability of its political life and the interorganizational competition which scarred the revolutionary elite, and has displayed an industrial effort which is one of the most dynamic and significant among the countries of the Third World. But, whether by calculation or lack of political direction, the state limited its effort to this sector and ignored the rest of society. Thus, two disjunctions have been created by selective socialism: first, between the new, expert, well-salaried industrial bureaucracy and the petty bourgeoisie, which surrounds the FLN party and the old administration; and secondly, between the same bureaucracy and the mass of peasants,

---

[60] Jamil Moulahidh, "Le Maroc dans l'inquietude," *Esprit,* no. 397 (November, 1970), pp. 783–804, reports the rural malaise, such as the insurrection of Settat in the summer of 1970, which resulted in six deaths and three hundred arrests and the deliberate destruction of irrigation channels and royal family farms by the rural youth. From a recent monograph, *Bulletin Economique et Social du Maroc,* 1969, we learn that "the youth's demands of society are such that it cannot possible satisfy them without transforming itself entirely. The survey reveals that their aggression is boundless, their criticism is radical when they are disappointed, and their determination is to live as the delinquent and the debauched in response to the ferocity of their society."

The July 10, 1971, bloody rebellion which Morocco suffered and the attempted coup of August 16, 1972, are, unfortunately, further proof of the corruption and hopelessness of the present Morocco situation.

lumpenproletariat, and Algerian immigrants forced to make their living abroad. As it grows increasingly homogeneous, the industrial bureaucracy might be expected to conflict with the traditional middle classes and might even call for land reform in order to render agriculture open to the products of industry. Indeed, by 1972, the regime's commitment to agrarian revolution became much more pronounced. But what is needed in the long run, more than economic alliances, is a political reorientation of the society, in which the cosmopolitan bureaucracy would play an instrumental role, and the building of institutions designed to integrate the political community as a whole.

For the time being, the absence of a genuine political order and political direction leaves important areas, such as ideology formation and mass media, to the scripturalists and the petty bourgeoisie, to the point that the government must refrain from any cultural change which would alienate these groups. In this disconnected society, one is struck by the socialist rhetoric disseminated to the outside and by the Puritanism embraced at home. Even within the society, the combination of technical buildup and complete avoidance of secular practices seems paradoxical to most observers. The most we can suggest at this point is that it will take Algeria some time to overcome the cultural inhibitions and heal the profound social wounds that are its colonial legacy. This also means that neither the army nor the administration, whatever their efficiency, will be able to effect reconciliation within the society and construct the foundation of a new political culture.

In Tunisia, the cost of the developmental effort was sustained from within, and consequently, the polarization was internal. It ranged from landowners' overt resistance to collectivization to serious disagreements among the national elites.[61] Although there are no total schisms within the political system, definite cleavages have appeared and have become more acute in the continuing crisis over the successor to President Bourguiba. The first movement to challenge Bourguiba was identified with Ben Salah and was systematically dismantled in 1969. Its elimination indicates the final tri-

[61] Hédi Nouira, "Discours Programme," presented to the National Assembly, *L'Action,* November 18, 1970; see also "Ben Salah et le développement tunisien (1961–1969)," document published in *Esprit,* no. 397 (November, 1970), pp. 805–817.

umph of reconciliatory leadership as well as a preference for moderate programs and mixed economy. It also attests to the structural incapability of the country to undertake, alone and in the absence of maghribi regional economic integration, the task of full industrialization. In the wake of this debate, a second movement appeared, which has been identified with Ahmed Mestiri. It called for more coherent institutional organization and greater decentralization of power in order to avoid the mistakes of the last decade. It even received strong backing by the party congress of October 1971, which decided to replace the old procedure of official nomination for each political office with the procedure of direct election of every political official.

The point that emerges from these recent events in Tunisia is that arguments in favor of the priority of economic development at any cost and those in favor of the priority of political institutionalization are expressed within one and the same political party, for no reform—social, economic, or political—can be formulated or implemented outside of the party's apparatus.

By being particularly sensitive to the society as a whole, responding to different sectors and alternating its orientation according to the existing equilibrium of forces, the party has undoubtedly been able to contain the conflictive tendencies of its elite members and to maintain a relatively high level of legitimacy. The commitment to national unity under the leadership of one party and one man was unquestionably instrumental in the past, but in view of the increasing differentiation in and the transformation of the Tunisian society after a decade of national mobilization, this formula has outlived its usefulness. To concentrate power in a mobilized and increasingly stratified society and to refuse to take the risk of making costly but necessary choices, in the name of national unity, is tantamount to imagining that development can proceed without alienating any social class and that the transformation of society can be accomplished without dividing it.

The challenges that will confront the Tunisian political system in the future will be those of power distribution and institutional reorganization. It is likely that these challenges will be met with such hesitation and slowness that the cleavages the party has been able to minimize until now will intensify and will more readily come to the surface. All in all, it seems that the Tunisian elite is in the process of losing its dynamizing and liberating powers, and that the political system has lost its equilibrium. One is led to believe that in contrast to the recent and remote past, Algeria is finally displacing Tunisia as the symbol of progress in the Maghrib.

These are the general outlines of the policies selected by maghribi political systems in the face of the pressing exigencies of today. Nothing in this profile suggests that one or another of the historical versions of industrialization (i.e., bourgeois-democratic, Fascist, or Communist) is being reenacted in North Africa. The propensity of many analysts to interpret nation building according to familiar forms and through prematurely constructed typologies can be indulged only by imposing ethnocentric categories upon a struggle among groups and nations that is still too problematic to be neatly packaged into discrete categories. The profiles of South America, where economic growth coexists with praetorian politics, and of India, where democracy is associated with economic backwardness, lead to similar conclusions. In the midst of societies undergoing changes that are unequal, involuted, and incoherent, and in which there is a compounding of challenges, leaders find themselves in a more precarious position than at any other time in the history of national societies. Their dependency upon the bloc of privileged nations is so profound as to preclude the objective possibility of past historical options.

Given the exhausted paths, the lost opportunities, and the texture of national and international constraints, there can only be a quest for alternative forms of development. For the time being, no national effort, not even that of China, has yet reached a definitely institutionalized and distinctly identifiable form. By comparing the North African societies' confrontations of similar institutional problems, it is hoped that the Maghrib has become more intelligible. It is further hoped that a step has been taken toward the formulation of a new methodology for the study of the formation and transformation of national societies.

EPILOGUE

On the subject of national development, which has been the impassioned concern of this book, I have remained skeptical as to the scientific worth of most preestablished theories. These theories, which have pretensions to universal applicability, have been generally elaborated in the sanctity of the office, far away from men's struggle for living and meaning. I find it more useful to present a paradigm that enables us to raise relevant questions and to build region-specific models as a first step to critical and scientific knowledge of new nations. The paradigm applied to North Africa seems to me appropriate for other national societies. It suggests fundamentally new ways of phrasing the questions and framing the problems, and especially suggests some research priorities.

(1) The conclusion must be drawn that modernization theory is a failure; it cannot explain backwardness, and it offers no practical remedy for underdevelopment.

(2) In order to comprehend variations in national development, social scientists must study historical backwardness and the specific consequences of world domination. For this task, there is no respectable shortcut that avoids historical analysis. This kind of study, which is historically grounded, saves us from two tempting pitfalls. The first is in line with a long-standing sociological tradition that considers social change as immanent in the society. It has led many scholars to focus exclusively on internal processes, to assume that most obstacles to development lie in people's attachment to traditional identities, and to perceive the endogenous culture as the major barrier to be overcome if change is to occur.[1] According to this perspective, imperialism, and its profound impact on these

[1] This tradition pervades the literature on North Africa, as can be seen from the following: John Waterbury writes, "It is my contention that this state of affairs [i.e., the political stalemate in Morocco] can be explained by a common Moroccan attitude toward power and authority and that this attitude is conceivably derived from the country's traditional social structure." John Waterbury, *The Commander of the Faithful: The Moroccan Political Elite—A Study in Segmented Politics.*

For the *reductio ad absurdum*, see David and Marina Ottoway's *Algeria: The Politics of a Socialist Revolution* (Berkeley and Los Angeles: Univer-

societies' internal developments, is considered merely a residual category. As a result, we find ourselves in a bizarre situation: Economists sell their discipline short in order to study the cultural restraints that hinder economic growth, and sociologists and anthropologists try to become experts in economics. Thus, the real processes by which societies evolve and the structure of dependency that makes genuine development questionable indeed are obscured. Instead, enlightened social scientists should assume that people of all origins, whatever their traditional culture and social structures, would respond favorably to political and economic opportunities. In fact, to analyze backwardness in the present world context as merely a cultural and local failure to "modernize" is no more than ideology disguised as science.

The second pitfall, which has trapped only a minority, involves placing the whole explanatory weight for underdevelopment upon imperialism. This perspective is based mainly upon two assumptions. The first is that new nations' leaders are nothing but liaison-elite providing linkages between the center and the periphery of the capitalist economy. The liaison-elite and their class basis are presumed to have internalized a legacy of dependency because they have a vested interest in its sustenance. By implication, the second assumption is that given the conditions obtaining for peripheral countries, development is unlikely within the confines of the international capitalist system, but possible through an integration of their economies with the socialist system.[2]

Briefly, these propositions should be the objectives of empirical investigation rather than being taken for granted. Although it is true that some political systems are client regimes, it is difficult, at best, to conceive indiscriminately of leaders, past or present, such

sity of California Press, 1970), pp. 6–9: "The nature of politics in Algeria today remains the same as it was in the time of Ibn Khaldun . . . a cyclical process of rise and fall of empires . . . a politics of clans and personalities."

[2] See Andre Gunder Frank, *Latin America: Underdevelopment or Revolution* (New York and London: Monthly Review Press, 1969); Theotonio Dos Santos, "The Structure of Dependence," *American Economic Review* (May, 1970), pp. 231–236. A European version of this debate takes place between Marxists whose internal factors are class antagonism and Marxists whose explanatory framework is the antagonism between nation building and imperialism. See Maxime Rodinson, "Dynamique Interne ou Dynamique Globale? L'exemple des pays musulmans," *Cahiers Internationaux de Sociologie*, XLII (1967), 27–47.

as Allende of Chile, Boumediène of Algeria, and Nasser of Egypt, as liaison-elites serving North Atlantic and European metropolises. Moreover, evidence from tropical Africa suggests that disengagement from the capitalist system may not, in itself, alter what Giovanni Arrighi calls the pattern of growth without development.[3] The significant point is that these nations must still face the problem of ending Balkanization and of capital accumulation. Fundamentally, the whole perspective is excessively economic, and in this instance, it is the national societies themselves that become residual categories.

(3) The external environment must be absolutely integrated as an additional determinant.[4] But it is by focusing our investigation on national societies that we can evaluate the differential capacities for rupturing the chains of dependency and achieving integration and institutional competence. One of the central recommendations in favor of this paradigm is precisely this essential perspective.

(4) A contextual analysis of national societies raises at least two important theoretical and methodological questions: What level of social reality and which societies should we study? Whatever the differences that exist among sociologists in conceptualizing nation building, a fruitful way to study its processes is to focus on those who are most responsible for shaping them—the leaders. This supposes a reorientation of present research. Without such a reorientation, we shall be embarrassed by the shortage of studies on elites, and we shall continue, without theoretical justification, to concentrate on workers, farmers, villages, and tribes.

Moreover, if we are to sustain the hope of cumulative knowledge and the formulation of more grounded theories, we must introduce criteria for selecting case studies, which up to now have been dictated more often by the biographies of individual scholars than by the requirements of the discipline. By identifying the four key problems confronting national societies, this paradigm also offers an

[3] "International Corporations, Labor Aristocracies, and Economic Development in Tropical Africa," in Robert I. Rhodes, ed., *Imperialism and Underdevelopment* (New York and London: Monthly Review Press, 1970), pp. 220–267.

[4] Much is to be learned from Neil Smelser's causal models in the analysis of social change, in *Essays in Sociological Explanation* (Englewood Cliffs, N.J.: Prentice-Hall, 1968).

idea of the required theoretical sampling for carefully selecting cases in a comparative perspective. For instance,

—One should compare nation building in societies that emerged from colonial empires with those whose distance from colonial empire and whose size permitted almost autonomous evolution.

—Societies in which national integration has taken place, e.g., North Africa, should be compared with others that have yet to face this task, e.g., Nigeria and Pakistan.

—Societies with significant economic opportunities (oil-producing countries) should be compared to civic societies without such opportunities, e.g., Tunisia and Chile.

These are some of the research strategies that can make us more sensitive to the range of variation in the national elites' responses to the basic problems of their societies, and that are indispensable for the elaboration of typologies and the foundation of grounded theories.

Finally, one of the advantages of this perspective is that the concentration on national dilemmas, policies, and the costs of alternatives pursued by national leadership makes the discipline relevant to new nations, and, as such, worthy of the expectations that, as it happens, they place in it.

SELECTED BIBLIOGRAPHY

In this brief bibliography, we list only the books and articles in Arabic, French, and English that we found useful for the elaboration of this work. The first part contains theoretical works relating in one way or another to the question of national development. The second body of references consists either of introductory or comparative works relating to the Maghrib as a whole. The third part lists case studies on Algeria, Morocco, and Tunisia. Students who seek information on contemporary North Africa should also consult the following journals:

1. *Revue Tunisienne des Sciences Sociales*. Tunis.
2. *Revue Algérienne des Sciences Juridiques, Politiques, et Economiques*. Algiers.
3. *Bulletin Economique et Social du Maroc*. Rabat.
4. *Maghreb*. Paris: Fondation nationale des sciences politiques and Documentation Francaise.
5. *L'Annuaire de l'Afrique du Nord*. Aix-en-Provence: Centre de Recherches et d'Etude sur les sociétés mediterranéennes.
6. *Encyclopedia of Islam*. New Edition. Leiden and London, (1960).

I. THEORETICAL WORKS

Abdel-Malek, Anouar. "Orientalism in Crisis," *Diogenes*, (Winter, 1963), no. 44, pp. 103–140.
———. "Esquisse d'une typologie des formations nationales dans les 'trois continents,'" *Cahiers Internationaux de Sociologie*, XLII (January–June 1967), 49–57.
Almond, Gabriel A., and G. Bingham Powell. *Comparative Politics: A Developmental Approach*. Boston: Little, Brown, 1966.
Almond, Gabriel A., and Sidney Verba. *The Civic Culture*. Boston: Little, Brown, 1963.
Apter, David E. *The Politics of Modernization*. Chicago: Chicago University Press, 1965.
Baran, Paul A. *The Political Economy of Growth*. New York and London: Monthly Review Press, Modern Reader Books, 1968.
Bellah, Robert N., ed. *Religion and Progress in Modern Asia*. New York: Free Press, 1965.
Bendix, Reinhard. *Nation-Building and Citizenship*. New York: John Wiley & Sons, 1964.

————. "Tradition and Modernity Reconsidered," *Comparative Studies in Society and History*, IX:3 (April, 1967), 292–346.

————, et al., eds. *State and Society: A Reader in Comparative Political Sociology*. Boston: Little, Brown, 1968.

Berger, Morroe. *Bureaucracy and Society in Modern Egypt*. Princeton, N.J.: Princeton University Press, 1954.

Binder, Leonard. *Iran: Political Development in a Changing Society*. Berkeley and Los Angeles: University of California Press, 1962.

Bonilla, Frank. *The Failure of Elites*. Cambridge, Mass.: M.I.T. Press, 1970.

————, and José Silva Michelena. *A Strategy for Research on Social Policy*. Cambridge, Mass.: M.I.T. Press, 1967.

Brunner, Ronald D., and Garry D. Brewer. *Organized Complexity: Empirical Theories of Political Development*. New York: Free Press, 1971.

Deutsch, Karl W. "Social Mobilization and Political Development," *APSR*, LV (September, 1961), 493–514.

Eisenstadt, S. N. *The Political Systems of Empires*. New York: Free Press, 1963.

————. *Modernization: Protest and Change*. Englewood Cliffs, N.J.: Prentice-Hall, 1967.

Emerson, Rupert. *From Empire to Nation*. Cambridge, Mass.: Harvard University Press, 1960.

Etzioni, Amitai. *Political Unification: A Comparative Study of Leaders and Forces*. New York: Holt, Rinehart and Winston, 1965.

————. *The Active Society: A Theory of Societal and Political Processes*. New York: Free Press, 1971.

Geertz, Clifford, ed. *Old Societies and New States: The Quest for Modernity in Asia and Africa*. New York: Free Press, 1963.

Gerschenkron, Alexander. *Economic Backwardness in Historical Perspective*. Cambridge, Mass.: Harvard University Press, 1962.

Halpern, Manfred. "The Revolution of Modernization in National and International Society," in Carl J. Friedrich, ed., *Revolution*, New York: Atherton Press, 1966.

Hopkins, Terence K., and Immanuel Wallerstein. "The Comparative Study of National Societies," *Social Science Information*, VI:5 (October, 1967), 25–58.

Huntington, Samuel P. "Political Development and Political Decay," *World Politics*, XVII (April, 1965), 384–430.

————. *Political Order in Changing Societies*. New Haven, Conn. and London: Yale University Press, 1968.

————. "The Change to Change: Modernization, Development and Politics," *Comparative Politics*, III:3 (April, 1971), 283–322.

———— and C. H. Moore, eds. *Authoritarian Politics in Modern Society*. New York: Basic Books, 1970.

Ibn Khaldun. *Al-Mouqaddimah*. Tunis: 1377. English translation: *Prolegomenon: An Introduction to History*, translated by Frantz Rosenthal. Princeton, N.J.: Princeton University Press, 1967. 3 vols.

Ilchman, Warren F., and Norman T. Uphoff. *The Political Economy of Change*. Berkeley and Los Angeles: University of California Press, 1969.

Kishimoto, Hideo. "Modernization versus Westernization in the East," *Cahiers d'Histoire Mondiale*, VII (1963), 871–874.

Kornhauser, William. "Rebellion and Political Development," in Harry Eckstein, ed., *Internal War: Problems and Approaches*. New York: Free Press, 1963.

Lasswell, Harold, and Daniel Lerner, eds. *World Revolutionary Elites: Studies in Coercive Ideological Movements*. Cambridge, Mass.: M.I.T. Press, 1965.

Lévi-Strauss, Claude. *La Pensée sauvage*. Paris: Plon, 1962.

Levy, Marion J., Jr. "Contrasting Factors in the Modernization of China and Japan," *Economic Development and Cultural Change*, II (October, 1953), 161–197.

Lockwood, David, "Social Integration and System Integration," in George K. Zollschan and Walter Hirsch, eds., *Explorations in Social Change*. Boston: Houghton Mifflin, 164, pp. 244–257.

Markov, Walter. "La Nation dans l'Afrique tropicale: Notion et Structure." Submitted to the Sixth World Congress of Sociology, 1966. Mimeographed.

Michelena, José A. Silva. *The Illusion of Democracy in Dependent Nations*. Vol. III of *The Politics of Change in Venezuela*. Cambridge, Mass.: M.I.T. Press, 1971.

Moore, Barrington, Jr. *Political Power and Social Theory*. New York: Harper & Row Torchbooks, 1965.

————. *Social Origins of Dictatorship and Democracy: Lord and Peasant in the Making of the Modern World*. Boston: Beacon Press, 1967.

Nisbet, Robert A. *Social Change and History: Aspects of the Western Theory of Development*. New York: Oxford University Press, 1969.

Parsons, Talcott. "On the Concept of Political Power," *Proceedings of the American Philosophical Society*, CVII (1963), 232–262.

Rhodes, Robert I., ed. *Imperialism and Underdevelopment.* New York and London: Monthly Review Press, Modern Reader Books, 1970.

Rodinson, Maxime. *Islam et Capitalisme.* Paris: Le Seuil, 1965.

———. "Dynamique interne ou dynamique globale? L'exemple des pays musulmans," *Cahiers Internationaux de Sociologie,* XLII (1967), 27–47.

Rokkan, Stein. "Models and Methods in the Comparative Study of Nation-Building," *Acta Sociologica,* XII:2 (June, 1969), 53–73.

Schurmann, H. F. *Ideology and Organization in Communist China.* Berkeley and Los Angeles: University of California Press, 1965.

Selznick, Philip. *Leadership in Administration: A Sociological Interpretation.* New York: Harper & Row, 1957.

Shils, Edward. *Political Development in the New States.* The Hague: Mouton, 1962.

Smelser, Neil J. *Social Change in the Industrial Revolution.* Chicago: University of Chicago Press, 1950.

———. *Theory of Collective Behavior.* New York: Free Press, 1963.

———. *Essays in Sociological Explanation: A Theoretical Statement on Sociology as a Social Science and Its Application to Processes of Social Change.* Englewood Cliffs, N.J.: Prentice-Hall, 1968.

Stinchcombe, Arthur L. "Social Structures and Organizations," in James G. March, ed., Chicago: Rand McNally, *Handbook of Organization.* 1965. Pp. 142–193.

———. *Constructing Social Theories.* New York: Harcourt, Brace and World, 1968.

———, et al. "Innovation in Industrial Bureaucracies." A Report of the Joint Center for Urban Studies of Harvard and M.I.T., 1970.

Touraine, Alain. *Sociologie de l'action.* Paris: Aux Editions du Seuil, 1965.

Whitaker, C. S. "A Dysrhythmic Process of Political Change," *World Politics* XIX (January, 1967), 190–217.

Wolin, Sheldon S. *Politics and Vision.* Boston: Little, Brown, 1960.

———. "Political Theory as a Vocation," *APSR* LXIII:4 (December, 1969), 1062–1082.

Worsley, Peter. *The Third World: A Vital Force in International Affairs.* London: Weidenfeld and Nicolson, 1964.

II. STUDIES ON THE AREA

A. General and Introductory

Al-Fasi 'Allal. *al-Harakah al-Istiqlaliyah fi el-Maghrib el-Arabi.* Cairo: 1948. English translations: *The Independence Movements in Arab*

North Africa, translated by Hazem Zahi Nuseibeh. Washington, D.C.: American Council of Learned Societies, 1954.

Barbour, Nevill, ed. *A Survey of North West Africa (The Maghreb)*. 2d ed. New York: Oxford University Press, 1962.

Bennabi, Malek. *Vocation de l'Islam*. Paris: Editions du Seuil, 1954.

Berque, Jacques. *Le Maghreb entre Deux Guerres*. Paris: Editions du Seuil, 1962.

———, Ben Barka, *et al. Reforme agraire au Maghreb*. Paris: Maspero, 1963.

Braudel, Ferdinand. *La Méditerranée et le monde méditerranéen à l'epoque de Philippe II*. 2d ed. Paris: Armand Colin, 1966.

Brown, Leon Carl, ed. *State and Society in Independent North Africa*. Washington, D.C.: The Middle East Institute, 1966.

Camau, Michel. *La Notion de démocratie dans la pensée des dirigeants maghrébins*. Paris-C. N. R. S., 1971

Debbasch, Charles, *et al. Mutations culturelles et coopération au Maghreb*. Paris: Editions Centre National de la Recherche Scientifique, Collection C.R.E.S.M., 1969.

———.*Pouvoir et Administration au Maghreb: Etudes sur les élites maghrébines*. Paris: Editions Centre National de la Recherche Scientifique, Collection C.R.E.S.M., 1970.

Dermenghem, Emile. *Le Culte des Saints dans l'Islam Maghrebin.* Paris: Gallimard, 1954.

Despois, Jean. *L'Afrique du Nord*. Paris: Presses Universitaires de France, 1958.

Dresch, J., *et al. Industrialisation au Maghreb*. Paris: Maspero, 1965.

Duclos, L. J., J. Duvignaud, and J. Leca. *Les Nationalismes maghrébins*. Paris: Fondation Nationale des Sciences Politiques, Etudes Maghrébines, no. 7, 1966.

Evans-Pritchard, Edward. *The Sanusi of Cyrenaica*. Oxford: Clarendon Press, 1949.

Favret, Jeanne, "La segmentarité au Maghreb," *L'Homme: Revue Française d'Anthropologie* (April–June 1966), pp. 105–111.

Flory, M., *et al. La succession d'Etat en Afrique du Nord*. Paris: Editions Centre National de la Recherche Scientifique, Collection C.R.E.S.M., 1967.

Galissot, René. *L'Economie de l'Afrique du Nord*. Paris: Presses Universitaires de France, 1961.

Gannun, A. *Ahadith 'an al-adab al-Maghribi al-Hadith* [Lectures on Contemporary Maghribi Literature]. Cairo: 1964.

Geertz, Clifford. "In Search of North Africa," *The New York Review of Books* (April 22, 1971), pp. 20–24.

Gellner, Ernest. *Saints of the Atlas.* Chicago: University of Chicago Press, 1969.

Gokalp, Ziya. *Turkish Nationalism and Western Civilization.* New York: Columbia University Press, 1959.

Gordon, David C. *North Africa's French Legacy, 1954–1962.* Cambridge, Mass.: Harvard University Press, 1962.

Hahn, Lorna. *North Africa: Nationalism to Nationhood.* Washington, D.C.: Public Affairs Press, 1960.

Hamon, Léo, ed. *Le Rôle Extra-Militaire de l'Armée dans le Tiers Monde.* Paris: Presses Universitaires de France, 1966.

Hopkins, J. F. P. *Medieval Muslim Government in Barbary until the Sixth Century.* London: Luzac, 1958

International Labor Organization. *Labor Survey of North Africa.* Geneva: 1960.

Julien, Charles-Andre. *L'Afrique du Nord en Marche.* Paris: Julliard, 1953.

Lacoste, Yves. *Ibn Khaldoun: naissance de l'histoire, passé du Tiers-Monde.* Paris: Maspero, 1966.

Lacouture, Jean. *Cinq Hommes et la France.* Paris: Editions du Seuil, 1961.

————. *Quatre Hommes et leurs Peuples: sur-pouvoir et sous-developpement.* Paris: Editions du Seuil, 1969.

Laroui, Abdallah. *L'Idéologie Arabe Contemporaine.* Paris: Maspero, 1967.

————. *L'Histoire du Maghreb; un essai de synthèse.* Paris: Maspero, 1970.

Le Tourneau, Roger. "North Africa: Rigorism and Bewilderment," in G. E. von Grunebaum, ed. *Unity and Variety of Muslim Civilization.* Chicago: University of Chicago Press, 1955. Pp. 231–260.

————. "Le developpement d'une classe moyenne en Afrique du Nord," in *Developpement d'une Classe Moyenne dans les Pays Tropicaux et Sub-Tropicaux.* Brussels: International Institute of Differing Civilizations, 1956. Pp. 103–111.

————. *Evolution Politique de l'Afrique du Nord, 1920–1961.* Paris: Armand Colin, 1962.

Mahdi, Muhsin. *Ibn Khaldun's Philosophy of History.* Chicago: University of Chicago Press, 1964.

Memmi, Albert. *Portrait du Colonisé.* Paris: Editions Pauvert, 1966.

Purtschet, Christian, and Andre Valentino. *Sociologie electorale en Afrique du Nord.* Paris: Presses Universitaires de France, 1966.

Rivlin, Benjamin. "Politics and Leadership in Tunisia and Morocco."

Washington, D.C.: Text of address to Fifteenth Annual Conference of the Mid-East Institute, May 7, 1961.

Rustow, Dankwart A. *Middle Eastern Political System.* Englewood Cliffs, N.J.: Prentice-Hall, 1971.

Souriau, Charles. *La presse maghrégine.* Paris: Editions Centre National de la Recherche Scientifique, Collection C.R.E.S.M., 1969.

Tocqueville, Alexis de. "Ecrits et Discours politiques." Vol. III of *Oeuvres Complètes.* Paris: Gallimard, 1962.

Valensi, Lucette. *Le Maghreb avant la prise d'Alger.* Paris: Flammarion, 1969.

Zartman, I. William, ed. *Man, State and Society in the Contemporary Maghreb.* New York: Praeger, January 1971.

B. Comparative Studies

Amin, Samir. *L'Economie du Maghreb.* Paris: Editions de Minuit, 1966. 2 vols.

————. *Le Maghreb moderne.* Paris: Editions de Minuit, 1970.

Ashford, Douglas E. *Second and Third Generation Elites in the Maghreb.* U.S. Department of State Pub., Policy Research Study. Washington, D.C.: Government Printing Office, 1964.

————. *Morocco—Tunisia: Politics and Planning.* National Planning Series, no. 3. New York: Syracuse University Press, 1965.

————. *National Development and Local Reform: Political Participation in Morocco, Tunisia and Pakistan.* Princeton, N.J.: Princeton University Press, 1967.

Beling, Willard A. "Mobilization of Human Resources in Developing Nations: Algeria, Tunisia and Egypt," in W. A. Beling and George O. Totter, eds., *Developing Nations in Quest for a Model.* New York: Van Nostrand Reinhold, 1970. Pp. 182–204.

Ben Youcef, A. *Population du Maghreb et Communauté économique à quatre.* Paris: Editions S.E.D.E.S., 1967.

Etienne, Bruno. "Maghreb et C.E.E." In *Les Economies Maghrébines: L'imdépendance à l'épreuve du développement économique.* Charles Debbasch, *et al.,* eds. Paris: Editions Centre National de la Recherche Scientifique, Collection C.R.E.S.M., 1971. Pp. 165–192.

Fischer, George. "Syndicats et Décolonisation," *Présence Africaine* (October 1960–January 1961), pp. 17–60.

Geertz, Clifford. *Islam Observed: Religious Development in Morocco and Indonesia.* New Haven, Conn.: Yale University Press, 1968.

Gellner, Ernest. "Tribalism and Social Change in North Africa," in *French-Speaking Africa: The Search for Identity,* W. H. Lewis, ed. New York: Walker, 1965. Pp. 107–118.

Halpern, Manfred. *The Politics of Social Change in the Middle East and North Africa*. Princeton, N.J.: Princeton University Press, 1963.

Kostic, C. "Transformations des communautés rurales en Algérie et en Yougoslavie," *Cahiers Internationaux de Sociologie* (July–December 1967), pp. 109–122.

Lerner, Daniel. *The Passing of Traditional Society: Modernizing the Middle East*. New York: Free Press, 1964.

Meynaud, Jean, and Anisse Salah Bey. *Le Syndicalisme Africain*. Paris: Editions Payot, 1963.

Moore, Clement Henry. *Politics in North Africa, Algeria, Morocco, and Tunisia*. Boston: Little, Brown, 1970.

———, and Arlie R. Hochschild. "Student Unions in North African Politics," *Daedalus*, Vol. 97, no. 1 (Winter, 1968), 21–50.

Poncet, Jean. *Le sous-développement vaincu? La lutte pour le développement en Italie méridionale, en Tunisie, et en Roumanie*. Paris: Editions Sociales, 1970.

Robert, Jacques. "Opposition and Control in Tunisia, Morocco, and Algeria," *Government and Opposition*, no. 3 (1965), pp. 389–404.

Tiano, André. *Le Maghreb entre les mythes*. Paris: Presses Universitaires de France, 1967.

III. CASE STUDIES

A. *Algeria*

1. BOOKS

Abbas, Ferhat, *La Nuit Coloniale*. Paris: Julliard, 1962.

Ageron, Charles R. *Les Algériens Musulmans et la France, 1870–1919*. Paris: Presses Universitaires de France, 1968. 2 vols.

Ait Ahmed, Hocine. *La Guerre et l'Après–Guerre*. Paris: Minuit, 1964.

Ait-Amara, A. "L'Autogestion Agricole en Algérie." Thesis, Ecole Pratique des Hautes Etudes, Paris, 1966.

Alleg, Henri, *La Question*. Paris: Minuit, Collection Documents, 1958.

Al-Madani, A. T. *Kitab al-Jaza ir*. Algiers: 1931.

Al Mili, Mubarik. *Tarikh al-Jaza ir fi-l- Qadim wa-l- Jadid*. Algiers: 1963. 2 vols.

Ben Khedda, Ben Youssef. "Contribution à l'historique du FLN." April, 1964. Mimeographed.

Bennabi, Malek. *Mémoires d'un témoin du siècle*. Algiers: Editions Nationales Algériennes, 1965.

Blair, Thomas L. *The Land to Those Who Work It: Algeria's Experi-*

ment in Worker's Management. New York: Doubleday Anchor Books, 1970.

Boudiaf, Mohamed. *Où Va l'Algérie?* Paris: Editions de l'Etoile, 1964.

Bourdieu, Pierre. *Sociologie de l'Algérie.* Paris: Presses Universitaires de France, Collection "Que Sais-Je?," 1963. Expanded version in Bourdieu's *The Algerians,* Boston: Beacon Press, 1962.

————, and Alain Darbel, *et al. Travail et Travailleurs en Algérie.* Paris: Mouton, 1963.

————, and Abdelmalek Sayad. *Le Déracinement: La Crise de l'Agriculture Traditionelle en Algérie.* Paris: Minuit, 1964.

————. "Le Désenchantement du Monde: Travail et Travailleurs en Algérie." Paris: Centre de Sociologie Européenne, 1966. Mimeographed.

Bourgès, Hervé. *L'Algérie à l'épreuve du pouvoir.* Paris: Grasset, 1967.

Camus, Albert. *Actuelles III: Chronique Algérienne, 1939-1958.* Paris: Gallimard, 1958.

Chaliand, Gérard. *L'Algérie est-elle socialiste?* Paris: Maspero, 1964.

Charnay, Jean-Paul, *La Vie Musulmane en Algérie d'après la Jurisprudence de la Première Moitié du XXe Siècle.* Paris: Presses Universitaires de France, 1965.

d'Arcy, François. *L'administration communale dans les communes rurales du département de Constantine.* Paris: Presses Universitaires de France, 1966.

d'Arcy, François, Annie Krieger, and Alain Marill. *Essais sur l'Economie de l'Algérie Nouvelle.* Paris: Presses Universitaires de France, 1965.

Descloitres, Robert, and Laid Debzi. *Système de Parenté et Structures Familiales en Algérie.* Paris: Collections du Centre Africain des Sciences Humaines Appliquées, 1965.

Douence, Jean Claude. *La Mise en place des institutions Algériennes.* Paris: Fondation Nationale des Sciences Politiques, 1964.

Emerit, Marcel. *Les Saint-Simoniens en Algérie.* Paris: Les Belles Lettres, 1941.

————. *L'Algérie à l'époque d'Abdelkader.* Paris: 1951.

Fanon, Frantz. *Les damnés de la terre.* Paris, Maspero, 1961.

————. *L'An V de la Révolution Algérienne.* 3d ed. Paris: Maspero, 1962.

Gordon, David C. *The Passing of French Algeria.* London: Oxford University Press, 1966.

Humbaraci, Arslan. *Algeria: A Revolution that Failed.* London: Pall Mall, 1966.

Julien, Charles-André. *Histoire de l'Algérie Contemporaine.* Vol. I of *La Conquête et les Débuts de la Colonisation, 1827–1871*. Paris: Presses Universitaires de France, 1964.

Lacheraf, Mostefa. *Algérie: Nation et Société*. Paris: Maspero, 1965.

Lacoste, Yves, André Nouschi, and A. Prenant. *L'Algérie, Passé et Présent*. Paris: Editions Sociales, 1960.

Launay, Michel. *Paysans Algériens*. Paris: Le Seuil, 1963.

Lentin, Albert-Paul. *L'Algérie Entre Deux Mondes*. Paris: Julliard, 1963. 3 vols.

Mandouze, Andre, ed. *La Révolution Algérienne par les textes*. Paris: Maspero, 1962.

Mazouni, Al. *Culture et enseignement en Algérie*. Paris: Maspero, 1969.

Merad, A. *La Réformisme musulman en Algérie de 1925 à 1940*. Paris: Mouton, 1968.

Miner, Horace M., and George De Vos. *Oasis and Casbah: Algerian Culture and Personality in Change*. Ann Arbor: University of Michigan Press, 1960.

Morizot, Jean. *L'Algérie kabylisée*. Paris: Peyronnet, 1962.

M'Rabet, Fadela. *La Femme Algérienne*. Paris: Maspero, 1964.

Noushi, André. *La naissance du nationalisme Algérien*. Paris: Editions Minuit, 1962.

Ottoway, David and Marina. *Algeria: The Politics of a Socialist Revolution*. Berkeley and Los Angeles: University of California Press, 1970.

Ouzegane, Amar. *Le Meilleur Combat*. Paris: Julliard, 1962.

Perroux, François, ed. *Problèmes de l'Algérie Indépendante*. Paris: Presses Universitaires de France, 1963.

Quandt, William B. *Revolution and Political Leadership: Algeria, 1954–1968*. Cambridge, Mass.: M.I.T. Press, 1969.

Raptis, Michel. *Le Dossier de l'Autogestion en Algérie*. Special Issue of *Autogestion: études, débats, documents*, Paris, *Cahier* no. 3 (September, 1967).

Remili, Abderrahmane. *Les institutions administratives Algériennes*. Algiers: Editions S.N.E.D., 1968.

Saadallah, Belkacem. "The Rise of Algerian Nationalism (1900–1930)." Ph.D. dissertation in history, University of Minnesota, July, 1965.

Sahli, Mohamed, *Décoloniser d'histoire*, Paris: Maspéro, 1965.

Teillac, Jean. *Autogestion en Algérie*. Paris: Paris University and J. Peyronnet, 1965.

Temmar, Hamid. "La Problématique Socialiste en Algérie (à Travers l'Experience de l'Autogestion dans l'Agriculture)." Thesis, Faculté de Droit, Paris, 1966.

Tidafi, Tami. *L'Agriculture Algérienne et ses perspectives du développement*. Paris: Maspéro, 1970

Turin, Yvonne. *Affrontements culturels dans l'Algérie coloniale*. Paris: Maspéro, 1970.

Viratelle, Gérard. *L'Algérie Algérienne*. Paris: Editions Sociales, 1970.

Wehr, Paul E. "Local Leadership and Problems of Rural Development in Algeria." Ph.D. dissertation, University of Pennsylvania, 1968.

2. ARTICLES

Ageron, Charles R. "Brève histoire de la politique d'assimilation en Algérie." *Revue Socialiste*, no. 95 (March, 1958).

Belloula, T. "Le Syndicalisme en Algérie." *Revue Algérienne du Travail*, VI (January, 1969), 54–64.

Berque, Jacques. "Les Hilaliens repentis ou l'Algérie rurale au XVe siècle d'après un manuscrit jurisprudentiel," *Annales Economies Sociétés Civilizations* [hereinafter cited as *Annales E.S.C.*], XXV: 5 (September–October, 1970), 1325–1353.

Bourdieu, Pierre. "The Sentiment of Honor in Kabyle Society," in J. G. Peristiany, ed. *Honour and Shame: The Values of Mediterranean Society*. Chicago: University of Chicago Press, 1968.

———. "The Berber House or the World Reversed," *Social Science Information*, IX:2 (April, 1970), 151–170.

Chaliand, Gérard. "De Ben Bella à Boumediène." *Partisans*, no. 23 (November, 1965).

———. "L'Algérie au Miroir Marxiste." *Partisans*, no. 21 (June–July–August, 1965).

De Bernis, G. Destanne. "L'Economie Algérienne depuis l'indépendance," in *Les Economies Maghrébines*, Charles Debbasch, *et al.*, eds. Paris: Centre National de la Recherche Scientifique, Collection C.R.E.S.M., 1971. Pp. 9–37.

Dumont, René. "Des Conditions de la Réussite de la Réforme Agraire en Algérie," in *Problèmes de l'Algérie Indépendante*, François Perroux, ed. Paris: Presses Universitaires de France, 1963.

Favret, Jeanne. "Le syndicat, les travailleurs et le pouvoir en Algérie," *Annuaire de l'Afrique du Nord*, III (1964), 45–62.

———. "Le traditionalisme par excès de modernité." *Archives Européennes de Sociologie*, VIII (1967), 71–93.

———. "Relations de dépendance et manipulation de la violence en Kabylie," *L'Homme*, VIII:4 (October–December, 1968), 18–44.

Hubert, Michel. "Les institutions politiques et la République Algérienne," *Revue de l'Occident Musulman*, no. 1 (1966).

Lazarev, Grigori. "Autogestion Agricole en Algérie: Institutions et Développement Agricole du Maghreb," *Tiers Monde* (1965).

Leca, Jean. "Remarques sur la réorganisation des structures du parti et les statuts provisoires du fonctionnement du FLN," *Revue Algérienne des Sciences Juridiques, Politiques, et Economiques*, V:3 (September, 1968), 787–797.

Mokrane, Mohamed. "Les changements dans les modèles d'autorité paternelle à Alger depuis l'indépendance." Paper delivered in Tunis, 1967.

Murray, Roger, and Tom Wengraf. "The Algerian Revolution," *New Left Review*, XXII (1963), 14–65.

Quandt, William B. "Algeria: The Revolution Turns Inward," *Middle-East—North Africa Review*, X:4 (August, 1970), 9–12.

Timsit, Gérard. "Le statut de la fonction publique Algérienne," *Revue Algérienne des Sciences Juridiques, Politiques et Economiques* (June, 1969), pp. 203–292.

B. Morocco

1. BOOKS

Al-Fasi, 'Allal. Al-Naqd al-Dhati [Self-Criticism]. 2d ed. Tetouan, n.d.

———. M'arakat al-yawm wal-Ghad [The Battle of Today and Tomorrow]. Rabat: 1965.

Ashford, D. E. *Political Change in Morocco*. Princeton, N.J.: Princeton University Press, 1961.

Ayache, A. *Le Moroc: Bilan d'une colonisation*. Paris: Editions Sociales, 1956.

Belal, Abd-el-Aziz. *L'Investissement au Maroc, 1912–1964*. Paris: Mouton, 1968.

Ben Barka, Mehdi. Al-Ikhtiyar al-Thawri fil-Maghrib [The Revolutionary Choice in Morocco]. Beirut: Dar Attali's, 1966.

Bernard, Stephane. *The Franco-Moroccan Conflict*. New Haven, Conn. and London: Yale University Press, 1968.

Berque, Jacques. *Structures Sociales du Haut-Atlas*. Paris: Presses Universitaires de France, 1955.

———. Al-Yousi: Problèmes de la culture marocaine au XVIIe siècle. Paris: Mouton, 1958.

Chamoux, Daniel. "L'Experience Marocaine (1955–1964): vers un essai d'entente entre le 'personnalisme' royal et le multipartisme parlementaire." Ph.D. dissertation, Institut d'Etudes Politiques, Aix-en-Provence, 1964.

Chenier, M. *The Present State of the Empire of Morocco*. New York: Johnson, 1967. 2 vols.

Couleau, J. *La paysannerie Marocaine*. Paris: Editions Centre National de la Recherche Scientifique, Collection C.R.E.S.M., 1968.

Gallisot, René. *Le Patronat Européen au Maroc, 1931–1942*. Rabat: 1964.

Gellner, Ernest. *Saints of the Atlas*. Chicago: University of Chicago Press, 1969.

Guillaume, Albert. *L'Evolution économique de la Société rurale Marocaine*. Paris: Librairie Générale de Droit et de Jurisprudence, 1947.

Halstead, John P. *Rebirth of a Nation: The Origins and Rise of Moroccan Nationalism*. Cambridge, Mass.: Harvard University Press, 1967.

Lacouture, Jean and Simone. *Le Maroc à l'épreuve*. Paris: Editions de Seuil, 1958.

Lahbabi, Muhamed. *Le Gouvernement Marocain à l'Aube du XXe Siècle*. Rabat: Editions Techniques Nord-Africaines, 1958.

Le Tourneau, Roger. *Fès avant le Protectorat*. Casablanca: IHEM, 1949.

Michaux-Bellaire, and Henry Gaillard. *L'Administration au Maroc: Le Makhzen, Etendue et Limites de son Pouvoir*. Tangier: 1909.

Miège, J. L. *Le Maroc et l'Europe*. Paris: Presses Universitaires de France, 1962. 4 vols.

————. *Documents d'histoire économique et sociale Marocaine au XIXe siècle*. Paris: Editions Centre National de la Recherche Scientifique, Collection C.R.E.S.M., 1969.

Montagne, Robert. *Les Berbères et le Makhzen dans le Sud du Maroc*. Paris: Alcan, 1930.

————, ed. *Naissance de Prolétariat Marocain*. Paris: Alcan, 1950.

————. *Révolution au Maroc*. Paris: France Empire, 1953.

Radi, Abdelwahad. "Naissance et Evolution des Mouvements de Jeunesse au Maroc." Diplôme d'Etudes Supérieures de Philosophie, Sorbonne, Paris, 1963–1964.

Raymond, Jean, *et al*. *Problèmes d'Edification du Maroc et du Maghreb: Quatre Entretiens avec Mehdi Ben Barka*. Paris: Plon, 1959.

Rézette, Robert. *Les Partis Politiques Marocains*. Paris: Armand Colin, 1955.

Schaar, Stuart. "Conflict and Change in Nineteenth Century Morocco." Ph.D. dissertation, Departments of Oriental Studies and History, Princeton University, November, 1965.

Stewart, Charles F. *The Economy of Morocco, 1912–1962*. Cambridge, Mass.: Harvard University Press, 1964.

Tiano, André. *La Politique Economique et Financière du Maroc Indépendant*. Paris: Presses Universitaires de France, Etudes Tiers Monde, 1963.

Waterbury, John. *The Commander of the Faithful: The Moroccan Political Elite—A Study in Segmented Politics.* New York: Columbia University Press, 1970.

Waterston, Albert. *Planning in Morocco.* Baltimore, Md.: Johns Hopkins Press, 1967.

2. ARTICLES

Aubin, Jules and Jim. "Le Maroc en Suspens," *Annuaire de l'Afrique du Nord,* III (1964), 73–88.

Belal, 'Abdel Aziz. "L'Orientation des investissements et les impératifs du développement national," *Bulletin Economique et Social du Maroc,* XXVIII (January–March, 1966), 41–58.

———, and Abdeljalil Agourram. "L'Economie Marocaine depuis l'indépendance," *Les Economies Maghrébines,* Paris: Centre National de la Recherche Scientifique, Collection C.R.E.S.M., 1971. Pp. 141–164.

Chambergeat, Paul. "L'Administration et le douar," *Revue de Géographie de Maroc,* no. 8 (1965), pp. 83–86.

Gellner, Ernest. "From Ibn Khaldûn to Karl Marx," *The Political Quarterly,* XXXII:4 (October–December, 1961), 385–392.

———. "The Struggle for Morocco's Past," *Middle East Journal* (Winter, 1961), pp. 79–90.

———. "Patterns of Rural Rebellion in Morocco: Tribes as Minorities," *Archives Européennes de Sociologie,* III:2, (1962), 297–311.

———. "The Great Patron: A Reinterpretation of Tribal Rebellions," *Archives Européennes de Sociologie,* X:1 (1969), 61–69.

Jamil Moulahidh. "Le Maroc dans l'inquietude," *Esprit,* no. 397 (November, 1970), pp. 783–804.

Lazarev, Gribori. "Le changement social et le développement dans les campagnes Marocaines," *Bulletin Economique et Social du Maroc,* XXX:109 (1968), 19–33.

Leveau, Rémy. "L'Administration locale et les élus du Maroc." Presented to the Fifth General Assembly of the Mediterranean Social Science Research Council, Beirut, September 12–16, 1966.

Lewis, W. H. "Feuding and Social Change in Morocco," *The Journal of Conflict Resolution,* V:1 (March, 1961), 43–54.

M. B. "Le Maroc," in Leo Hamon, ed., *Le Rôle Extra-Militaire de l'Armée dans le Tiers-Monde.* Paris: Presses Universitaires de France, 1966. Pp. 31–55.

Marais, Octave. "La classe dirigeante au Maroc," *Revue Française de Science Politique,* XIV:4 (August, 1964), 709–737.

———. "Les relations entre la monarchie et la classe dirigeante au

Maroc," *Revue Française de Science Politique*, XIX:6 (December, 1969), 1172–1186.

————, and John Waterbury. "Thèmes et Vocabulaire de la propagande des élites politiques au Maroc," *Annuaire de l'Afrique du Nord*, VII (1969), 57–78.

Miner, H. "Le déclin des corporations de Fès vus sous l'angle d'une théorie des conflits." *Bulletin Economique et Social du Maroc*, XXX:109 (April–June, 1968), 81–94.

Nicolas, Georges. "La Sociologie rurale au Maroc pendant les cinquante dernières années." *Tiers Monde*, II:8, (October–December, 1961), 527–543.

Pascon, Paul. "Birth Control: dialogue de sourds." *Lamalif*, no. 3 (May, 1966), pp. 16–20.

————. "Désuétude de la Jma's dans le Haouz de Marrakech." *Les Cahiers de Sociologie*, no. 1 (September–October–November, 1965), pp. 67–78.

Poncet, Jean. "Grands projets et difficultés Marocaines," *Tiers Monde*, XI:41 (January–March, 1970), 197–218.

Vinogradov, Amal, and John Waterbury. "Situations of Contested Legitimacy in Morocco: An Alternative Framework," *Comparative Studies in Society and History*, XIII:1 (January, 1971) 32–59.

Waterbury, John. "Marginal Politics and Elite Manipulation in Morocco," *Archives Européennes de Sociologie*, VIII:1 (1967), 94–111.

C. Tunisia

1. Books

Al-Balhawan, Ali. *Tunus ath-Tha'ira*. Cairo: Lajnat Tahrir al-Maghrib al-'arabi, 1954.

Al-Haddad, Tahir. *Al-'Ummal al-Tunusiyyun Wa Dhuhur al-Harakat al-Naqabiyya*. Tunis: 1927.

————. *Imraatuna fi al-Shari'ah wal-Mujtama'*. Tunis: Imprimerie d'Art, 1930. For an analysis in French of its content, see Al-Haddad, *Revue d'Etude Islamique*, IX (1935) 201–230.

Ath-Taalbi, Abd-el-Aziz. *La Tunisie Martyre*. Paris: Ch. Jouve, 1920.

Aydalot, Philippe. *Essai sur les problèmes de la stratégie de l'industrialisation en économie sous-développée. L'exemple tunisien.* C.E.R.E.S., Tunis University, 1968.

Bardin, Pierre. *La Vie d'un douar: Essai sur la vie rurale la haute Medjerda*. Paris: Mouton, 1965.

Beling, Willard A. *Modernization and African Labor: A Tunisian Case Study*. New York: Praeger, 1965.

Ben Ashur, M. al-Fadhil. *Al-Haraka al-Adabiya wal-fikriya fi Tunus.* Cairo: 1956.

Bistolfi, Robert. "Structure économique et décolonisation monétaire, le cas tunisien." Thesis, Paris: Sorbonne, 1964.

Bouhdiba, Abdelwahab. *Criminalité et Changements Sociaux en Tunisie.* Tunis: Tunis University, 1965.

Bourguiba, Habib. *La Tunisie et la France.* Paris: Julliard, 1954.

Brown, Leon Carl. "Tunisia Under the French Protectorate: A History of Ideological Change." Ph.D. dissertation, Harvard University, 1962.

Brugnes, M. P. *Investissements industriels et développement en Tunisie.* C.E.R.E.S., Tunis University, 1966.

Cuisenier, Jean. *L'Ansarine.* Paris: Presses Universitaires de France, 1966.

Eqbal, Ahmed. "Politics and Labor in Tunisia." Ph.D. dissertation, Princeton University, May, 1967.

Ganiage, Jean. *Les Origines du Protectorat Français en Tunisie, 1861–1881.* Paris: Presses Universitaires de France, 1959.

Guen, Moncef. *La Coopération en Tunisie.* Tunis: 1964.

Hermassi, Elbaki. "Le Mouvement Ouvrier en Société Coloniale: la Tunisie entre les deux guerres." Ph.D. dissertation submitted to the Sorbonne, 1966.

Ibn Abi Dhiyaf. *Ithaf.* Tunis: 1963. 6 vols.

Khairallah, Chedly. *Le Mouvement Evolutioniste Tunisien.* Tunis: 1935. 3 vols.

————. *Le Mouvement Jeune-Tunisien.* Tunis: Imprimerie Bonici, 1957.

Khayr ad-Din. *Aqwam al-Masalik li-ma'rifat ahwal al-Mamalik.* Tunis: 1867. French edition, Paris: 1868. English translation, L. C. Brown, *The Surest Path,* Cambridge, Mass.: Harvard University Press, 1967.

Ling, Dwight L. *Tunisia: From Protectorate to Republic.* Bloomington: Indiana University Press, 1967.

Makhlouf, Ezzedine. *Structures agraires et modernisation de l'agriculture dans les plaines du Kef.* C.E.R.E.S., Tunis University, 1968.

Micaud, Charles A., *et al. Tunisia: The Politics of Modernization.* New York: Praeger, 1964.

Moalla, Mansour. *L'Etat Tunisien et l'Indépendance.* Ph.D. dissertation, University of Paris, 1957.

Moore, Clement H. *Tunisia Since Independence: the Dynamics of One-Party Government.* Berkeley and Los Angeles: University of California Press, 1965.

Poncet, Jean. *La Colonisation et l'agriculture européennes en Tunisie depuis 1881.* Paris: Mouton, 1961.

Rudebeck, Lars. *Party and People: A Study of Political Change in Tunisia.* Stockholm: Almquist and Wiksell, 1967.

Sebag, Paul. *La Tunisie: Essai de monographie.* Paris: Editions Sociales, 1951.

Slama, Bice. *La Révolte de 1864.* Tunis: 1967.

Thamir, al-Habib. *Hadihi Tunis.* Cairo: Matba' at al-Risalah, 1948.

Ziyadeh, N. *Origins of Nationalism in Tunisia.* Beirut: 1962.

2. ARTICLES

Abdallah, Ridha. "Le néo-Destour Depuis l'Indépendance." *Revue Juridique et Politique d'Outre-Mer,* XVII:4 (October–December, 1963), 573–657.

———. "Structure et Evolution du néo-Destour," *Revue Juridique et Politique d'Outre-Mer,* XVII:3 (July–September, 1963), 358–428.

Ben Salah, Ahmed. "Décolonisation et Politique Sociale," *Esprit* (June, 1957).

Bouhdiba, Abd-el-Wahab. "Dialogue et Politique, à propos des Congrès des cellules du P.S.D.," *Institut des Belles Lettres Arabes,* Tunis (1969), pp. 51–70.

Calamitsis, E. "Stabilization problems and policies in Tunisia," *Finance and Development,* VII:3 (Summer, 1970), 43–48.

Cherif, Mohammed Hedi. "Les Mouvements paysans de la Tunisie du XIXe siècle," in *Mouvements Nationaux d'Independance . . . ,* Paris: A. Colin, 1971.

Ennafaa, Mohammed. "Situation et perspective du développement de la Tunisie," *Economie et Politique,* no. 106 (May, 1963), pp. 54–65.

Lacouture, Jean. "Habib Bourguiba Prophète d'une Bourgeoisie Nationale," in *Quatre Hommes et Leurs Peuples.* Paris: Le Seuil, 1969. Pp. 135–188.

Montety, Henri de. "Le Développement des Classes Moyennes en Tunisie" in *Développement d'une Classe Moyenne dans les Pays Tropicaux et Sub-Tropicaux* (Brussels: INCIDI, 1956).

———. "Le Jaillissement Occidental de la Tunisie," *Etudes Mediterranéennes,* no. 3 (1958), pp. 57–66.

———. "Vieilles Familles et Nouvelle Elite en Tunisie," *Documents sur l'Evolution du Monde Musulman,* no. 3 (August 8, 1940). Paris: Centre des Hautes Etudes d'Administration Musulmane.

Poncet, Jean. "l'Economie Tunisienne depuis l'Indépendance," in *Les Economies Maghrébines.* Paris: Editions Centre National de la Recherche Scientifique, Collection C.R.E.S.M., 1971. Pp. 89–110.

Rivlin, Benjamin. "The Tunisian Nationalist Movement: Four Decades of Evolution." *Middle Eastern Journal*, VI (1952), 167–193.

Simmons, John L. "Agricultural Cooperatives and Tunisian Development," *Middle Eastern Journal* (Winter, 1971), pp. 45–57.

Zghal, Abdelkader. "La participation de la paysannerie Maghrébine à la construction nationale," *Revue Tunisienne de Sciences Sociales*, no. 22 (July, 1970), pp. 125–161.

INDEX